Experiencing Choral Music

TENOR/BASS

Developed by

HAL•LEONARD®
CORPORATION

McGraw Hill Glencoe

New York, New York   Columbus, Ohio   Chicago, Illinois   Peoria, Illinois   Woodland Hills, California

Send all inquiries to:
Glencoe/McGraw-Hill
21600 Oxnard Street, Suite 500
Woodland Hills, CA 91367

ISBN 0-07-861114-8 (Student Edition)
ISBN 0-07-861115-6 (Teacher Wraparound Edition)

1 2 3 4 5 6 7 8 9   045   09 08 07 06 05 04

Table of Contents

Contents Teacher Wraparound Edition T3

Program at a Glance T4

National Standards T6

Introduction T8

Program Philosophy T8

Organization and Flexibility T10

Intermediate Tenor/Bass—Lesson Objectives T11

Student Text T13

Teacher Wraparound Edition T14

Teacher Resource Binder T15

Effective Teaching Checklist T16

SECTION			National Standards								
Selection	**Concepts and Skills**		**1**	**2**	**3**	**4**	**5**	**6**	**7**	**8**	**9**
LESSONS											
This Land Is Your Land	Sing expressively in G major; rhythmic patterns in cut time; American heritage.		b, c				b	c	a, b		a, b
Spotlight On Posture	Performance techniques—posture.		b								
Be Cool	Identify and perform accidentals; perform swing rhythms; cool jazz style.		a, b, c, e				c	a, c	a, b		a
Spotlight On Arranging	Arrange melodic and rhythmic phrases.					b					
Red River Valley	Sing a cappella music in three-part harmony; use dynamics; American and Texas heritage.		b, c, d, e				a		a		
Codfish Shanty	Define staccato and accent; dotted eighth and sixteenth notes; sea chantey.		b, c			a	c		a, b		
Festival Procession	Perform music in Mixolydian mode; 6/4 meter; create a percussion arrangement.		a, c, d, e	b		a	a, b		b		
Soldier's Hallelujah	Identify and describe form in music; interpret dynamics; perform a cappella music in two parts		a, d				c	a	a	a	
Light The Candles Of Hanukkah	Major and minor tonality; sing adequate breath support; music from Jewish culture.		a, b, c			a	c	c	b		
The Shepherd's Spiritual	Perform expressively in solo and ensemble singing; syncopation; African American spiritual.		b, c	b			a, b		b		
Spotlight On Vowels	Performance techniques—vowels.		b								
Now Is The Month Of Maying	Homophony and polyphony; sing a madrigal; describe and perform music from the Renaissance period.		c, e			a	a	a	a		
Der Herr segne euch	Identify and perform music written in counterpoint; proper German diction; describe and perform music from the Baroque period.		b,d					b	b	b	a
Ave Verum Corpus	Legato phrases and proper breath support; sing Latin text; describe and perform music from the Classical period.		a, b, e					b	a	a	
Da unten im Tale	Harmony with intervals of a third; dotted quarter notes; describe and perform music from the Romantic period.		b			a	a	b		a	
MUSIC & HISTORY											
Renaissance, Baroque, Classical, Romantic and Contemporary periods	Describe, listen to and analyze music from the five main historical periods.							a, b, c, d, e, f		a, b, c, d, e	a, c, d, e
Spotlight On Diction	Performance techniques—diction.		a								

SECTION		National Standards								
Selection	Concepts and Skills	1	2	3	4	5	6	7	8	9
CHORAL LIBRARY										
The Battle Cry Of Freedom	Melodies with step-wise and skip-wise motion; dotted eighth and sixteenth note patterns; American heritage.	a, b, c d, e				a, b, c	c	b		a, b, c
Spotlight On Careers In Music	Describe music-related vocations and avocations.									c
Come Travel With Me	Dynamic markings in music; triplets; relate music to poetry.	a, b, d, e				a, b, c	c	a, b	b	
Spotlight On Concert Etiquette	Apply concert etiquette in a variety of settings.							a, b		
Frog Went A-Courtin'	Pentatonic scale; describe octave and unison; American folk song.	a, b, c, d				d	c	b	a, b	b
Guantanamera	Spanish diction with clarity and proper syllabic stress; music of Cuban heritage; relate music to history and culture.	a, b, c, d					a, b, c	a, b	b	a
Joshua! (Fit The Battle Of Jericho)	Creating an arrangement; African American spiritual.	a, b, c, d			c		b, c	b		a
Spotlight On Breath Management	Sing accurately with good breath control.	b								
Leave Her, Johnny	Staggered breathing; identify and describe dissonance; relate music to writing.	a, b, c, d					a, b, c	b	b	
New River Train	Identify standard notation for rhythm; sight-sing in F major; relate music to history.	a, b, c, d		a, b, c		a, b, c	b, c	b		a, b
Spotlight On Improvisation	Create rhythmic and melodic phrases. Improvise melodic embellishments.	a, b, c		a, b, c						
On The Deep, Blue Sea	Describe and perform chords in tune; sing expressively in a spirited style; read rhythms in cut time.	a, b, c, d				a, b, c	a, c	b	b	
Spotlight On Changing Voice	Describe characteristics of vocal timbre individually and in groups.	b								
Pretty Saro	Read notation in 3/4 meter; write a pentatonic scale; American folk music.	a, b, c, d		c		a, b, c, d		a, b		b
Santa Lucia	Read and perform rhythmic patterns in 3/8 meter; sing expressively with rubato; Neapolitan barcarole.	b, c, e				b	b	a		
Sing To The Lord	Distinguish between unison and two-part singing; dotted quarter notes; relate music to other subjects.	a, b, c, d				a	a, b	a, b	b	
Spotlight On Vocal Production	Performance techniques—vocal production.	b								
You Gentlemen Of England	Perform expressively from memory; symbols referring to dynamics; define writing techniques (sequence and contrary motion).	a, b, d				c	a	a, b		

National Standards Middle School Grades 5–8

The National Standards for Music Education were developed by the Music Educators National Conference. Reprinted by permission.

MUSIC

The period represented by grades 5–8 is especially critical in students' musical development. The music they perform or study often becomes an integral part of their personal musical repertoire. Composing and improvising provide students with unique insight into the form and structure of music and at the same time help them develop their creativity. Broad experience with a variety of music is necessary if students are to make informed musical judgments. Similarly, this breadth of background enables them to begin to understand the connections and relationships between music and other disciplines. By understanding the cultural and historical forces that shape social attitudes and behaviors, students are better prepared to live and work in communities that are increasingly multi-cultural. The role that music will play in students' lives depends in large measure on the level of skills they achieve in creating, performing and listening to music.

Every course in music, including performance courses, should provide instruction in creating, performing, listening to and analyzing music, in addition to focusing on its specific subject matter.

1. **Content Standard:** Singing, alone and with others, a varied repertoire of music
   Achievement Standard:
   Students
   a. sing accurately and with good breath control throughout their singing ranges, alone and in small and large ensembles.
   b. sing with *expression and *technical accuracy a repertoire of vocal literature with a *level of difficulty of 2, on a scale of 1 to 6, including some songs performed from memory.
   c. sing music representing diverse *genres and cultures, with expression appropriate for the work being performed.
   d. sing music written in two and three parts.
   Students who participate in a choral ensemble
   e. sing with expression and technical accuracy a varied repertoire of vocal literature with a level of difficulty of 3, on a scale of 1 to 6, including some songs performed from memory.

2. **Content Standard:** Performing on instruments, alone and with others, a varied repertoire of music
   Achievement Standard:
   Students
   a. perform on at least one instrument[1] accurately and independently, alone and in small and large ensembles, with good posture, good playing position and good breath, bow or stick control.
   b. perform with expression and technical accuracy on at least one string, wind, percussion or *classroom instrument a repertoire of instrumental literature with a level of difficulty of 2, on a scale of 1 to 6.
   c. perform music representing diverse genres and cultures, with expression appropriate for the work being performed.
   d. play by ear simple melodies on a melodic instrument and simple accompaniments on a harmonic instrument.
   Students who participate in an instrumental ensemble or class
   e. perform with expression and technical accuracy a varied repertoire of instrumental literature with a level of difficulty of 3, on a scale of 1 to 6, including some solos performed from memory.

3. **Content Standard:** Improvising melodies, variations and accompaniments
   Achievement Standard:
   Students
   a. improvise simple harmonic accompaniments.
   b. improvise melodic embellishments and simple rhythmic and melodic variations on given pentatonic melodies and melodies in major keys.
   c. improvise short melodies, unaccompanied and over given rhythmic accompaniments, each in a consistent *style, *meter and *tonality.

4. **Content Standard:** Composing and arranging music within specified guidelines
   Achievement Standard:
   Students
   a. compose short pieces within specified guidelines,[2] demonstrating how the elements of music are used to achieve unity and variety, tension and release, and balance.
   b. arrange simple pieces for voices or instruments other than those for which the pieces were written.

c. use a variety of traditional and nontraditional sound sources and electronic media when composing and arranging.

5. **Content Standard:** Reading and notating music
   Achievement Standard:
   Students
   a. read whole, half, quarter, eighth, sixteenth and dotted notes and rests in 2/4, 3/4, 4/4, 6/8, 3/8 and *alla breve meter signatures.
   b. read at sight simple melodies in both the treble and bass clefs.
   c. identify and define standard notation symbols for pitch, rhythm, *dynamics, tempo, *articulation and expression.
   d. use standard notation to record their musical ideas and the musical ideas of others.

6. **Content Standard:** Listening to, analyzing and describing music
   Achievement Standard:
   Students
   a. describe specific music events[3] in a given aural example, using appropriate terminology.
   b. analyze the uses of *elements of music in aural examples representing diverse genres and cultures.
   c. demonstrate knowledge of the basic principles of meter, rhythm, tonality, intervals, chords and harmonic progressions in the analyses of music.

7. **Content Standard:** Evaluating music and music performances
   Achievement Standard:
   Students
   a. develop criteria for evaluating the quality and effectiveness of music performances and compositions and apply criteria in their personal listening and performing.
   b. evaluate the quality and effectiveness of their own and others' performances, compositions, arrangements and improvisations by applying specific criteria appropriate for the style of the music and offer constructive suggestions for improvement.

8. **Content Standard:** Understanding relationships between music, the other arts and disciplines outside the arts
   Achievement Standard:
   Students
   a. compare in two or more arts how the characteristic materials of each art (that is, sound in music, visual stimuli in visual arts, movement in dance, human interrelationships in theatre) can be used to transform similar events, scenes, emotions or ideas into works of art.
   b. describe ways in which the principles and subject matter of other disciplines taught in the school are interrelated with those of music.[4]

9. **Content Standard:** Understanding music in relation to history and culture
   Achievement Standard:
   Students
   a. describe distinguishing characteristics of representative music genres and styles from a variety of cultures.
   b. classify by genre and style (and, if applicable, by historical period, composer and title) a varied body of exemplary (that is, high-quality and characteristic) musical works and explain the characteristics that cause each work to be considered exemplary.
   c. compare, in several cultures of the world, functions music serves, roles of musicians[5] and conditions under which music is typically performed.

Terms identified by an asterisk (*) are explained further in the glossary of *National Standards for Arts Education,* published by Music Educators National Conference, © 1994.

1. E.g., band or orchestra instrument, *fretted instrument, electronic instrument
2. E.g., a particular style, form, instrumentation, compositional technique
3. E.g., entry of oboe, change of meter, return of refrain
4. E.g., language arts: issues to be considered in setting texts to music; mathematics: frequency ratios of intervals; sciences: the human hearing process and hazards to hearing; social studies: historical and social events and movements chronicled in or influenced by musical works
5. E.g., lead guitarist in a rock band, composer of jingles for commercials, singer in Peking opera

INTRODUCTION

Experiencing Choral Music is a four-level series designed to build music literacy and promote vocal development for all students and voice categories in grades 6–12. The series is a multitextbook program supported with print materials and audio listening components that enable students to develop music skills and conceptual understanding, and provides teachers with a flexible, integrated program.

Experiencing Choral Music presents beginning, intermediate, proficient and advanced literature for various voice groupings: unison, 2-part/3-part, mixed, treble, and tenor/bass. All selections in *Experiencing Choral Music* are recorded three ways: full performance with voices, accompaniment only, and individual part-dominant recordings. The program also includes companion *Sight-Singing* textbooks that present a sequential approach to musical literacy and is directly correlated to the literature books. This comprehensive choral music program includes student texts, teacher wraparound editions, teacher resource binders, and rehearsal and performance audio recordings designed to enhance student learning while reducing teacher preparation time.

Experiencing Choral Music is a curriculum that provides your students with a meaningful, motivating choral music experience, and will help you and your students build choral music knowledge and skills. For example:

Experiencing Choral Music connects to . . . the National Standards

The National Standards are correlated to each lesson for quick-and-easy identification and reference. The performance standards related to singing and reading notations are explicit in each lesson, and by using the extension activities, teachers can connect the musical elements through improvisation and composition. Analysis and evaluation are an active and consistent component of lessons throughout the series. Additional student activities connect the lessons to the other arts, as well as provide a consistent historical and cultural context.

Experiencing Choral Music connects to . . . Skill Development

Through the Links to Learning exercises, students build vocal, theory and artistic expression skills necessary to perform each piece. Rhythmic, melodic and articulation skills are developed as needed for expressive interpretation. Students are encouraged to develop listening skills and use their perceptions to improve individual and group performance.

Experiencing Choral Music connects to . . . Creative Expression/Performance

Student performance provides opportunities for young musicians to demonstrate musical growth, to gain personal satisfaction from achievement, and to experience the joy of music making. To help develop skills, *Experiencing Choral Music* provides vocal, theory and artistic expression exercises which help prepare students to successfully sing each piece. Conceptual understanding is built throughout the teaching/learning sequence, as the performance is prepared.

Experiencing Choral Music connects to . . . Historical and Cultural Heritage

Experiencing Choral Music provides a vehicle to help students gain knowledge and understanding of historical and cultural contexts across the curriculum. These concepts are presented in the Getting Started section of each lesson. Also, historical connections through art, history, timelines, performance practices and listening examples are made in Music & History.

Experiencing Choral Music connects to . . . the Arts and Other Curriculum Areas

Choral music provides a rich opportunity to connect the musical experience to other art disciplines (dance, visual arts, theater), and to enhance the learning in other subject areas.

PROGRAM PHILOSOPHY

Responding to New Trends in Choral Music Education

Experiencing Choral Music is consistent with current educational philosophy that suggests:

- Performance is a product that should be the end result of a sound educational process, building conceptual understanding and skills as the performance is prepared.
- Students are motivated through materials and concepts that are connected to their own lives and interests, and should be exposed to high-quality, challenging musical literature.
- Students learn best when they are active participants in their learning, and when they clearly understand and help set the goals and objectives of the learning outcome.
- Students understand concepts better when they have background information and skills that allow them to place their learning into a larger context.
- Students need to actively manipulate musical concepts and skills through improvisation and/or composition in order to fully assimilate and understand them.

- Students improve when they receive fair, honest and meaningful feedback on their success and failures.
- Students should be encouraged to assess themselves individually and as a group, learning to receive and process constructive criticism, leading to independent self-correction and decision making.

Scope and Depth of Music Literature

Most students are capable of performing more difficult material than they can sight-read. Therefore, the literature in *Experiencing Choral Music* is drawn from many periods and styles of music. The wide range of composers and publishers ensures variety, and allows for various skills and concepts to be developed as each new piece is encountered. The high standards set in *Experiencing Choral Music* provide selections that are inherently powerful and exciting for students. The *Sight-Singing* textbooks provide additional literature for sight-singing purposes. Written in a sequential manner, this component will present students with a developmental process for learning to read music.

Addressing the National Standards

The National Standards for Arts Education, published in 1994, launched a national effort to bring a new vision to arts education for all students. The National Standards provide a framework for achievement in music, with outcomes suggested for grades 4, 8, and 12. *Experiencing Choral Music* addresses the National Standards in several ways.

The most obvious and predominant National Standards addressed in choral ensemble are: (1) singing and (5) reading and notation. However, good performance requires musical understanding that only occurs when all aspects of musical experience are incorporated. The preparation of vocal performance is enriched and deepened by involvement in all nine of the National Standards.

As you teach with *Experiencing Choral Music*, there will be frequent opportunities to deepen or extend student learning through: (2) playing through creating accompaniments, (3) improvisation, (4) composition and arranging, (6) analyzing, (7) assessing, (8) linking with other arts and other academic disciplines, and (9) understanding historical and cultural contexts. The National Standards identified for each lesson and the Extension activities provided in the Teacher Wraparound Edition help you become aware of the National Standards, and the depth of learning that will occur as you implement this choral music program.

Promoting Music Literacy

Experiencing Choral Music promotes music literacy throughout the lessons. Literacy includes oral and aural aspects of music communication—reading, writing, singing and listening. Each lesson begins with Getting Started that (1)

connects the song to the student, and (2) frames the historical and cultural aspect of the music to be performed. From there the students are directed to the Links to Learning that is divided into three categories: Vocal, Theory and Artistic Expression. These exercises emphasize reading development and artistic expression. These may be rhythmic, melodic, harmonic or a combination thereof; and are directly related to the objectives of the lesson. The exercises lead directly into the musical selection. Students are encouraged to sight-sing in every lesson. Sight-singing is approached as a challenge and a means to musical independence for the student.

Literacy goes beyond simply reading pitch and rhythm, extending to the expressive elements of music and appropriate interpretation. Through Artistic Expression, students will be asked to explore interpretive aspects of music making, and are encouraged to suggest their own ideas for phrasing, dynamics, and so on. Through careful listening and constructive critique of their own work, they will gradually become more discriminating about the quality of performance and the impact of that performance on the audience.

Including Authentic Student Assessment

The assessment in *Experiencing Choral Music* is systematic, objective and authentic. There is ongoing informal assessment by teacher observation throughout the lessons. The text is written as a series of action steps for the student, so there are many opportunities for the director to hear and see the level of accomplishment.

Students will find objectives at the beginning of each lesson, and evaluation activities at the end. The Evaluation questions and activities are always related directly to the lesson objectives, and allow students to demonstrate their understanding. By answering the questions, and demonstrating as suggested, students are involved in *self-assessment*. Many times students are involved in their own assessment, constructing rubrics or critiquing their performance to determine what level of success has been achieved, and identifying the next challenge.

The *Teacher Wraparound Edition* includes lesson objectives, and each lesson is taught so the concepts and skills are experienced, labeled, practiced and reinforced, then measured through *formal assessment*. These assessment tasks match the lesson objectives, allowing students to demonstrate understanding of concepts and skills through performance, composition, or writing. Students are frequently required to produce audio- or videotapes. This authentic assessment keeps testing of rote learning to a minimum, and allows measurement of higher-level application of knowledge and skills. A portfolio can be constructed for individual students, groups, or the whole ensemble, demonstrating growth over time.

Connecting the Arts and Other Curriculum Areas

Lessons in *Experiencing Choral Music* integrate many appropriate aspects of musical endeavor into the preparation of a piece. Students compose, improvise, conduct, read, write, sing, play, listen/analyze and assess on an ongoing basis that builds understanding, as well as high standards. In this way, the many aspects of music are integrated for deeper learning.

As one of the arts, music can be linked to other arts through similarities and differences. Throughout the text, and particularly in the historical section, music is compared and contrasted with other arts to determine aspects of confluence and the unique features of each art.

As one way of knowing about the world, music can be compared with concepts and skills from other disciplines as seemingly different as science or mathematics. The integrations between music and other disciplines are kept at the conceptual level, to maintain the integrity of both music and the other subjects. For example, mathematical sets of 2, 3, 4, 5 and 6 might be explored as a link to pieces with changing meter; or the text of a piece might become a starting point for exploration of tone painting. In Music & History, a time line connects music to social studies, and a list of authors for each period provides a link to language and literature.

Providing a Variety of Student Activities

Experiencing Choral Music begins with the choral experience, and builds understanding through active participation in a range of activities including singing, playing, improvising, composing, arranging, moving, writing, listening, analyzing, assessing and connecting to cultures, periods or disciplines. Lessons are written with the heading "Direct students to . . ." so there is always an emphasis on learning by doing. In this way the teacher becomes a guide and places the responsibility for learning on the student. When students are engaged in meaningful and challenging activity, they are more likely to learn.

Fitting Your Classroom Needs

With *Experiencing Choral Music*, your students will be clear about purpose and direction, have multiple routes to success, and be involved in their own learning. The lessons will guide you and your students to share in the excitement of music making, and help you to grow together. The lessons are written the way you teach, and allow you to maintain and strengthen your routines, while adding flexibility, variety and depth.

ORGANIZATION AND FLEXIBILITY

Each *Experiencing Choral Music* text is divided into the following sections:
- Lessons
- Music & History
- Choral Library

Lessons

The Lessons are designed to be taught over a period of time. They are divided into three categories: Beginning of the Year, Mid-Winter, and Concert/Festival. Each lesson is developed around a piece of authentic and quality music literature. The lesson includes background information, vocal examples, sight-reading and rhythmic or melodic drills, all of which are directly related to preparation of the piece. Objectives are clearly stated, and a motivational opening activity or discussion is provided. The Teacher Wraparound Edition outlines a carefully sequenced approach to the piece and clear assessment opportunities to document achievement and growth.

Music & History

Music & History provides narrative and listening experiences for each of the five main historical periods. A *narrative lesson* provides a brief and interesting exposition of the main characteristics of the period outlining the achievements and new styles that emerged. A time line guides the student to place the musical characteristics into a larger historical and cultural context. The listening lesson includes both vocal and instrumental *listening selections* from the period, with a guide to student listening. A listing of the historical pieces to be sung from the period are cross-referenced from the Music & History divider page. Combined, these components give historical context of the period across the arts, then apply the context to musical literature.

Choral Library

The Choral Library provides the same comprehensive student lesson featured in the Lessons. The additional literature features multicultural selections, patriotic and seasonal selections, American folk music, African American spirituals, Broadway show tunes, and light concert pieces that can be used to enhance the repertoire of your choral music performance.

Overview of Lesson Objectives

Each lesson has objectives that emphasize and build conceptual understanding and skills across the lessons. The objectives in this book are:

LESSON OBJECTIVES	
Title	**Objective**
This Land Is Your Land	• Sing a melody expressively in G major tonality. • Read and perform rhythmic patterns in cut time. • Perform music representing the American heritage.
Be Cool	• Identify and perform musical symbols (accidentals) found in music. • Identify and perform swing-style rhythms. • Perform music representing cool jazz style.
Red River Valley	• Sing a cappella music in three-part harmony. • Use dynamics to sing expressively. • Perform music representing American heritage.
Codfish Shanty	• Define *staccato* and *accent*. Perform music that contains both. • Read and perform dotted eighth- and sixteenth-note patterns. • Perform music representing the sea chantey.
Festival Procession	• Identify and perform music in a modal key (Mixolydian). • Read and perform music in 6/4 meter. • Create an original percussion arrangement.
Soldier's Hallelujah	• Identify and describe form in music. • Interpret dynamics when performing. • Perform a cappella music in two parts.
Light The Candles Of Hanukkah	• Distinguish between major and minor tonality. • Sing with adequate support. • Perform music representing the Jewish culture.
The Shepherd's Spiritual	• Perform expressively in both solo and ensemble singing. • Read and perform rhythmic patterns that contain syncopation. • Perform music representing the African American spiritual.
Now Is The Month Of Maying	• Describe and perform *homophony* and *polyphony*. • Sing music in a madrigal style. • Perform music representing the Renaissance period.
Der Herr segne euch	• Identify and perform music written in counterpoint. • Demonstrate musical artistry through the use of proper German diction. • Describe and perform music from the Baroque period.
Ave Verum Corpus	• Sing with legato phrasing and proper breath support. • Sing a Latin text with comprehension and expression. • Describe and perform music from the Classical period.
Da unten im Tale	• Perform harmony with intervals of a third. • Read and perform dotted quarter notes. • Describe and perform music from the Romantic period.

LESSON OBJECTIVES	
Title	**Objective**
The Battle Cry Of Freedom	• Identify and perform melodies with step-wise and skip-wise motion. • Read and perform dotted eighth- and sixteenth-note rhythmic patterns. • Sing music representing American heritage.
Come Travel With Me	• Identify dynamic markings in music. • Read and perform rhythmic patterns that contain triplets. • Relate music to other subjects (poetry).
Frog Went A-Courtin'	• Perform music based on the pentatonic scale. • Use standard terminology to describe octave and unison. • Perform music that represents an American narrative folk song.
Guantanamera	• Perform Spanish diction with clarity and proper syllabic stress. • Perform music that represents the Cuban heritage. • Relate music to history, culture and literature.
Joshua! (Fit The Battle Of Jericho)	• Describe techniques used in creating an arrangement. • Perform music representing the African American spiritual.
Leave Her, Johnny	• Sing phrases expressively using staggered breathing. • Identify and describe the music terminology for dissonance. • Relate music to writing (poetry and short stories).
New River Train	• Identify standard music symbols for rhythm. • Sight-sing music. • Relate music to history.
On The Deep, Blue Sea	• Describe and perform chords in tune. • Sing expressively in a spirited style. • Read rhythms in cut time.
Pretty Saro	• Read music notation in 3/4 meter. • Write a pentatonic scale. • Perform music representing American folk music.
Santa Lucia	• Read and perform rhythmic patterns in 3/8 meter. • Sing expressively using rubato. • Perform music that represents the Neopolitan barcarole.
Sing To The Lord	• Distinguish between unison singing and part-singing. • Read and perform rhythmic patterns that contain dotted quarter notes. • Relate music to other subjects.
You Gentlemen Of England	• Perform expressively from memory. • Interpret music symbols referring to dynamics when performing. • Define musical symbols and writing techniques found in music.

STUDENT TEXT

The comprehensive student lessons are structured as follows:

- **FOCUS** ... tells the student the main concepts and skills addressed in the lesson. By having only a few main goals, students and teacher will keep focused on these objectives as work progresses.

- **VOCABULARY** ... gives the student an opportunity to build a musical vocabulary essential for clarity of thought in communicating about music to others.

- **LINKS TO LEARNING**

  Vocal ... allows the student to explore the melodic and vocal skills that are directly related to some aspect of the upcoming musical selection. Also includes melodic sight-singing examples.

  Theory ... builds rhythmic, theory and basic reading skills through exercises that are directly related to the musical selection about to be learned. Through sight-reading practice every day, students gain confidence and skills to become independent readers.

  Artistic Expression ... provides interpretive aspects of music making, such as phrasing, dynamics, stylistic performance practices, movement, and artistic expression through drama, writing and the visual arts. Through interest and active participation, the student is then led logically into the piece.

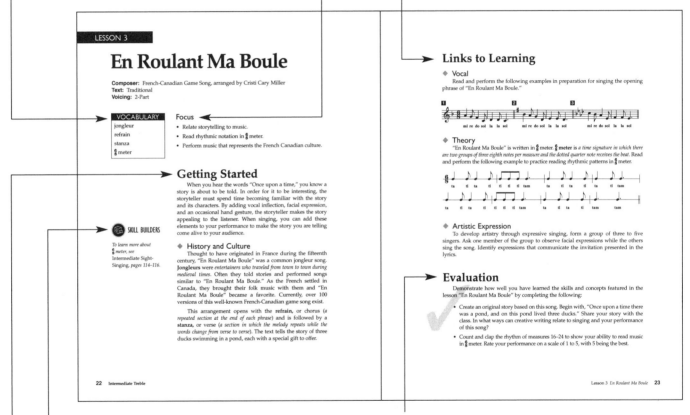

- **SIDEBAR REFERENCES** ... provide additional information about the lesson through:
  Skill Builders ... reference to *Sight-Singing* textbook
  Music & History ... reference to the History section
  Spotlights ... reference to a featured Spotlight page

- **GETTING STARTED**... provides a motivating introduction to the piece of music, related to the student's perspective. The History and Culture provides background information on the selection, the composer and/or the cultural context.

- **EVALUATION** ... gives the student ways to assess accomplishment, growth and needs, for both self and group. Through careful listening and constructive critique of their own work, they will gradually become more discriminating about the quality of performance and the impact of that performance on the audience.

Lessons

The student lessons, through which students systematically build musical skills and conceptual understanding, comprise the first twelve selections of the text. They are presented in three general categories: Beginning of the Year, Mid-Winter, and Concert/Festival.

Music & History

The Historical section of the text provides a survey of Western music history through exploration of the culture and music of the five overarching periods: Renaissance, Baroque, Classical, Romantic and Contemporary. Each period is addressed in the following ways:

- **Historical Narrative Lesson** . . . provides a brief, student-oriented historical context of the period through visual art, architecture, historical events, musical developments, artistic characteristics, musical personalities and listening selections.
- **Historical Listening Lesson** . . . provides one choral and one instrumental listening selection to give students an aural experience with the styles, sounds and forms of the period. Recordings are provided to aid student learning.

Choral Library

The Choral Library maintains the same comprehensive lesson format of the Lessons and comprises the final twelve selections of the text. The additional literature features multicultural selections, patriotic and seasonal selections, American folk music, African American spirituals, Broadway show tunes and light concert pieces.

Glossary

The glossary provides brief, accurate definitions of musical terms used in the text.

TEACHER WRAPAROUND EDITION

National Standards Connections

Experiencing Choral Music affords multiple opportunities to address the National Standards. Correlations among lesson content, extension activities and bottom-page activities are listed to make obvious the relationship between lesson activities and the standards.

Suggested Teaching Sequence

Each lesson is organized to follow a logical progression from Getting Started through Evaluation, while providing maximum flexibility of use for your individual situation. Each lesson is linked to one musical selection, and provides learning opportunities based on the inherent concepts and skills required to understand and perform the piece. The lessons of the Teacher Wraparound Edition are structured as follows.

- **Overview** . . . Gives the teacher a brief analysis of the music being taught, including composer, text, voicing, key, meter, form, style, accompaniment, programming ideas and vocal ranges for each voice part.
- **Objectives** . . . Two or three concrete, measurable objectives form the skeletal structure for the lesson, allowing an interconnected approach to lesson segments.
- **Vocabulary** . . . Vocabulary terms are those used during the lesson and music terms used in the music to build understanding and skills.
- **Links to Learning** . . . The Links to Learning of the lesson includes exercises that focus on vocal, theory and artistic expression elements of the upcoming song. It provides rhythm and vocal, as well as sight-singing exercises. They are designed to sequentially develop vocal and sight-singing skills, and lead directly into the upcoming piece. These exercises may all be done before the piece is introduced, or they may be presented cumulatively, one each day, and concurrent with developing understanding of the piece.
- **The Lesson Plan: Suggested Teaching Sequence** . . . The Suggested Teaching Sequence is divided into three section: Introduce, Rehearse, and Refine. At the end of each section, Progress Checkpoints are provided for quick informal assessment of the materials covered to that point. Introduce often refers to the Links to Learning exercises on the student page and provides meaningful ways to introduce a new song to students. Rehearse includes a list of recommended steps to teach the piece through a variety of teaching techniques. Refine puts it all together and prepares the students for performance of the piece. The Performance Tips provide teachers with the polishing nuances that transform the notes on the page into an expressive performance experience.

Informal Assessment, Student Self-Assessment, and Individual and Group Performance Evaluation

Informal Assessment is done by teacher observation during the lesson. Each objective is observable, and the text indicates the checkpoint for teacher assessment.

Student Self-Assessment is accomplished through student evaluation of their individual performance based on an established set of criteria.

Individual and Group Performance Evaluation requires the student to demonstrate a skill or understanding through individual or group evaluation. This is directly related to the Evaluation found in the student lesson. Individual and Group Performance Evaluation can be done by the teacher, student, peers or a combination thereof. Frequent audio- or videotaping is suggested as an effective means of evaluation. The tapes may be compiled into a portfolio that shows growth and developing understanding over time.

Bottom-Page Activities

Bottom-page activities in each lesson afford a plethora of background information, teaching strategies and enrichment opportunities.

- *Teacher 2 Teacher* provides a brief description of the main features of the lesson.
- *Enrichment activities* provide musical activities that go beyond the basic lesson including composition, improvisation, and so forth.
- *Extension activities* expand the lesson to the other arts or other disciplines.
- *Teaching strategies* reinforce concepts or skills presented in the lesson, or elaborate on classroom management techniques.
- *More about* boxes provide background historical, cultural, and/or biographical information.
- *Curriculum connections* provide strategies to help students build bridges between music and other disciplines.
- *Vocal development strategies* give detailed information about specific techniques that facilitate vocal production and style.
- *Music literacy strategies* help students expand their ability to read and analyze music.
- *Cultural connections* provide cultural information related to the lesson.
- *Connecting to the arts* boxes provide strategies to help students connect music to the other arts.
- *Community connections* provide activities that extend into the community.
- *Careers in music* boxes provide information about career opportunities in music.
- *Online* directs students and teachers to **music.glencoe.com**, the website for *Experiencing Choral Music*.

TEACHER RESOURCE BINDER

The *Teacher Resource Binder* contains teaching materials designed to reduce teacher preparation time and maximize students' learning. The following categories are provided to assist with meeting the individual needs and interests of your students.

- **Teaching Masters.** The *Teaching Masters* support, extend and enhance the musical concepts and skills presented in the text lessons. Included are strategied focusing on composing, arranging, evaluating, analyzing, writing, multi-arts, culture and language pronunciation guides.
- **Evaluation Masters.** The *Evaluation Masters* provide performance assessment criteria, rubrics and other pages to help teachers and students with individual group, and ensemble assessment.
- **Music & History.** The *Music & History Masters* include full-color overhead transparencies of the visual art pieces introduced in each of the historical sections. They also include characteristics of the period, biographies of composers and other teaching strategies.
- **Vocal Development Masters.** The *Vocal Development Masters* provide important information about the voice. Included are numerous warm-up exercises that may be used throughout the year. Each exercise is recorded and included on the *Sight-Singing CD*.
- **Skill Builders Masters.** The *Skill Builders Masters* reinforce the development of fundamental skills, knowledge and understanding in areas such as rhythm, notation, music symbols, conducting patterns, improvisation, Kodály hand signs, time signatures and meter.
- **Sight-Singing Masters.** The *Sight-Singing Masters* are directly correlated to the *Sight-Singing* textbooks. They provide reproducible evaluation activity sheets for assessment and review.
- **Kodály, Dalcroze, Interdisciplinary.** Teaching strategies with a focus on Kodály, Dalcroze and Interdisciplinary are presented in this section.
- **Reference Resources.** The *Reference Resource Masters* serve as a resource bank for the teacher and provides a library of resource materials useful in supporting instruction.
- **Listening Selections CD.** *Listening Selections CD* provides full recordings of the vocal and instrumental historical listening lessons from the student text.
- **Sight-Singing CD.** The *Sight-Singing CD* provides a piano accompaniment track for practice songs and sight-singing exercises found in the student text of *Experiencing Choral Music: Sight-Singing*. The CD also includes the accompaniment track to the vocal warm-up exercises in the Vocal Development section.

EFFECTIVE TEACHING CHECKLIST

Teaching can be a rewarding as well as a challenging experience. The following is a compilation of suggestions and tips from experienced teachers. Review this list often.

Preparation

- Good planning leads to a successful rehearsal.
- Establish high expectations from the start – students want to succeed.
- Establish a routine and basic standards of behavior – and stick to it!
- Follow your planned routine every rehearsal (e.g. opening cue that rehearsal has begun, warm-up, sight-reading, repertoire, evaluation). Younger choirs in particular respond well to structure in a rehearsal.
- Plan, plan, plan.
- Develop long-range planning (the entire year's goals and activities, the semester, the month) and short-range planning (weekly plans and the daily lesson as they fit within the entire year's goals).
- Vary teaching strategies: modeling, peer coaching, large group, small group, cooperative learning, individual instruction, student conductors, independent practice.
- Study the score well. Anticipate problem areas.
- Be able to sing any one part while playing another.
- Know the vocal ranges of each member of the chorus.
- Select appropriate music to fit those vocal ranges.
- Remember: out-of-range results in out-of-tune singing.
- Select music of appropriate difficulty for the group.
- Plan evaluation techniques in advance.
- Have all necessary supplies and equipment ready (music in folders or ready to pass out, tapes cued, director's folder handy, recording equipment set, etc.) before the lesson begins.
- Plan to make beautiful music at least once during every rehearsal.

Presentation

- Begin each lesson with singing rather than talking.
- Make all parts of the lesson musical—including warm-ups and sight-reading.
- Rehearse a cappella. Use the piano as little as possible.
- Remember: Delivering information is not necessarily teaching.
- Display a positive attitude.
- Communicate effectively and concisely.
- Enthusiasm is essential.
- Make learning an enjoyable experience.
- Respect legitimate effort on the part of every student.
- Be the best musician you can be.
- Laugh often.

Pacing

- Be 30 seconds mentally ahead of the class at all times.
- Know where the lesson is going before it happens.
- Vary activities and standing/sitting positions.
- Plan a smooth transition from one activity to the next.
- Avoid "lag" time.
- If a "teachable" moment occurs, make the most of it.
- Avoid belaboring any one exercise, phrase, or activity—come back to it at another time.
- Always give students a reason for repeating a section.
- Provide at least one successful musical experience in every rehearsal.

Evaluation

- Assess student learning in every lesson (formally or informally).
- Vary the assessment activities.
- Consider evaluating individual as well as group effort.
- Tape the rehearsals often (audio and/or video).
- Study the rehearsal tapes: (1) to discover where overlooked errors occur, (2) to assist in planning the next rehearsal, or (3) to share findings with the students.
- Provide students with opportunities to evaluate themselves.
- Teach critical listening to the students by asking specific students or a group of students to listen for a specific thing (balance of parts in the polyphonic section, a correct uniform vowel sound on a particular word or words, rise and fall of phrase, and so forth).
- Constantly evaluate what's really happening. (We often hear what we want to hear!)
- Listen, listen, listen.

TEACHER WRAPAROUND EDITION
INTERMEDIATE

Experiencing Choral Music

TENOR/BASS

Developed by

HAL•LEONARD® CORPORATION

Mc Graw Hill **Glencoe**

New York, New York   Columbus, Ohio   Chicago, Illinois   Peoria, Illinois   Woodland Hills, California

The portions of the National Standards for Music Education included here are reprinted from *National Standards for Arts Education* with permission from MENC–The National Association for Music Education. All rights reserved. Copyright © 1994 by MENC. The complete National Standards and additional materials relating to the Standards are available from MENC, 1806 Robert Fulton Drive, Reston, VA 20191 (telephone 800-336-3768).

A portion of the sales of this material goes to support music education programs through programs of MENC–The National Association for Music Education.

 **Glencoe**

The **McGraw·Hill** Companies

Printed in the United States of America.

Send all inquiries to:
Glencoe/McGraw-Hill
21600 Oxnard Street, Suite 500
Woodland Hills, CA 91367

ISBN 0-07-861114-8 (Student Edition)
ISBN 0-07-861115-6 (Teacher Wraparound Edition)

1 2 3 4 5 6 7 8 9   045   09 08 07 06 05 04

Credits

LEAD AUTHORS

Emily Crocker
Vice President of Choral Publications
Hal Leonard Corporation, Milwaukee, Wisconsin
Founder and Artistic Director, Milwaukee Children's Choir

Michael Jothen
Professor of Music, Program Director of Graduate Music Education
Chairperson of Music Education
Towson University, Towson, Maryland

Jan Juneau
Choral Director
Klein Collins High School
Spring, Texas

Henry H. Leck
Associate Professor and Director of Choral Activities
Butler University, Indianapolis, Indiana
Founder and Artistic Director, Indianapolis Children's Choir

Michael O'Hern
Choral Director
Lake Highlands High School
Richardson, Texas

Audrey Snyder
Composer
Eugene, Oregon

Mollie Tower
Coordinator of Choral and General Music, K-12, Retired
Austin, Texas

AUTHORS

Anne Denbow
Voice Instructor, Professional Singer/Actress
Director of Music, Holy Cross Episcopal Church
Simpsonville, South Carolina

Rollo A. Dilworth
Director of Choral Activities and Music
   Education
North Park University, Chicago, Illinois

Deidre Douglas
Choral Director
Labay Junior High, Katy, Texas

Ruth E. Dwyer
Associate Director and Director of Education
Indianapolis Children's Choir
Indianapolis, Indiana

Norma Freeman
Choral Director
Saline High School, Saline, Michigan

Cynthia I. Gonzales
Music Theorist
Greenville, South Carolina

Michael Mendoza
Professor of Choral Activities
New Jersey State University
Trenton, New Jersey

Thomas Parente
Associate Professor
Westminster Choir College of Rider University
Princeton, New Jersey

Barry Talley
Director of Fine Arts and Choral Director
Deer Park ISD, Deer Park, Texas

CONTRIBUTING AUTHORS

Debbie Daniel
Choral Director, Webb Middle School
Garland, Texas

Roger Emerson
Composer/Arranger
Mount Shasta, California

Kari Gilbertson
Choral Director, Forest Meadow Junior High
Richardson, Texas

Tim McDonald
Creative Director, Music Theatre International
New York, New York

Christopher W. Peterson
Assistant Professor of Music Education (Choral)
University of Wisconsin-Milwaukee
Milwaukee, Wisconsin

Kirby Shaw
Composer/Arranger
Ashland, Oregon

Stephen Zegree
Professor of Music
Western Michigan State University
Kalamazoo, Michigan

EDITORIAL

Linda Rann
Senior Editor
Hal Leonard Corporation
Milwaukee, Wisconsin

Stacey Nordmeyer
Choral Editor
Hal Leonard Corporation
Milwaukee, Wisconsin

Table of Contents

Introductory Materials . . . . i–viii

Lessons

1 **This Land Is Your Land • TB** 2
   Woody Guthrie, arranged by Donald Moore

   Spotlight On Posture 13

2 **Be Cool • Unison Voices** 14
   Bob Chilcott

   Spotlight On Arranging 21

3 **Red River Valley • TB/TTB** 22
   Traditional American Cowboy Song,
   arranged by Emily Crocker

4 **Codfish Shanty • TB** 26
   Traditional Sea Chantey, arranged by Vijay Singh

5 **Festival Procession • TB** 34
   Notre Dame Conductus, arranged by Emily Crocker

6 **Soldier's Hallelujah • TB** 42
   Vijay Singh

7 **Light The Candles Of Hanukkah • TB** 48
   George L. O. Strid

8 **The Shepherd's Spiritual • TB** 56
   American Spiritual, arranged by Donald Moore

   Spotlight On Vowels 65

9 **Now Is The Month Of Maying • TTB** 66
   Thomas Morley, arranged by Sherri Porterfield

10 **Der Herr segne euch • TB** 74
   Johann Sebastian Bach, arranged by Barry Talley

11   **Ave Verum Corpus • TTB** 86
        Wolfgang Amadeus Mozart, arranged by Joyce Eilers

12   **Da unten im Tale • TB** 94
        Johannes Brahms, arranged by Barry Talley

Music & History

Renaissance Period 99

Baroque Period 100

Classical Period 104

Romantic Period 112

Contemporary Period 116

Spotlight On Diction 120

Choral Library

The Battle Cry Of Freedom • TB 122
    George Frederick Root, arranged by Patti DeWitt

Spotlight On Careers In Music 127

Come Travel With Me • TTB 128
    Scott Farthing

Spotlight On Concert Etiquette 139

Frog Went A-Courtin' • TB 140
    Traditional Folk Song, arranged by Audrey Snyder

Guantanamera • TB 152
    Cuban Folk Song, arranged by John Higgins

Joshua! (Fit The Battle Of Jericho) • TTB 158
    Traditional Spiritual, arranged by Kirby Shaw

Spotlight On Breath Management 169

Leave Her, Johnny • TB/TTB 170
    Traditional Sea Chantey, arranged by Emily Crocker

New River Train • TB 174
    American Spiritual, arranged by Donald Moore

Spotlight On Improvisation 183

On The Deep, Blue Sea • TTB 184
    Mary Donnelly, arranged by George L.O. Strid

Spotlight On Changing Voice 197

Pretty Saro • TTB 198
    American Folk Song, arranged by Jennifer B. Scoggin

Santa Lucia • TB 206
    Teodoro Cottrau, arranged by Henry Leck

Sing To The Lord • TTB 212
    Emily Crocker

Spotlight On Vocal Production 217

You Gentlemen Of England • TB 218
    Time of Elizabeth, arranged by Barry Talley

Glossary 225

Classified Index 239

Index of Songs and Spotlights 241

TO THE STUDENT

Welcome to choir!

By singing in the choir, you have chosen to be a part of an exciting and rewarding adventure. The benefits of being in choir are many. Basically, singing is fun. It provides an expressive way of sharing your feelings and emotions. Through choir, you will have friends that share a common interest with you. You will experience the joy of making beautiful music together. Choir provides the opportunity to develop your interpersonal skills. It takes teamwork and cooperation to sing together, and you must learn how to work with others. As you critique your individual and group performances, you can improve your ability to analyze and communicate your thoughts clearly.

Even if you do not pursue a music career, music can be an important part of your life. There are many avocational opportunities in music. **Avocational** means *not related to a job or career*. Singing as a hobby can provide you with personal enjoyment, enrich your life, and teach you life skills. Singing is something you can do for the rest of your life.

In this course, you will be presented with the basic skills of vocal production and music literacy. You will be exposed to songs from different cultures, songs in many different styles and languages, and songs from various historical periods. You will discover connections between music and the other arts. Guidelines for becoming a better singer and choir member include:

- Come to class prepared to learn.
- Respect the efforts of others.
- Work daily to improve your sight-singing skills.
- Sing expressively at all times.
- Have fun singing.

This book was written to provide you with a meaningful choral experience. Take advantage of the knowledge and opportunities offered here. Your exciting adventure of experiencing choral music is about to begin!

Lessons

Lessons for the Beginning of the Year

1   This Land Is Your Land 2

2   Be Cool 14

3   Red River Valley 22

4   Codfish Shanty 26

Lessons for Mid-Winter

5   Festival Procession 34

6   Soldier's Hallelujah 42

7   Light The Candles Of Hanukkah 48

8   The Shepherd's Spiritual 56

Lessons for Concert/Festival

9   Now Is The Month Of Maying 66

10 Der Herr segne euch 74

11 Ave Verum Corpus 86

12 Da unten im Tale 94

This Land Is Your Land

OVERVIEW

Composer: Woody Guthrie, arranged by Donald Moore

Text: Woodie Guthrie

Voicing: TB

Key: G major

Meter: Cut Time

Form: AA'AA'BACoda

Style: Patriotic

Accompaniment: Piano

Programming: Thematic Programming, Concert Closer, Community Concert

Vocal Ranges:

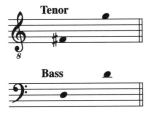

OBJECTIVES

After completing this lesson, students will be able to:

• Perform expressively from notation.

• Perform independently with accurate rhythm.

• Perform music of American heritage.

VOCABULARY

Have students review vocabulary in student lesson. Introduce terms found in the music. A complete glossary of terms is found on page 226 of the student book.

LESSON 1

This Land Is Your Land

Composer: Woody Guthrie, arranged by Donald Moore

Text: Woody Guthrie

Voicing: TB

VOCABULARY

arrangement

major tonality

cut time

SPOTLIGHT

To learn more about arranging, see page 21.

Focus

• Sing a melody expressively in G major tonality.

• Read and perform rhythmic patterns in cut time.

• Perform music representing American heritage.

Getting Started

Here are some of America's spectacular natural wonders. In which states are they located?

The Grand Canyon	The Great Smoky Mountains
The Everglades	Mount McKinley
Old Faithful	Niagara Falls

"This Land Is Your Land" is a tribute to the natural beauty of America. It's easy to show your pride, admiration and appreciation of our country as you perform this popular song.

◆ History and Culture

Woody Guthrie (1912–1967), who composed "This Land Is Your Land" in 1940, is considered one of the most influential songwriters of the twentieth century. He wrote songs about what he saw and experienced as he traveled across America from the 1930s to the 1950s. Besides writing prose, poetry and children's songs, Guthrie wrote songs of social, political and spiritual justice and injustice. Born in Oklahoma, he spent much of his adult life in California and New York.

"This Land Is Your Land" is an example of a choral **arrangement,** or *a piece of music in which a composer takes an existing song and adds extra features or makes changes in some way.* Contemporary composer Donald Moore uses several phrases of "America The Beautiful" to complement Guthrie's original melody.

2 Intermediate Tenor/Bass

RESOURCES

Beginning Sight-Singing

Intermediate Sight-Singing

Sight-Singing in G Major, pages 82–85, 89–90

Reading Rhythms in 2/2 Meter and Cut Time, page 140

Beat, Quarter Note/Rest, Half Note/Rest, pages 1–9

Teacher Resource Binder

Evaluation Master 1, *Accuracy in Performance*

Skill Builder 12, *Constructing Major Scales*

Skill Builder 22, *Reading Ties and Slurs*

Reference 16, *My Music Dictionary*

For additional resources, see the TRB Table of Contents.

Links to Learning

◆ **Vocal**

Perform the following example to establish G **major tonality** *(a song that is based on a major scale with* do *as its keynote, or hometone)*. Can you feel the G major tonality and the notes leading you to the pitch *do*?

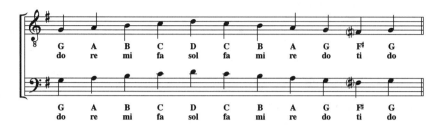

	G	A	B	C	D	C	B	A	G	F♯	G
	do	re	mi	fa	sol	fa	mi	re	do	ti	do

	G	A	B	C	D	C	B	A	G	F♯	G
	do	re	mi	fa	sol	fa	mi	re	do	ti	do

◆ **Theory**

This arrangement is written in **cut time (¢),** or *the time signature in which there are two beats per measure and the half note receives the beat.* Perform the following example by having one group chant the steady beat "1, 2, 1, 2," while the other group claps the rhythm. Switch roles.

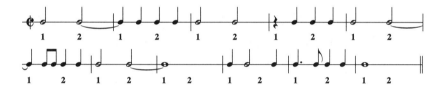

Evaluation

Demonstrate how well you have learned the skills and concepts featured in the lesson "This Land Is Your Land."

• Sing your voice part expressively in measures 4–11 on the correct solfège syllables. Ask a classmate to check for accuracy.

• With one singer on each part, chant the words in rhythm in measures 69–85, keeping a steady beat in cut time. How well did you do?

LINKS TO LEARNING

Vocal

The Vocal section is designed to prepare students to sing in the tonality of G major.

Have students:

• Sing the Vocal exercise using letter names.

• Sing the Vocal exercise using solfège syllables.

Theory

The Theory section is designed to prepare students to:

• Sing various rhythmic patterns in cut time.

• Maintain a steady beat while performing.

Have students:

• Divide into two equal groups. One group will chant a steady beat ("1, 2, 1, 2") while the other group claps the written rhythms.

• Switch roles so that each group has an opportunity to experience both rhythms.

RESOURCES

Intermediate Tenor/Bass Rehearsal/Performance CD

CD 1:1 Voices

CD 1:2 Accompaniment Only

CD 3:1 Vocal Practice Track—Tenor

CD 4:1 Vocal Practice Track—Bass

National Standards

1. Singing, alone and with others, a varied repertoire of music. **(b, c)**

5. Reading and notating music. **(b)**

LESSON PLAN

Suggested Teaching Sequence and Performance Tips

1. Introduce

Direct students to:

- Read and discuss the information found in the Getting Started section on page 2.
- Practice singing in the tonality of G major as shown in the Vocal section on page 3. Relate the ascending first four pitches of the exercise *(do, re, mi, fa)* to the opening phrase of the piece (measures 4–5).
- Practice performing rhythmic patterns in cut time as shown in the Theory section on page 3. Be mindful of the notes that are tied across the barline. Relate to rhythm patterns found in the opening section of the piece.

Progress Checkpoints

Observe students' progress in:

✓ Singing in the tonality of G major.

✓ Singing rhythmic patterns in cut time.

This Land Is Your Land

For TB and Piano

Arranged by
DONALD MOORE (ASCAP)

Words and Music by WOODY GUTHRIE (1912–1967)
Quoting America The Beautiful
Music by SAMUEL WARD (1848–1903)
Words by KATHARINE LEE BATES (1859–1929)

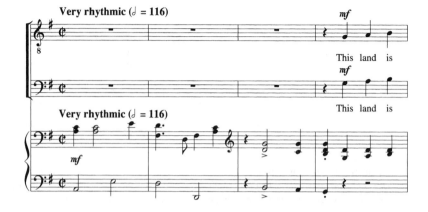

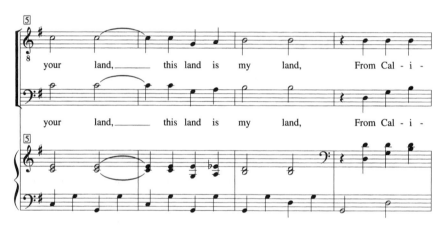

4   Intermediate Tenor/Bass

TEACHER 2 TEACHER

"This Land Is Your Land" serves as a wonderful piece to teach students about composer Woodie Guthrie and the American popular folk tradition. This particular arrangement will also expose students to singing in cut time and sustaining tied rhythms across the barline. Also in this arrangement, singers will explore a portion of "America The Beautiful."

2. Rehearse

Direct the students to:

- Label measures 4–19 as "Chorus." Sight-sing this passage on a neutral syllable. Notice where the pitches move by step and when they move by a skip or a leap. When pitches are secure, add text and practice.

- Label measures 21–35 as "Verses." Sight-sing this section with text with the understanding that the notes are similar to that of the "Chorus."

- Label measures 36–51 as "Chorus." Sight-sing this passage. Notice that the melody in the Bass voice part is the same as before. It is the Tenor voice part that now sings harmony.

TEACHING STRATEGY

2/2 Meter (Cut Time)

To help familiarize students with the half-note pulse, place eight "beat bars" (horizontal line each of the same length) on the board, prefaced by a cut time meter signature. Have students:

- Pat once for each beat bar as you point.
- Place a half note above each beat bar, and them clap once on each beat as you point.
- Substitute two quarter notes for some of the half notes and clap as you point.
- Substitute other rhythms from the piece into the rhythm, and then clap it.
- Continue to play with the rhythms in cut time until they become familiar.

- Measures 53–68 contain an arrangement of "America the Beautiful." Sight-sing this section. Notice that both Tenor and Bass voice parts sing the melody in unison and divide on the word "his" in measure 58. The Bass part continues with the melody.

- Label measures 69–97 as "Chorus." Sight-sing this passage with text. As before, the Bass voice part sings the melody. The Tenor part sings new material in the form of a descant. In the final two measures of the piece, it may be necessary to rehearse parts separately in order to secure the three-part harmony.

Progress Checkpoints

Observe students' progress in:

✓ Singing the correct pitches, especially where the Tenor and Bass parts are not in unison.

✓ Singing rhythms accurately, especially in places where notes are tied across the barline.

MORE ABOUT

Arranger Donald Moore

Donald Moore is the secondary choral director at North Olmsted Middle School in North Olmsted, Ohio. He received his B.M. and M.A. from Kent State University and did additional work at Ohio and Ashland Universities. Mr. Moore has over 400 music publications, including eight music education books, music collections, organ and piano works, cantatas and choral music. He is a member of the MENC, AGO, NEA, ACDA and OMEA organizations. From 1989–1998, Mr. Moore received the ASCAP Standard Composers Award.

TEACHING STRATEGY

Sight-Singing Intervals

Have students practice singing in the tonality of G major as indicated in the Vocal section until all pitches can be securely sung in sequence. Vary the exercise by having students sing every other note in the sequence, sometimes using pitch names, and sometimes using solfège syllables. The resulting pattern is a G major arpeggio. Point to various pitches on the scale and ask the students to sing as you point. Begin with step-wise motion, and gradually increase the difficulty level by initiating skips and leaps. Specifically, use this exercise to reinforce intervals that will be found in the piece.

3. Refine

Direct the students to:

- Go back to the beginning of the piece. Sing the entire song using solfège syllables. For the lowered sixth (E♭) that occurs in the Tenor part (measures 38 and 46), use the solfège syllable *"le"* (pronounced "lay").
- Carefully examine all of the dynamic markings in the score. Make sure that all markings are observed during performance.
- Review all pitches to make certain that intonation is accurate.
- Chant the text of the piece in rhythm. Be certain that all consonants are crisp and that all vowels are tall and unified. As you chant the text, make sure that all attacks and releases are together.
- Perform the piece with pitches and text, keeping in mind all of the concepts that were explored during the refining process.

Progress Checkpoints

Observe students' progress in:

✓ Performing all dynamic markings as written in the score.

✓ Singing all of the pitches correctly.

✓ Unifying all consonants, vowels, attacks, and releases.

ASSESSMENT

Informal Assessment

In this lesson, students showed the ability to:

- Sing expressively in the tonality of G major.
- Read and perform rhythmic patterns in cut time.
- Perform music representing American heritage.

Student Self-Assessment

Have students evaluate their individual performances based on the following:

- Phrasing
- Diction
- Accurate Pitches
- Accurate Rhythms
- Correct Part-Singing

Have each student rate his/her performance of this song in the areas above on a scale of 1–5, 5 being the best.

8   Intermediate Tenor/Bass

MORE ABOUT

Composing from Experience

Like many composers, Woodie Guthrie often wrote songs based upon his personal experiences. In the mid-1930s, Guthrie migrated west to California from his hometown—as did many poor farmers and unemployed workers—in search of work and a better life. Upon arriving in California, Guthrie experienced much hatred and discrimination from those who did not welcome outsiders. Such challenging experiences inspired Guthrie to write songs such as "I Ain't Got No Home" and "Goin' Down The Road Feelin' Bad."

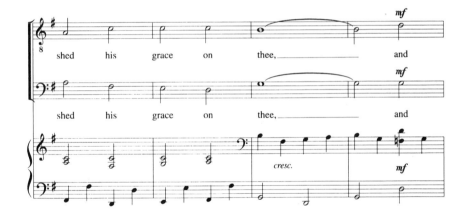

TEACHING STATEGY

Expressive Elements and Phrasing

To help students expand their music literacy, have them:

- Read the text of "This Land Is Your Land" and "America The Beautiful," identifying where the natural phrase breaks are and where they should breathe.
- Look through the notation, finding all dynamic and tempo markings.
- Sing through the phrases, following the dynamic and tempo markings.
- Contrast the longer rhythms *(half notes and whole notes)* against the shorter rhythms *(quarter notes and eighth notes)* in the piece. Decide how these different rhythms will be treated with respect to the phrase and the text.

ENRICHMENT

Small Ensemble Performances

Have students:

1. Prepare solos and small ensembles for performance or competition.

2. Interpret music symbols and terms referring to dynamics, tempo and articulation during the performance.

3. Evaluate the quality of the performance using standard termination.

MORE ABOUT

Songs as Social Commentary

Woodie Guthrie also composed songs that commented on political and social concerns. His song lyrics could speak out against corruption or injustice, sometimes in an angry tone, and sometimes in a humorous one. This type of songwriting technique was prevalent in musical styles that preceded Guthrie's rise to prominence (such as the spiritual and the blues), and certainly there are musical styles of today that embody this technique (including country-western and rap).

EXTENSION

Advanced Phrasing Technique

As your students mature musically, try some advanced phrasing techniques. For example, in this piece, many of the tied notes have the stressed part of the word on the shorter note of the tie and the unstressed part with a longer note. It is the unstressed part of the word that will require a more sensitive phrasing technique. Tell the students to perform the same method of stress and unstressed syllables, but this time after the decrescendo of the unstressed syllable, add a crescendo. Isolate words like "forest," "waters," "walking" with this concept. Once the students have mastered speaking these words, put them back in the song and sing them. Ask the students to decide how this technique affects the performance of the phrase.

MORE ABOUT

America, the Beautiful

Katharine Lee Bates (1859–1929) wrote the words to "America The Beautiful" in its original version in 1893. She wrote a second version in 1904 and a final version in 1913. Similar to Guthrie, Bates was inspired to write this piece through personal experience. Here is her personal testimony: "One day some of the other teachers and I decided to go on a trip to 14,000-foot Pikes Peak. We hired a prairie wagon. Near the top we had to leave the wagon and go the rest of the way on mules. I was very tired. But when I saw the view, I felt great joy. All the wonder of America seemed displayed there, with sea-like expanse."

Music, Society and Culture

Have students perform additional songs representing diverse cultures, including American and Texas heritage. Go to **music.glencoe.com**, the Web site for Glencoe's choral music programs, for additional music selections students can perform.

Additional National Standards

The following National Standards are addressed through the Assessment, Extension, Enrichment, and bottom-page activities:

6. Listening to, analyzing and describing music. **(c)**

7. Responding to and evaluating musical performances. **(a, b)**

9. Understanding music in relation to history and culture. **(a, b)**

SPOTLIGHT

Posture

Posture is important for good singing. By having the body properly aligned, you are able to breathe correctly so that you have sufficient breath support needed to sing more expressively and for longer periods of time.

To experience, explore and establish proper posture for singing, try the following:

Standing

- Pretend someone is gently pulling up on a thread attached to the top of your head.
- Let out all of your air like a deflating balloon.
- Raise your arms up over your head.
- Take in a deep breath as if you were sipping through a straw.
- Slowly lower your arms down to your sides.
- Let all your air out on a breathy "pah," keeping your chest high.
- Both feet on floor, shoulder-width apart.
- Chest high, shoulders relaxed.
- Neck relaxed, head straight.

Sitting

- Sit on the edge of a chair with your feet flat on the floor while keeping your chest lifted.
- Hold your music with one hand and turn pages with the other.
- Always hold the music up so you can easily see the director and your music.

Spotlight *Posture* **13**

RESOURCES

Teacher Resource Binder

Vocal Development 13, *Posture and Breathing*
Reference 16, *My Music Dictionary*

National Standards

1. Singing, alone and with others. **(b)**

POSTURE

Objectives

- Demonstrate basic performance techniques including proper singing posture.

Suggested Teaching Sequence

Direct students to:

- Read the Spotlight On Posture on student page 13 and identify the importance of proper posture in singing.
- Perform the exercise for standing posture as presented on page 13.
- Perform the exercise for sitting posture as presented on page 13.
- Compare the concept of proper posture to basic performance techniques and the effect posture has on breath support, tone quality and overall stage presence.

Progress Checkpoints

Observe students' progress in:

- ✓ Their ability to stand in correct singing posture.
- ✓ Their ability to sit using correct singing posture.
- ✓ Their ability to explain the importance of proper posture in singing.

Be Cool

OVERVIEW

Composer: Bob Chilcott
(b. 1955)

Text: Bob Chilcott

Voicing: Unison

Key: D minor

Meter: 4/4

Form: Intro, ABC, Interlude, ABC, Coda

Style: Jazz

Accompaniment: Piano

Programming: Small Ensemble, School Assembly, Community Concert, Spring Concert

Vocal Ranges:

Tenor/Bass*

* Sing in appropriate octave

OBJECTIVES

After completing this lesson, students will be able to:

- Use standard terminology to describe in detail music notation.
- Perform independently with accurate rhythm.
- Perform a varied repertoire representing styles from diverse cultures.

VOCABULARY

Have students review vocabulary in student lesson. Introduce terms found in the music. A complete glossary of terms is found on page 226 of the student book.

Be Cool

Composer: Bob Chilcott (b. 1955)
Text: Bob Chilcott
Voicing: Unison

VOCABULARY

Jazz

Contemporary period

accidental

flat

natural

MUSIC & HISTORY

To learn more about the Contemporary period, see page 114.

Focus

- Identify and perform musical symbols (accidentals) found in music.
- Identify and perform swing-style rhythms.
- Perform music representing cool jazz style.

Getting Started

- In the past one hundred years, the earth has warmed by 1°F. Scientists predict that the average global temperature may increase by 2–6°F over the next hundred years.

This is not cool!

- Little changes in the climate can result in big changes for all people on Earth. These changes can affect the level of the oceans, the land we use for crops, the air we breathe and the water we drink.

This is not cool!

- We can make big differences in little ways! We can turn off the lights and save electricity. We can recycle bottles and cans. We can plant trees. We can ride our bikes or walk.

Now this is cool!

◆ History and Culture

The song "Be Cool" is a cool way to remind your audience about global warming. **Jazz** is *a popular style of music characterized by strong meter, improvisation and syncopated rhythms* that was developed during the **Contemporary period** *(1900–present)*. Cool jazz emerged in the 1950s as a reaction to a complex, improvised jazz style of the 1940s called bebop. "Be Cool" is written in a cool jazz style that uses a less complicated melody and rhythm than bebop. You will astound your audience with your cool sounds of vocal jazz.

Now this is cool!

14 Intermediate Tenor/Bass

RESOURCES

Intermediate Sight-Singing

Sight Singing in D Minor, pages 63–64, 78–80

Reading Rhythms in 4/4 Meter, pages 2–6

Reading Tied Notes, pages 32, 44

Reading Triplets and Duplets, pages 135–136

Teacher Resource Binder

Teaching Master 1, *Cool Jazz and "Be Cool"*

Evaluation Master 2, *Analyzing Pitch Accuracy*

Skill Builder 30, *Solfège Hand Signs*

Music and History 23, *Robert Chilcott, a "Contemporary" Composer*

For additional resources, see TRB Table of Contents.

Links to Learning

◆ **Vocal**

An **accidental** is *any sharp, flat or natural that is not included in the key signature of the piece.* A **flat** (♭) is *a symbol that lowers the pitch of a given note one half step,* and a **natural** (♮) is *a symbol that cancels a previous sharp or flat.* Read and perform the following example to hear and sing the difference between *mi* and *me*.

◆ **Artistic Expression**

Perform "Be Cool" in a cool jazz style by treating the dotted rhythmic patterns like a swing triplet. To prepare to do this, first chant the traditional triplet pattern (example 1). Then, chant the swing eighth pattern (example 2). Finally, the dotted eighth and sixteenth note patterns found in "Be Cool" should be performed in the swing eighth pattern (example 3).

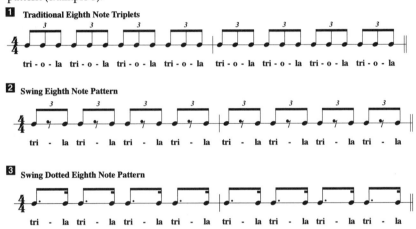

Evaluation

Demonstrate how well you have learned the skills and concepts featured in the lesson "Be Cool" by completing the following:

- Locate three examples of accidentals in the music. How did they alter the pitch?
- Sing measures 4–19 to demonstrate the difference between the pitches *mi* and *me*. Can you sing both pitches in tune?
- Perform measures 21–22 to demonstrate your ability to sing swing-style rhythms. Evaluate how well you did.

RESOURCES

Intermediate Tenor/Bass Rehearsal/Performance CD	National Standards
CD 1:3 Voices **CD 1:4** Accompaniment Only **CD 3:2** Vocal Practice Track—Unison	1. Singing, alone and with others, a varied repertoire of music. **(b, c)** 6. Listening to, analyzing, and describing music. **(c)**

LINKS TO LEARNING

Vocal

The Vocal section is designed to prepare students to practice the minor tonality of the piece, including accidentals.

Have students sing the Vocal exercise using solfège syllables.

Artistic Expression

The Artistic Expression section is designed to prepare students to practice reading and performing swing rhythms.

Have students:

- Practice each exercise separately and then one after another without stopping.
- Discover that example 2 and example 3 are performed exactly the same way.

LESSON PLAN

Suggested Teaching Sequence and Performance Tips

1. Introduce

Direct students to:

- Read and discuss the information found in the Getting Started section on page 14.
- Practice the rhythmic examples found in the Artistic Expression section on page 15. Discuss swing rhythms as contrasted to even, or straight rhythms.
- Listen to the CD recording of "Be Cool" and identify if the rhythms are more even or swing *(swing)*.
- Practice the rhythmic patterns again and listen to the CD recording once more.

Progress Checkpoints

Observe students' progress in:

✓ Their ability to perform "swing" rhythms.

✓ Their ability to differentiate between "swing" and straight rhythms.

For Peter Coulianos and the New York Children's Chorus

Be Cool

from *Green Songs*

For Unison Voices and Piano

Words and Music by
BOB CHILCOTT

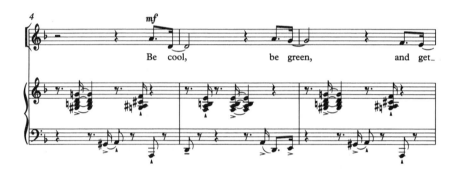

16 Intermediate Tenor/Bass

TEACHER 2 TEACHER

A "cool" performance of this piece can be enhanced by helping students to exhibit an "aloof, removed, distant " stage presence. The use of theatrical "role-playing" scenarios in rehearsal can assist in this process.

not al - ways seen.___ Be cool,___

be kind,___ get some peace of mind,___

and leave___ a bet - ter world be - hind.

Look here, look_ there,

Lesson 2 *Be Cool* **17**

2. Rehearse

Direct students to:

- Practice singing the vocal exercise in the Vocal section on page 15. *(Young tenors may have to leave out pitches or even sections of "Be Cool" which are out of their range. You may also consider adding the upper octave to out-of-range pitches. Practice and decide how to best adapt the ranges to your group.)*

- Listen to the CD and begin to read and sing individual swing rhythms using the score.

- Discuss the form and organization of "Be Cool." Label measures 4–11 as section A. Read and sing this section. Practice as needed, working for stylistic rhythmic treatment and pitch accuracy.

- Listen to measures12–20 and discuss how the music changes *(some melodic material pitched higher, some rhythmic changes)*. Identify this music as section B.

- Read and sing section B with and without the CD. You may need to listen and perform several times in order to capture the style.

- Describe the challenges found in section B *(accidentals, pitch and range)*. Focus on tuning accidentals and accuracy of pitch.

- Perform sections A and B unaccompanied, using the CD and the CD performance track to secure the voice part. Isolate and practice counting rests and singing rhythmic patterns accurately.

TEACHING STRATEGY

Audience Etiquette

Discuss with students different concert settings (rock, classical, pep band, school concert, church choir, etc.). What changes would be present in the audience as they listened to the music? How would the performers change their presence on the stage?

To assess students, have them sing "Be Cool" in small groups while other members of the class observe. Copy and distribute the Resource Master 5, *Concert Etiquette Quiz* (TRB) to assist observers in discussing audience expectations in live and video settings as well as the stage "coolness" of the performers.

- Analyze and then identify sections A and B later in the music *(measures 31–38 and measures 39–47)*.

- Sing sections A and B with the accompaniment CD. Emphasize accuracy in performing the swing rhythm and pitch.

- Identify section C *(measures 21–28 and 48–55)*.

- Read and sing section C in a swing style and with pitch accuracy. Work the head voice to assure pitch accuracy in changed voices. Encourage unchanged voices to lead here, as this section is in their best range.

- Discuss the Coda, noting how the style is a fade-out, the music simply fading away.

Practice counting and singing the Coda section.

- Sing "Be Cool" with the accompaniment CD.

Progress Checkpoints

Observe students' progress in:

✓ Singing chromatic accidentals in tune.

✓ Maintaining a "swing" style throughout.

✓ Adapting to vocal range as needed.

18   Intermediate Tenor/Bass

MORE ABOUT...

Chromatics

The English word *chromatic* derives from the Greek word *khroma*, meaning color. In music, besides facilitating the functional harmonic aspects of enabling harmonic changes, chromatics may be used to "color" various scale tones.

In certain musical styles such as jazz and popular, performers are expected to color their performances by chromatically bending or sliding into notated or correct scale pitches. In vocal/choral music from the Renaissance however, chromatics would be much more inappropriate.

to clear_ the at - mos - phere.

It's good_ to meet_ where the

air is sweet,_ sit back,_ re - lax,_

turn down the heat._ Look here,

Lesson 2 Be Cool **19**

3. Refine

Direct the students to:

- Practice singing section C with appropriate dynamics, accented articulation, defined consonant sounds.

- Sustain the energy of the vowel sound to the end of all tied rhythm values.

- Sustain a slow, laid-back tempo while sounding at times ahead of the beat.

- Re-read and discuss the information found in the Getting Started and History and Culture sections on page 15 concerning "cool jazz."

- Establish a stage presence, that is "cool" in character. Exactly how does one go about acting "cool"? Compile a list of "cool" characters from rock groups, television shows and movies. Discuss what makes them fit the term "cool." Include facial gestures, body stance and other ways an attitude is conveyed.

- Sing "Be Cool" using your cool attitude.

Progress Checkpoints

Observe students' progress in:

✓ Singing the sections with musical contrast.

✓ Singing with consistent pitch accuracy and overall musical style throughout.

✓ Performing with a "cool" attitude.

TEACHING STRATEGY

Swing Style

If students are not familiar with the swing style, and are a bit stiff, have them:

- Listen to swing music.
- Move to swing music.
- Watch video footage of swing-style performance.
- Attend a dance-band performance.

19

ASSESSMENT

Informal Assessment

In this lesson, students showed the ability to:

- Sing expressively in a "cool jazz" style by demonstrating those musical attributes.
- Analyze musical form by labeling sections of the music correctly.
- Establish and demonstrate stage presence effective in communicating the musical style of "cool jazz."

Student Self-Assessment

Have students evaluate their individual performances based on the following:

- Phrasing
- Expressive Singing
- Intonation
- Accurate Pitches
- Accurate Rhythms

Have each student rate his/her performance of this song in the areas above on a scale of 1–5, 5 being the best.

Individual and Group Performance Evaluation

To further measure growth of musical skills presented in this lesson, direct students to complete the Evaluation section on page 15:

- Develop performance criteria appropriate to evaluating in-class performances by individuals and groups.
- Select a favorite song not in a "cool" style and present it to the class in a "cool" style.
- Create and present a "cool" song, poem, or story. Perform it for the class and discuss what makes it "cool."

20   Intermediate Tenor/Bass

Additional National Standards

The following National Standards are addressed through the Assessment, Extension, Enrichment and bottom-page activities:

1. Singing, alone and with others, a varied repertoire of music. **(a, e)**

5. Reading and notating music. **(c)**

6. Listening to, analyzing, and describing music. **(a)**

7. Evaluating music and music performances. **(a, b)**

9. Understanding music in relation to history and culture. **(a)**

SPOTLIGHT

Arranging

In music, an **arrangement** is *a composition in which a composer takes an existing melody and adds extra features or changes the melody in some way.* An **arranger** is *a composer who writes an arrangement by changing an existing melody to fit certain musical parameters.* The arranger has the following things to consider:

- Pitch—What is the range of the melody?
- Tempo—What is the speed of the beat?
- Instrumentation—Is the music for voices, instruments or both?
- Accompaniment—What will be used for accompaniment (piano, guitar, etc.), if anything?
- Harmony—What type of chords will be used for the harmony?
- Melody/Countermelody—Will harmony be added by use of a **countermelody** *(a separate vocal line that supports and contrasts the primary melody)*?

Read and perform the familiar melody "Hot Cross Buns."

Hot cross buns,   hot cross buns.   One a pen-ny, two a pen-ny,   hot cross buns.

Now you are ready to write your own arrangement. Using "Hot Cross Buns" as the existing melody, decide which element or elements you wish to change to compose your arrangement. You can try one or more of the ideas listed below:

- Pitch—Start the song higher or lower than currently written.
- Tempo—Alter the tempo in some manner (faster or slower).
- Instrumentation—Play the melody on different instruments.
- Accompaniment—Use a piano, guitar or other instrument to accompany your melody.
- Harmony—Add harmony notes from the chords and play them on an instrument or sing them with the melody.
- Melody/Countermelody—Compose a second melody or countermelody that fits musically with the existing melody.

Spotlight *Arranging* **21**

ARRANGING

Objectives

- Arrange melodic and rhythmic phrases.

Suggested Teaching Sequence

Direct students to:

- Read the Spotlight On Arranging on student page 21 and discuss the difference between an arranger and an arrangement.
- Identify the six elements an arranger must consider in writing an arrangement.
- Sing "Hot Cross Buns," then write an arrangement of "Hot Cross Buns" following the guidelines listed on page 21.
- Perform the arrangement for the class.
- Compare an arrangement to an original composition and find examples of arrangements in this book.

Progress Checkpoints

Observe students' progress in:

✓ Their ability to identify the six components to consider in arranging.
✓ Their ability to write a simple arrangement of "Hot Cross Buns."

Red River Valley

OVERVIEW

Composer: Traditional Cowboy Song, arranged by Emily Crocker
Text: Traditional
Voicing: TB/TTB
Key: B♭ major
Meter: 4/4
Form: Strophic with Coda
Style: American Cowboy Song
Accompaniment: Unaccompanied
Programming: Americana Concert, Small Ensemble

Vocal Ranges:

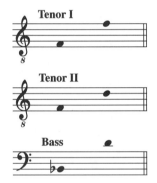

OBJECTIVES

After completing this lesson, students will be able to:

- Sing in groups a varied repertoire of music.
- Perform expressively from notation.
- Perform music representative of diverse cultures, including American heritage.

VOCABULARY

Have students review vocabulary in student lesson. Introduce terms found in the music. A complete glossary of terms is found on page 226 of the student book.

Red River Valley

Composer: Traditional American Cowboy Song, arranged by Emily Crocker
Text: Traditional
Voicing: TB/TTB

VOCABULARY

stage presence
folk song
dynamics
melody
chord

Focus

- Sing a cappella music in three-part harmony.
- Use dynamics to sing expressively.
- Perform music representing American heritage.

Getting Started

When you hear the words "Once upon a time," you know a story is about to be told. The storyteller often adds vocal inflection, facial expression and an occasional hand gesture to make the story appealing to the listener. As a singer, you must make your song appealing to the listener. You can raise the quality of your performance through enhanced facial expression, proper vocal production and good **stage presence** (*one's overall appearance on stage*).

🔺 **SPOTLIGHT**

To learn more about the changing voice, see page 195.

◆ **History and Culture**

A **folk song** is *a song that was originally passed down from generation to generation through oral tradition and often describes a certain place or event.* The folk song "The Red River Valley," so popular with the American cowboy, is based on a nineteenth-century tune "In the Bright Mohawk Valley."

During the late 1800s, cattle drives from Texas to Kansas were important in the American Southwest. Texas cowboys could get a higher price for their cattle in Kansas than they could in Texas. The large cattle drives would take several months to reach their final destination. The Red River, forming the Oklahoma and Texas border, served as one of the markers along the way. Stampedes, changing weather, disease and river crossings often made life dangerous on the trail. But in the evenings gathered around a campfire, the cowboys would sing songs of adventure, humor and love.

Dynamics (*symbols in music that indicate how loud or soft to sing*) can change the character of a song or give it expressiveness. After you have learned "Red River Valley," experiment with different dynamic markings to create another interpretation of the song.

22 Intermediate Tenor/Bass

RESOURCES

Intermediate Sight-Singing

Sight-Singing in B♭ Major, pages 121–129
Reading Rhythms in 4/4 Meter, pages 2–6

Teacher Resource Binder

Teaching Master 3, *Developing Stage Presence*
Teaching Master 4, *Performing "Red River Valley" with Stage Presence*
Evaluation Master 14, *Performance Evaluations: Part Singing*
For additional resources, see TRB Table of Contents.

Links to Learning

◆ **Vocal**

The **melody** *(a logical succession of musical tones)* is usually very prominent in folk songs. However, in this arrangement, the melody moves from line to line. To hear the complete melody, sing the following example in a comfortable range for your voice.

From this val - ley they say you are go - ing. We will
miss your bright eyes and sweet smile, for they say you are tak - ing the
sun - shine that has bright - ened our path for a - while.

◆ **Theory**

A **chord** is *a combination of three or more notes sung together at the same time.* The harmony in "Red River Valley" is created when the three voice parts move from chord to chord. Perform the following example to practice singing chords.

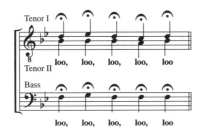

Evaluation

Demonstrate how well you have learned the skills and concepts featured in the lesson "Red River Valley" by completing the following:

- In a trio with one singer on each part, perform measures 1–8. Evaluate how well you were able to sing a cappella in three-part harmony.
- Sing measures 9–18 alone or with others to show how you can express the meaning of the text through your stage presence and use of dynamics. How well did you do?

RESOURCES

Intermediate Tenor/Bass Rehearsal/Performance CD

CD 1:5 Voices
CD 1:6 Accompaniment Only
CD 3:3 Vocal Practice Track—Tenor I
CD 3:4 Vocal Practice Track—Tenor II
CD 4:2 Vocal Practice Track—Bass

National Standards

1. Singing, alone and with others, a varied repertoire of music. **(b, c, d, e)**
5. Reading and notating music. **(a)**
7. Evaluating music and music performances. **(a)**

LINKS TO LEARNING

Vocal

The Vocal section is designed to prepare students to practice singing the melody.

Have students:

- Sing the melody in a range comfortable for their voices.
- Find the flow of the melody line in the music.

Theory

The Theory section is designed to prepare students to read three-part music.

Have students:

- Learn each part before dividing into three sections to sing all parts at the same time.
- Hold each chord until in tune before moving to the next.
- Find these chords in the music.

23

LESSON PLAN

Suggested Teaching Sequence and Performance Tips

- Read and discuss the information found in the Getting Started section on page 22.
- Discuss how the singer can convey these emotions to the audience (*raised eyebrows and focused attention to the conductor, tall vowels and legato singing*).
- Sight-sing the parts separately for measures 1–8.
- Compare measures 9–16, noting that they are the same as the first eight measures.
- Sing entire song using solfège syllables.
- Discuss diphthongs (*smile, sunshine, while*). Stress the first vowel sound (AH) and lightly add the other one only as moving to the next word.
- Outline the phrase groupings (*two bars, two bars then four bars*). Sing with tall, lifted vowels, particularly on longer note values.

Progress Checkpoints

Observe students' progress in:
- ✓ Creating facial expressions to convey the meaning of the song.
- ✓ Singing dipthongs correctly.
- ✓ Phrasing music as dictated by text.

Red River Valley

For TB or TTB, a cappella

Arranged by
EMILY CROCKER

Traditional American Cowboy Song

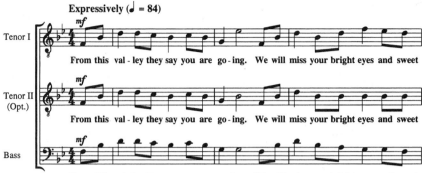

24   Intermediate Tenor/Bass

TEACHER 2 TEACHER

"Red River Valley" is an ideal selection for choirs working to master two- or three-part singing. The parts often create parallel thirds, a fundamental harmony in choral music.

love me. Do not hast - en to bid me a - dieu, but re -

love me. Do not hast - en to bid me a - dieu,_____ but re -

love me. Do not hast - en to bid me a - dieu, but re -

mem - ber the Red Riv - er Val - ley, and the cow - boy who loved you so

mem - ber the Red Riv - er Val - ley, and the cow - boy who loved you so

mem - ber the Red Riv - er Val - ley, and the cow - boy who loved you so

true. A - dieu, a - dieu.

true. A - dieu, a - dieu.

true. A - dieu,_____ a - dieu.

MUSIC, SOCIETY AND CULTURE

Have students perform additional songs representing diverse cultures, including American and Texas heritage. Go to **music.glencoe.com**, the Web site for Glencoe's choral music programs, for additional music selections students can perform.

ASSESSMENT

Informal assessment

In this lesson, the students showed the ability to:

- Sing independently in three-part harmony.
- Sing expressively with contrasting dynamics.
- Create a smooth, legato line using proper word stress treatment of diphthongs.
- Identify and perform strophic form with Coda.

Student Self-Assessment

Have students evaluate their individual performances based on the following:

- Breath Management
- Phrasing
- Tall Vowels
- Expressive Singing
- Correct Part-Singing

Have each student rate his/her performance of this song in the areas above on a scale of 1–5, 5 being the best.

Individual and Group Performance Evaluation

To further measure growth of musical skills presented in this lesson, direct students to complete the Evaluation section on page 23:

- After singing measures 1–8 as trios, evaluate the performances by asking, "How confident was each singer? Were the pitches and rhythms accurate?"
- After singing measures 9–18 individually, review each performance by asking, "Did the singer express the meaning of the text clearly?"

Codfish Shanty

OVERVIEW

Composer: Traditional, arranged by Vijay Singh
Text: Traditional Sea Chantey
Voicing: TB
Key: E♭ major
Meter: 2/4 and 4/4
Form: Strophic
Style: Traditional Sea Chantey
Accompaniment: Piano
Programming: Concert, Festival

Vocal Ranges:

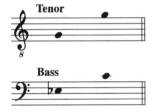

Objectives

After completing this lesson, students will be able to:

- Interpret music terms and symbols referring to articulation when performing.
- Perform independently with accurate rhythm.
- Perform music representative of diverse cultures.

VOCABULARY

Have students review vocabulary in student lesson. Introduce terms found in the music. A complete glossary of terms is found on page 226 of the student book.

Codfish Shanty

Composer: Traditional, arranged by Vijay Singh
Text: Traditional Sea Chantey
Voicing: TB

VOCABULARY

sea chantey
articulation
staccato
accent

Focus

- Define *staccato* and *accent*. Perform music that contains both.
- Read and perform dotted eighth and sixteenth note patterns.
- Perform music representing the sea chantey.

Getting Started

When it comes to cleaning your room at home, which description best fits you?

1. You love to clean and go right to work.
2. You do not enjoy cleaning, but if you play music or sing, the work gets done.

If you relate to the second statement, you have something in common with eighteenth-century sailors. "Codfish Shanty" is a **sea chantey,** or *a song sung by sailors in the rhythm of their work.* When you notice that the word *chantey* was transformed into *shanty,* you will not be surprised to learn that there are many different versions of this song.

◆ History and Culture

The work aboard early sailing ships included pulling the ropes, hoisting the sails and raising the anchor. The work was often repetitive and took a long time to complete. Sometimes the sailors created upbeat chanteys to pass the time that included improvised, humorous verses. This was probably the case with "Codfish Shanty." The various versions of this song refer to different towns and different situations. Every version, however, pokes fun in a good-natured way at the home ports of the sailors. After you learn this song, you might want to sing it while you clean your room.

Arranger Vijay Singh is a teacher and composer at Central Washington University, where he directs the University Choir and heads the vocal jazz program.

SPOTLIGHT

To learn more about careers in music, see page 125.

26 Intermediate Tenor/Bass

RESOURCES

Intermediate Sight-Singing

Sight-Singing in E♭ major, pages 141–143

Reading Eighth Note Rhythms, pages 26–27

Reading Dotted Note Rhythms, pages 45, 48, 49

Teacher Resource Binder

Evaluation Master 13, *Judging Stage Presence*

Skill Builder 23, *Rhythm and Kodály*

Skill Builder 25, *Rhythm Challenge in 2/4 Meter*

Dalcroze 12, *Moving to the Beat and Beat Subdivisions*

For additional resources, see the TRB Table of Contents.

Links to Learning

◆ Vocal

Articulation *(the amount of separation or connection between notes)* is used in music to show a singer how to sing the notes. A **staccato** marking (♪) is *a symbol that indicates to sing a note short and detached.* An **accent** (♪) is *a symbol that indicates that a note should receive extra emphasis or stress.* Perform the following example to demonstrate your understanding of staccato and accent markings.

◆ Theory

Read and perform the following rhythmic patterns, making sure there is a clear distinction between the groupings of two eighth notes and groupings of dotted eighth and sixteenth notes.

◆ Artistic Expression

To show artistry through performance practices, chant the words of "Codfish Shanty" from measures 8–24. Use facial expression, vocal inflections, and other gestures to emphasize the text. Use these expressions when performing the piece.

Evaluation

Demonstrate how well you have learned the skills and concepts featured in the lesson "Codfish Shanty" by completing the following:

- Define *staccato* and *accent.* Identify these articulation markings in the music and perform them appropriately. Evaluate how well you were able to perform them differently.

- Compose a four-measure rhythmic pattern in $\frac{2}{4}$ meter using eighth notes and dotted eighth and sixteenth note combinations. Perform your composition on a rhythm instrument for another student. Check each other's work for rhythmic accuracy.

RESOURCES

Intermediate Tenor/Bass Rehearsal/Performance CD

CD 1:7 Voices
CD 1:8 Accompaniment Only
CD 3:5 Vocal Practice Track—Tenor
CD 4:3 Vocal Practice Track—Bass

National Standards

1. Singing, alone and with others, a varied repertoire of music. **(b, c)**
5. Reading and notating music. **(c)**

LINKS TO LEARNING

Vocal

The Vocal section is designed to prepare students to:
- Sing staccato articulations.
- Sing accent articulations.

Have students:
- Sing the Vocal exercise, paying close attention to all articulation and dynamic markings.
- Locate all of the staccato *(measures 39, 40)* and accent *(measures 8, 11, 14, 15, 17, 19, 21, 23, 33, 36, 37, 41, 42, 55, 57, 59, 63)* markings in the score.

Theory

The Theory section is designed to prepare students to distinguish between groupings of eighth notes and groupings of dotted eighth and sixteenth notes.

Have students:
- Perform the rhythm in the first two measures and then the rhythm in the last two measures.
- Divide the students into two groups and have those two rhythms performed at the same time with several repetitions.

Artistic Expression

The Artistic Expression section is designed to prepare students to chant the words found in measures 8–24 with rhythmic accuracy and using appropriate expressive facial and vocal gestures.

Have students:

- Practice appropriate facial expressions reflecting the meaning of the text.
- Divide into pairs facing each other as students practice the facial expressions as they sing measures 8–24.

LESSON PLAN

Suggested Teaching Sequence and Performance Tips

1. Introduce

Direct students to:

- Read and discuss the information found in the Getting Started section on page 26.
- Practice singing the intervals as shown in the Vocal section on page 27. Relate this exercise to measures 39–42 of the score on page 31.

Codfish Shanty

TB and Piano

Arranged by
VIJAY SINGH (ASCAP)

Traditional

TEACHER 2 TEACHER

"Codfish Shanty" is an excellent selection for developing male voices. This two-part arrangement contains occasional unison singing that will assist the singers with intonation. This piece is also filled with dynamic and articulation markings that will challenge the singers to perform expressively.

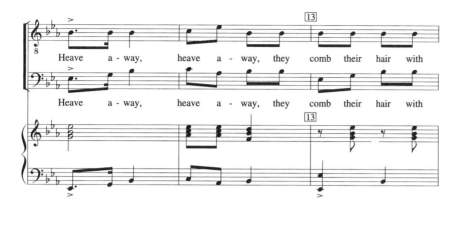

- Find all the measures in the score that contain staccato and accent markings (answers previous).
- Practice performing the rhythm patterns as shown in the Theory section on page 27. Relate this exercise to measures in the piece that contain both eighth-note groupings and dotted eighth- and sixteenth-note groupings.
- Chant the text in measures 8–24 as shown in the Artistic Expression section on page 27. Be sure to use gestures that are appropriate for the text and character of the piece.

Progress Checkpoints

Observe students' progress in:
- ✓ Their ability to chant the text using the correct rhythms.
- ✓ Their ability to identify all of the staccato and accent markings in the piece.
- ✓ Their ability to use facial and vocal gestures that are appropriate.

TEACHING STRATEGY

Staccato Versus Accent Markings

Review with students the difference between a staccato marking and an accent. Remember that accented notes are not necessarily sung short like staccato notes unless a staccato marking accompanies the accent mark. Therefore, make sure that students practice chanting and singing all accented rhythms while maintaining a legato, connected motion.

2. Rehearse

Direct students to:

- Label measures 8–16 as Verse 1. Review the rhythm patterns in this passage as outlined in the Theory section on page 27. Sight-sing measures 8–16. Rehearse parts separately if necessary. Notice the similarities between measures 9–11 and measures 13–15. When pitches are secure, chant the text for these measures (without pitches). Add dynamics to the chant. Finally, sing the section (measures 8–16) with pitches, text, and dynamics.

- Chant the rhythm patterns from measure 17–24. Label this section as Chorus. Next, chant the text in rhythm for this section, adding all expression markings. Practice the pitches for the Tenor part, followed by pitches for the Bass part. Combine parts and secure the two-part harmony.

- Rehearse measures 8–24. Ask students to identify the places in this section where both parts are singing the same pitches (*measure 8–"Oh," measure 9–"girls they," measure 10–"have" and "combs," measure 11–"-way," measure 12–"heave," "-way," "they," measure 13–"hair with," measure 14–"cod-," "bones," "we're," measure 15–"South"*).

30   Intermediate Tenor/Bass

MORE ABOUT...

"Codfish Shanty"

The song "Codfish Shanty" is derived from another sailor sea chantey entitled "South Australia." Below are the opening stanzas to "South Australia." Notice that the similarity in structure.

In South Australia I was born!
Heave away! Haul away!
South Australia round Cape Horn!
We're bound for South Australia!

Heave away, you rolling king,
Heave away! Haul away!
All the way you'll hear me sing
We're bound for South Australia!

30

- Label measures 30–42 as Verse 2. Sight-sing the section on a neutral syllable, paying close attention to pitch similarities between this verse and the first verse. When pitches are secure, add the text and dynamics.

- Label measures 47–54 as Verse 3. Sight-sing the section on a neutral syllable. When pitches are accurate, chant the text. Combine pitches and text, paying close attention to all expression markings.

- Label measures 55–65 as Chorus. Notice the similarities between this section and the Chorus beginning at measure 17. Sight-sing all pitches on a neutral syllable. When pitches are secure, add text and dynamics.

Progress Checkpoints

Observe students' progress in:
- ✓ Singing pitches and rhythms with accuracy.
- ✓ Interpreting the dynamics and articulation markings in the score.

TEACHING STRATEGY

Interpreting the Text

Have each student read the text of "Codfish Shanty." Generate a discussion with the class about the mood and main idea of the piece. Imagine the type of work that the sailors might be doing while singing this particular song. Generate a list of possible activities on the board. Ask the students to visualize themselves engaged in these activities while performing the song. Discuss how this visualization process affects the overall performance of the piece.

3. Refine

Direct students to:

- Return to the beginning of the piece. Read the text aloud in rhythm, incorporating all the expressive markings. Discuss and decide what gestures are most appropriate for performance based upon the character and mood of the text.
- Identify the performance markings at measures 47, 51, and 53. Discuss these markings and how they will impact the overall performance of the piece.
- Sing through the piece with energy and artistic expression.

Progress Checkpoints

Observe students' progress in:

- ✓ Observing all expression markings in the score.
- ✓ Using vocal and facial gestures that are appropriate for the text.

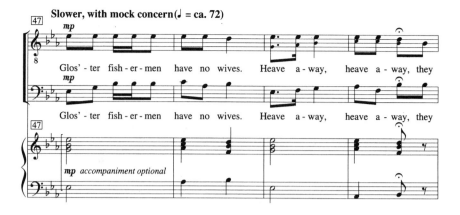

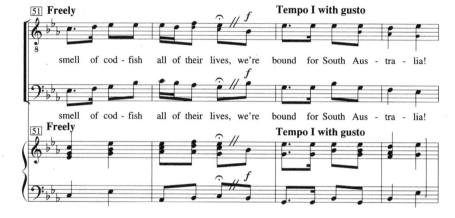

CURRICULUM CONNECTIONS

Writing Lyrics

Direct students to:

- Gather in small groups and write additional verses to "Codfish Shanty."
- Students may choose to keep the same subject for each set of verses (Glos'ter girls, Glos'ter boys and Glos'ter fisherman) or not. The text should fit the rest of the words in the song.

Have students evaluate their composition using the following criteria:

- Appropriateness of text
- Text follows a rhyme scheme

Additional National Standards

The following National Standards are addressed through the Assessment, Extension, Enrichment, and bottom-page activities:

4. Composing and arranging music within specified guidelines. **(a)**

7. Responding to and evaluating musical performances. **(a, b)**

ASSESSMENT

Informal Assessment

In this lesson, students showed the ability to:

- Sing with good intonation and rhythmic accuracy.
- Identify and observe all dynamic and articulation markings in the score.
- Sing with expression, using appropriate vocal and facial gestures.

Student Self-Assessment

Have students evaluate their individual performances based on the following:

- Diction
- Expressive Singing
- Accurate Pitches
- Accurate Rhythms
- Correct Part-Singing

Have each student rate his/her performance of this song in the areas above on a scale of 1–5, 5 being the best.

Individual and Group Performance Evaluation

To further measure growth of musical skills presented in this lesson, direct students to complete the Evaluation section on page 27.

- After performing "Codfish Shanty," ask the students, "Can you clearly distinguish between the staccato and accent articulations?"
- After composing the rhythmic pattern, ask students to choose a partner, and check each other's work for accuracy.

Festival Processional

OVERVIEW

Composer: Notre Dame Conductus, arranged by Emily Crocker
Text: Anonymous Latin Text, English text by Emily Crocker
Voicing: TB
Key: G Mixolydian
Meter: 6/4
Form: IntroABCB'C'B'C'BCA'
Style: Medieval French Procession
Accompaniment: Percussion
Programming: Festival, Concert Opener

Vocal Ranges:

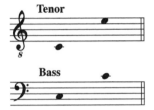

OBJECTIVES

After completing this lesson, students will be able to:

- Sight-sing music in various keys.
- Sight-sing music in various meters.
- Create music within specified guidelines.

Have students review vocabulary in student lesson. Introduce terms found in the music. A complete glossary of terms is found on page 226 of the student book.

Festival Procession

Composer: Emily Crocker
Text: Anonymous Latin Text, English text by Emily Crocker
Voicing: TB

VOCABULARY
conductus
mode
Mixolydian scale
$\frac{6}{4}$ meter

Focus

- Identify and perform music in a modal key (Mixolydian).
- Read and perform music in $\frac{6}{4}$ meter.
- Create an original percussion arrangement.

SKILL BUILDERS

To learn more about modes and modal scales, see Intermediate Sight-Singing, *page 168.*

Getting Started

Have you ever been in a processional? You may have seen a processional at a school graduation as the graduates filed into the auditorium, or at a wedding as the bridal party walked down the aisle. "Festival Procession" is a musical processional intended to be sung at the beginning of a concert. Composer Emily Crocker suggests using banners, percussion or other instruments as you sing and walk to make your processional festive.

◆ **History and Culture**

You only have to learn the first four measures of "Festival Procession" to discover that the song has a very distinctive sound. This is because Emily Crocker has set words from a medieval Latin text to music adapted from a **conductus,** or *a thirteenth-century song for two, three or four voices.* "Festival Procession" is in two parts. Because there is not a third note in each chord, the resulting harmony has an open and hollow sound. When you tune your notes carefully and sing with rhythmic precision, your processional will be very dramatic even if you are standing still.

The English translation of the Latin text is:

Novus annus hodie monet nos letitie laudes inchoare.

Today a new year urges us joyful praises to begin.

Eya rex nos adiuva qui gubernas omnia.

Ah! King, help us, who governs all.

Intermediate Sight-Singing
Sight-Singing Modes, pages 168–170
Reading Tied Notes, pages 32, 44
Reading Rhythms in Compound Meter, pages 114–116

Teacher Resource Binder
Teaching Master 5, *Pronunciation Guide for "Festival Procession"*
Teaching Master 6, *Creating a Percussion Accompaniment for "Festival Procession"*
Skill Builder 23, *Rhythm and Kodály*
Skill Builder 31, *Time Signatures in Music*
For additional resources, see TRB Table of Contents.

Links to Learning

◆ Vocal

A **mode** is *an early system of pitch organization that was used before major and minor keys were developed.* The **Mixolydian scale** is *a modal scale that follows the pattern of* sol *to* sol. "Festival Procession" is based on the G Mixolydian scale and uses the notes G, A, B, C, D, E F, G. To locate "G" on the piano, find any set of three black keys. "G" is the white key just to the left of the middle black key. Using the keyboard below as a guide, play the G Mixolydian scale.

The G major scale is similar to the G Mixolydian scale. The G major scale uses an F♯ *(ti)*; however, in the G Mixolydian mode, the F♯ *(ti)* is lowered to F natural *(te)*. Perform the following examples to compare the G major and G Mixolydian scales.

◆ Theory

"Festival Procession" is written in $\frac{6}{4}$ **meter**, *a meter in which there are two groups of three quarter notes per measure and the dotted half note receives the beat.* Read and clap the following example to practice rhythmic patterns in $\frac{6}{4}$ meter.

Evaluation

Demonstrate how well you have learned the skills and concepts featured in the lesson "Festival Procession" by completing the following:

- In a small group, sing measures 26–33 to show that you can sing in tune in a modal tonality. Evaluate how well you were able to sing in tune.
- Using what you have learned about $\frac{6}{4}$ meter, write an original percussion arrangement that can be played as you sing "Festival Procession." Check your work for rhythmic accuracy.

Lesson 5 *Festival Procession* **35**

RESOURCES

Intermediate Tenor/Bass Rehearsal/Performance CD

CD 1:9 Voices

CD 1:10 Accompaniment Only

CD 3:6 Vocal Practice Track—Tenor

CD 4:4 Vocal Practice Track—Bass

National Standards

4. Composing and arranging music within specific guidelines. **(a)**

5. Reading and notating music. **(b)**

LINKS TO LEARNING

Vocal

The Vocal section is designed to prepare students to:

- Learn about modes.
- Recognize and sing the Mixolydian scale.
- Compare scales and modes.

Have students:

- Play the Mixolydian scale on a keyboard.
- Sing the G major scale.
- Sing the Mixolydian scale.
- Compare the difference of the seventh degree of the scales (F♯ *versus* F).

Theory

The Theory section is designed to prepare students to:

- Read and clap a rhythm in 6/4 meter.
- Practive rhythm syllables.

Have students:

- Chant the rhythm syllables.
- Divide into two groups. One half claps the 2-beat pulse, while the other half chants the rhythm.
- Find the same rhythm in measures 43–46 in the score and sing it.

LESSON PLAN

Suggested Teaching Sequence and Performance Tips

1. Introduce

Direct students to:

- Read and discuss the information found in the Getting Started section on page 34.

- Practice singing the portions of the G major and G Mixolydian scales in the Vocal section on page 35 using solfège syllables.

- Practice clapping the rhythm in the Theory section on page 35. Transfer that rhythm to an unpitched rhythm instrument once it is clapped with confidence.

Progress Checkpoints

Observe students' progress in:

✓ Singing a G major and G Mixolydian scale.

✓ Clapping a rhythm in 6/4 meter.

For the Haltom High School Men's Chorus
Fort Worth, Texas
1996 TMEA Honor Choir
Stuart Younse, Director

Festival Procession

For TB, a cappella with Optional Percussion

Anonymous Latin Text (Munich clm 20153)
English Lyrics by EMILY CROCKER

Notre Dame Conductus
(Music adapted from 13th Century)
Arranged by EMILY CROCKER

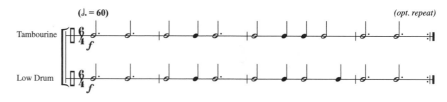

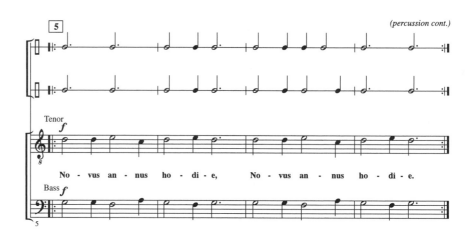

Percussion part found at end of song.

36   Intermediate Tenor/Bass

TEACHER2TEACHER

This very singable processional is a great way to introduce some new elements to a performance—banners, percussion, instruments—you determine how festive it should be. The two-part voicing is a great way to introduce modal singing to your choir. The piece would sight-sing easily in the key of C major or could also be read in the key of G major, using a lowered *ti (teh)*, as there is no F♯.

No-vus an-nus ho-di-e_____ mon-et nos le-ti-ti-e

lau-des in-cho-a-re. E-ya rex nos a-diu-va,

E-ya rex nos a-diu-va qui gu-ber-nas___ om-ni-a.

Joy-ful, joy-ful sing we___ all_____ on this hap-py___ morn-ing. Play the drum,___ come ye-all,___ join us in___ our___ sing-ing. Why this hap-py ju-bi-lee with

Lesson 5 *Festival Procession* **37**

2. Rehearse

Direct students to:

- Chant the text in measures 5–8 in rhythm. Practice singing the Tenor part with the text. Practice singing the Bass part with the text. Combine both parts.
- Practice pronouncing the text in measures 9–24. Chant the text in rhythm once the pronunciation is correct.
- Sing the Tenor part in measures 9–24 and then the Bass part. Combine parts once each section is confident in singing their part.
- Play measures 26–33 on the piano. Ask the students, "Have you heard a similar section previously?" (*measures 9–16*) Sing measures 26–33 in parts with the text.
- Play measures 34–41 on the piano. Ask the students, "Have you heard a similar section previously?" (*measures 19–24*) Sing measures 34–41 in parts with the text.
- The pitches in measures 43–75 are very similar to previous music (*measures 43–50 same as measures 26–33, measures 51–58 same as measures 34–42*). Challenge the students to sight-sing measures 43–75 with the new text.

TEACHING STRATEGY

Diction

Clear pronunciation requires attention to both vowels and consonants. Have students:

- Identify the need for clear diction so the audience will know what the piece is about.
- Discuss what choral techniques will produce clear diction. (unified vowels, crisp beginning and ending consonants, quick mouth movement to shape sounds)
- Sing through slowly with only vowels, keeping the jaw lowered, blending the vowels.
- Add the consonants, keeping the vowels blended.
- Sing through the piece attending to clear diction.

- Measures 60–75 is the same as measures 9–24. Sight-sing measures 60–75 with this in mind.

- Measures 76–79 are the same as measures 5–8. Discuss this with students before sight-singing the section. Practice singing the parts separately in measures 80–82 and then combine the parts.

Progress Checkpoints

Observe students' progress in:

✓ Singing the correct pitches and rhythms.

✓ Sight-singing similar musical material.

✓ Singing two parts at the same time with independence.

MORE ABOUT...

Arranger Emily Crocker

Emily Crocker, Director of the Milwaukee Children's Choir is recognized nationally as one of the leading experts in children's choirs. After a successful 15-year career as a music teacher and choral director in her native Texas, she joined the music publishing industry, and now holds the position of Vice President of Choral Publications for Hal Leonard Corporation in Milwaukee and is Senior Author and Editor of the *Essential Elements for Choir* textbook series. She holds degrees from the University of North Texas and Texas Woman's University, and has done additional study at UNT (choral conducting), Westminster Choir College (conducting and voice-building), TWU (vocal pedagogy) and Sam Houston State University (Kodály methods).

3. Refine

Direct students to:

- Sing the entire song using solfège syllables and correct rhythms.
- Combine the singing with the percussion parts.
- Sing with tall, lifted vowels. Sustain vowels and do not allow consonants to enter too early.
- Articulate the text cleanly and encourage active facial motion.
- Retain rounded vowels, particularly on "o" vowels in words such as "Novus" and "hodie."

Progress Checkpoints

Observe students' progress in:

✓ Performing with accurate rhythms in the vocal and percussion parts.

✓ Using clean diction throughout with beautiful vowel sounds and crisp consonants.

TEACHING STRATEGY

Intervals

Help students remember intervals by relating them to the first two pitches of familiar songs. Major 2nd—"Frère Jacques"; Major 3rd—"Taps"; Perfect 4th—"Here Comes the Bride"; Perfect 5th —"Twinkle, Twinkle, Little Star"; Major 6th—"My Bonny Lies Over the Ocean"; Octave—"Somewhere, Over the Rainbow." Have students:

- Challenge one another in pairs, one singing an interval, the other telling what interval was heard.
- Check any disagreements with another pair.

Take turns singing intervals.

ASSESSMENT

Informal Assessment

In this lesson, students showed the ability to:

- Sing the G Mixolydian mode with correct pitches.
- Sight-sing sections of music with similar pitches.

Create a percussion accompaniment within guidelines.

Student Self-Assessment

Have students evaluate their individual performances based on the following:

- Diction
- Foreign Language
- Tall Vowels
- Intonation
- Accurate Rhythms

Have each student rate his/her performance of this song in the areas above on a scale of 1–5, 5 being the best.

Individual and Group Performance Evaluation

To further measure growth of musical skills presented in this lesson, direct students to complete the Evaluation section on page 35.

- After singing measures 26–33 in small ensembles, evaluate the performance by asking, "How well in tune were the parts? Which section of the ensemble was better in tune?"
- After writing percussion parts in 6/4 meter, perform them as the choir sings "Festival Procession." Ask, "Were the new percussion parts rhythmically correct? Did they serve as a good accompaniment to the singing? Why or why not?"

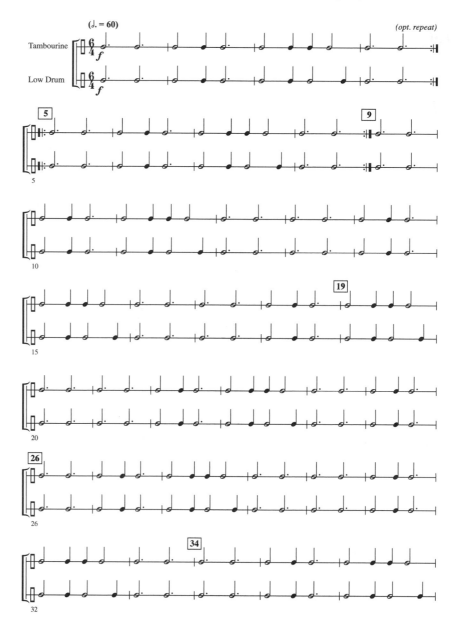

Festival Procession

Anonymous Latin Text (Munich clm 20153)
English Lyrics by EMILY CROCKER

Notre Dame Conductus
(Music adapted from 13th Century)
Arranged by EMILY CROCKER

40   Intermediate Tenor/Bass

TEACHING STRATEGY

Unified Vowels

Vowels are the fundamental building blocks of tone production, intonation, and blend. A pure vowel is one that does not change when sung. When the pure vowels *ee, ay, ah, oh,* and *oo* are sung identically by all singers, there is a magical musical resonance and blend that can occur.

Why is it important? The unity of vowels when sung by a chorus is the key to resonance and blend. The choral instrument should sound as one voice. Try singing identical vowels, and have one or more singers sing the same vowel slightly differently. Ask: Can you hear the difference?

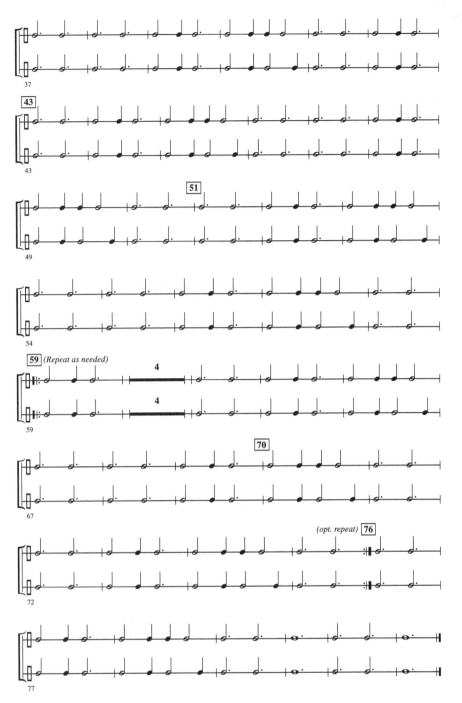

EXTENSIONS

Composing

Identify the characteristics of a canon or round. Compose a round or canon using the melody from one of the voice lines. Perform the round in pairs or small groups.

Performing from Memory

Have students:

1. Memorize this piece by learning shorter phrases at a time.
2. Perform it from memory on a program or in competition.
3. Further develop memorization skills by memorizing other songs and solos to perform for the class informally or at formal concerts.

Music, Society and Culture

Have students perform additional songs representing diverse cultures, including American and Texas heritage. Go to **music.glencoe.com**, the Web site for Glencoe's choral music programs, for additional music selections students can perform.

Additional National Standards

The following National Standards are addressed through the Assessment, Extension, Enrichment and bottom page activities.

1. Singing, alone and with others, a varied repertoire of music. **(a, c, d, e)**

2. Performing, alone and with others, a varied repertoire of music. **(b)**

5. Reading and notating music. **(a)**

7. Evaluating music and music performances. **(b)**

Soldier's Hallelujah

OVERVIEW

Composer: Vijah Singh
Text: Vijah Singh
Voicing: TB
Key: E♭ Dorian
Meter: 4/4
Form: AA′BA″B′A‴CA⁗A″
Coda
Style: Contemporary American Anthem
Accompaniment: Snare and Tenor Drums (opt.)
Programming: Christmas, Processional

Vocal Ranges:

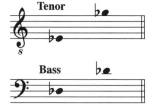

OBJECTIVES

After completing this lesson, students will be able to:

- Identify music forms presented through music notation.
- Interpret music symbols referring to dynamics when performing.
- Demonstrate appropriate small-ensemble performance techniques.

Soldier's Hallelujah

Composer: Vijay Singh
Text: Vijay Singh
Voicing: TB

VOCABULARY

form
phrase
coda
accidental
dynamics

Focus

- Identify and describe form in music.
- Interpret dynamics when performing.
- Perform a cappella music in two parts.

Getting Started

If you presently sing in a male choir, you have joined a very prestigious and historical choral tradition. Male choirs can trace their origins to the early medieval days of the church. Throughout history, male choirs have played significant roles in many cultures and countries. For instance, the Vienna Boys Choir and boarding school have been musical fixtures in Vienna, Austria, for over 500 years. In addition, every small mining town in Wales seemed to have a thriving male chorus made up of community members and miners at the beginning of the twentieth century. And today in America, many cities support boys' choirs that are patterned after their European counterparts. Given all this male singing history, a song called "Soldier's Hallelujah" seems quite natural.

◆ History and Culture

Form *(the design and structure of a composition)* is as important in music as it is in visual art. Without an organized form, a piece of music cannot present a cohesive musical idea. The American composer Vijay Singh wrote "Soldier's Hallelujah" in nine 4-measure **phrases** *(musical ideas with a beginning and an end)* and a **coda** *(a concluding portion of a composition)*. Singh's three principal melodies, introduced in measures 1, 9 and 25, define the three contrasting phrases of the piece and are called sections A, B and C. In what order does Singh use sections A, B and C for the nine phrases?

SKILL BUILDERS

To learn more about accidentals, see Intermediate Sight-Singing, *page 156 and 157.*

RESOURCES

Intermediate Sight-Singing

Sight-Singing Modes, pages 168–170

Reading Rhythms in 4/4 Meter, pages 2–6

Reading Sixteenth Notes, pages 57–60, 89–90

Teacher Resource Binder

Evaluation Master 7, *Evaluating Musical Expression*

Skill Builder 20, *Naming Intervals*

Vocal Development 8, *Articulation*

Reference 1, *At-a-Glance: Music Terms and Symbols*

Reference 16, *My Music Dictionary*

For additional resources, see TRB Table of Contents.

Links to Learning

◆ **Vocal**

An **accidental** is *any sharp, flat or natural sign that is not included in the key signature of a piece of music.* When singing "Soldier's Hallelujah," both voice parts must use *fi* instead of *fa* in sections A and B. Sing the following examples, first with *fa* and then with *fi*, to become familiar with the altered sound. Find these examples in the music.

mi mi sol fa mi re mi   mi mi sol fi mi re mi

mi fa sol fa mi re mi   mi fi sol fi mi re mi

◆ **Theory**

To analyze the form of this song, identify and label the nine sections and coda found in "Soldier's Hallelujah." You will discover that section A appears six times. Describe how Singh varied each repetition.

◆ **Artistic Expression**

Dynamics are *symbols in music used to indicate how loud or soft to sing a passage.* Review measures 29–40 in the music. Since the only word used is "Hallelujah," it is the changes in dynamics that create the artistic shape of this section. Locate the dynamic markings *mp* (medium soft), *f* (loud), *sub. p* (suddenly soft), *molto cresc.* (gradually getting louder), and *ff* (very loud). Observe these dynamic markings.

Evaluation

Demonstrate how well you have learned the skills and concepts featured in the lesson "Soldier's Hallelujah" by completing the following:

• Using visual arts (drawing, painting, sculpture, graph, etc.), design a piece of artwork that represents the form of "Soldier's Hallelujah." Show each variation of section A in a different manner. Share your work with the class. Critique how well the artwork represents the music.

• Record yourself singing measures 29–40 into a microphone. Listen to the recording and evaluate how well you were able to perform the dynamic markings indicated.

Lesson 6 Soldier's Hallelujah **43**

RESOURCES

Intermediate Tenor/Bass Rehearsal/Performance CD

CD 1:11 Voices

CD 1:12 Accompaniment Only

CD 3:7 Vocal Practice Track—Tenor

CD 4:5 Vocal Practice Track—Bass

National Standards

1. Singing, alone and with others, a varied repertoire of music. **(a)**

5. Reading and notating music. **(c)**

6. Listening to, analyzing, and describing music. **(a)**

LINKS TO LEARNING

Vocal

The Vocal section is designed to prepare students to:

• Recognize accidentals.

• Sing pitches from the E♭ Dorian scale.

Have students:

• Sing the first measure to hear *fa*.

• Sing second measure changing *fa* to *fi*.

• Practice until secure in switching from *fa* to *fi*.

Theory

The Theory section is designed to prepare students to analyze the form.

Have students locate and describe the six uses of the A theme *(measures 1–4, 5–8, 13–16, 21–24, 29–32, 33–36; Coda measures 37–41).*

Artistic Expression

The Artistic Expression section is designed to introduce students to dynamic symbols.

Have students:

• Locate the dynamic marks listed *(measures 21, 5, 38, 39, 41).*

• Identify the dynamic markings indicated.

• Locate markings in music.

LESSON PLAN

Suggested Teaching Sequence and Performance Tips

1. Introduce

Direct students to:

- Read and discuss the information found in the Getting Started section on page 42.

- Practice singing pitches from the E♭ Dorian scale as instructed in the Vocal section on page 43. Relate this exercise to the melody.

- Analyze the form and label the sections and coda as described in the Theory section on page 43. Locate statements of the 4-measure "Hallelujah" refrain as beginning at measures 1, 5, 13, 21, 29, and 33. Label as the verses the passages that begin at measures 9, 17, and 25.

- Be aware of the various dynamic levels they will encounter as presented in the Artistic Expression section on page 43.

Progress Checkpoints

Observe students' progress in:

- ✓ Singing pitches from the E♭ Dorian scale.
- ✓ Their ability to label the correct form.
- ✓ Their ability to locate varied dynamic marks in the score.

Soldier's Hallelujah

For TB, a cappella, with Optional Snare and Tenor Drum

Words and Music by
VIJAY SINGH

Optional Snare and Tenor Drum ostinato (continues throughout). Ostinato may begin four measures before voices enter; drums at last measure of piece should play the rhythm of the baritone melody.

44   Intermediate Tenor/Bass

TEACHER 2 TEACHER

Vijay Singh has written a rousing piece that will be a favorite with your choir! The optional snare and tenor drum ostinato contribute to the medieval feel of the song and are particularly useful when the song is used as a processional.

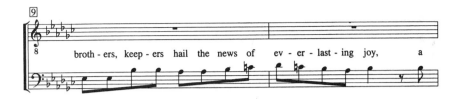

broth - ers, keep - ers hail the news of ev - er - last - ing joy, a

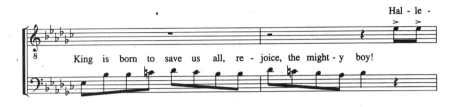

King is born to save us all, re - joice, the might - y boy!

Hal - le -

Hal - le - lu - jah, hal - le - lu - jah, hal - le - lu, hal - le - lu - jah!

lu! Hal - le - lu - jah!

Hal - le - lu - jah, hal - le - lu - jah, hal - le - lu - jah! We

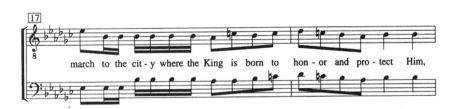

march to the cit - y where the King is born to hon - or and pro - tect Him,

Lesson 6 Soldier's Hallelujah **45**

2. Rehearse

Direct students to:

- Begin to learn the refrains by counting the rhythms and then adding pitches. Notice that the Baritones retain the melody in every repetition while the Tenors provide a harmony part that varies. Specifically, the Tenors' harmony at measure 5 repeats two refrains later at measure 21; and measure 13 repeats at measure 33.

- Learn the verses by counting the rhythms and learning the pitches. Chant the lyrics in rhythm before singing them to work on clear diction.

- Focus on the final measures, noticing that measures 36–38 are identical. Also notice that the final "Hallelujah" is a lengthened repetition of measures 36–38 with inner harmony parts added to thicken the texture.

Progress Checkpoints

Observe students' progress in:

- ✓ Their ability to count rhythms correctly and to sing accurate pitches.
- ✓ Singing together with accurate intonation for the frequent parallel perfect fifths between the Tenor and Bass parts.
- ✓ Using clear pronunciation of the text in the verses, particularly through the sixteenth notes.
- ✓ Their ability to sing correctly the final measures.

TEACHING STRATEGY

Form

Tell students that the form of a piece is shown in alphabetical order, with each new section being named by the next letter. The first section is always A, and any identical section will also be called A. If a section is nearly identical, it will become A′ (A prime). The second section will be called B, the next C, and so on. Common forms are AB (verse-refrain), ABA (ternary), ABACA (rondo). These forms are frequently modified by the composer and may have introductions, interludes, and codas as well. Have students list the characteristics of the A and B sections of "Soldier's Hallelujah." Compare the lists, discussing any contrast between the two sections.

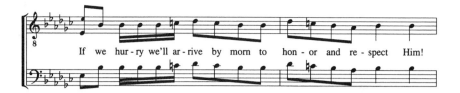

3. Refine

Direct students to:

- Focus on a proper pronunciation of the word "Hallelujah" with pure, round, vowel sounds.

- Apply the dynamic markings as provided in the score to give an artistic shaping to the piece.

Progress Checkpoints

Observe students' progress in:

✓ Their ability to sing "Hallelujah" with pure vowels.

✓ Their ability to sing audible differences between dynamic levels.

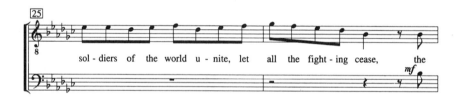

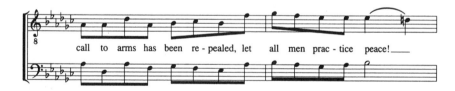

46 Intermediate Tenor/Bass

MORE ABOUT...

Modes

Modes are an ancient set of scales whose history is quite complex. The common major and minor scales are only two of many modes, the two that gained and maintained musical prominence. Other than Gregorian chant, modes are most often encountered in folk music and in composed music meant to evoke an older style of music. Three commonly known songs in Dorian mode are "Scarborough Faire," "I Wonder as I Wander," and "What Wondrous Love Is This." Allow the choir to listen to these and other songs in Dorian mode.

Lesson 6 *Soldier's Hallelujah* **47**

ASSESSMENT

Informal Assessment

In this lesson, students showed the ability to:
- Sing a melody in E♭ Dorian.
- Correctly analyze the form of a song.
- Observe dynamic marks and perform accordingly.

Student Self-Assessment

Have students evaluate their individual performances based on the following:
- Diction
- Tall Vowels
- Intonation
- Accurate Pitches
- Correct Part-Singing

Have each student rate his/her performance of this song in the areas above on a scale of 1–5, 5 being the best.

Individual and Group Performance Evaluation

To further measure growth of musical skills presented in this lesson, direct students to complete the Evaluation section on page 43.

- After analyzing the form of "Soldier's Hallelujah," create a form diagram of the piece representing the organization of refrains and verses.

- After recording measures 29–40 evaluate the performance by asking, "How clearly were the dynamic levels? Did they reflect what was written in the score?"

Additional National Standards

The following National Standards are addressed through the Assessment, Extension, Enrichment and bottom-page activities:

1. Singing, alone and with others, a varied repertoire of music. **(d)**

7. Evaluating music and music performances. **(a)**

8. Understanding relationships between music, the other arts, and disciplines outside the arts. **(a)**

Light The Candles Of Hanukkah

OVERVIEW

Composer: George L. O. Strid
Text: Mary Donnelly
Voicing: TB
Key: G harmonic minor
Meter: 4/4
Form: IntroABCA'BC'Coda
Style: Contemporary American Song
Accompaniment: Piano
Programming: Winter Concert

Vocal Ranges:

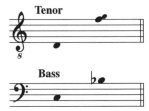

OBJECTIVES

After completing this lesson, students will be able to:

• Use standard terminology to describe in detail music notation.

• While performing, demonstrate fundamental skills.

• Perform a varied repertoire of music representing styles from diverse cultures.

VOCABULARY

Have students review vocabulary in student lesson. Introduce terms found in the music. A complete glossary of terms is found on page 226 of the student book.

LESSON 7

Light The Candles Of Hanukkah

Composer: George L. O. Strid
Text: Mary Donnelly
Voicing: TB

VOCABULARY

breath support

harmonic minor scale

relative minor scale

🔺 **SPOTLIGHT**

To learn more about breath management, see page 167.

Focus

• Distinguish between major and minor tonality.

• Sing with adequate support.

• Perform music representing the Jewish culture.

Getting Started

Holidays are a time for family traditions, unique foods and no school! Holidays often include special music. For instance, what holiday goes with each of these famous tunes?

1. "America the Beautiful"
2. "Auld Lang Syne"
3. "Deck The Halls"
4. "Ma'oz Tzur"

If you had difficulty in identifying the last one, it's because the song and holiday are not quite as well known as the others. "Ma'oz Tzur" ("Rock of Ages") is sung during Hanukkah, the Jewish festival of lights. Hanukkah begins on the Hebrew date of the 25th of Kislev and lasts for eight days in late November or December.

◆ History and Culture

Hanukkah means "dedication" and commemorates the victory of the outnumbered Maccabees (led by Judah) over a much larger army of Syrian Greeks (led by King Antiochus IV) in 165 B.C. The victory was considered a miracle. But once the temple in Jerusalem had been reclaimed, it had to be rededicated. According to legend, only one jar of sacramental oil was found, enough to light a flame for only one day. Miraculously, the oil burned for eight days, thus the eight days of Hanukkah.

Although not a traditional song, "Light The Candles Of Hanukkah" has a holiday tune that you may find yourself humming all year long.

48 Intermediate Tenor/Bass

RESOURCES

Intermediate Sight-Singing

Sight-Singing in G Minor, pages 133–136

Reading Rhythms in 4/4 Meter, pages 2–6

Reading Dotted Notes, pages 45, 48, 49

Teacher Resource Binder

Teaching Master 7, *Evaluating Breath Support in "Light the Candles of Hanukkah"*

Skill Builder 13, *Constructing Minor Scales*

Skill Builder 18, *Major and Minor Scales*

Skill Builder 30, *Solfège Hand Signs*

For additional resources, see TRB Table of Contents.

Links to Learning

◆ Vocal

When you perform the following example, you must maintain adequate **breath support** (*a constant airflow necessary to produce sound for singing*) to sing one word for two notes. Practice singing very smoothly with lots of breath support so there is no "H" sound when you change pitches.

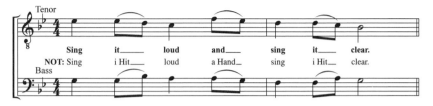

Sing	**it**	**loud**	**and**	**sing**	**it**	**clear.**
NOT: Sing	i Hit	loud	a Hand	sing	i Hit	clear.

◆ Theory

"Light The Candles Of Hanukkah" uses major and minor scales. Read and perform the B♭ major scale and G **harmonic minor scale** (*a minor scale that uses a raised seventh note; si is raised from sol*). G minor is called the **relative minor scale** to B♭ major because it is *a minor scale that shares the same key signature as its corresponding major scale*. Sing in your appropriate octave or range. When the notes feel high, change to your **falsetto** voice (*the light upper range of male singers*).

B♭ Major Scale

B♭	C	D	E♭	F	G	A	B♭	A	G	F	E♭	D	C	B♭
do	re	mi	fa	sol	la	ti	do	ti	la	sol	fa	mi	re	do

G Harmonic Minor Scale

G	A	B♭	C	D	E♭	F♯	G	F♯	E♭	D	C	B♭	A	G
la	ti	do	re	mi	fa	si	la	si	fa	mi	re	do	ti	la

Evaluation

Demonstrate how well you have learned the skills and concepts featured in the lesson "Light The Candles Of Hanukkah" by completing the following:

- Play the "major/minor" game with a friend. Sing example 1 or example 2 from the Theory section above on a neutral syllable. Ask a friend to identify if you are singing a major or minor scale. Switch roles. How well did you do?

- Sing your voice part in measures 38–45. Evaluate how well you are able to sing with adequate breath support and not allow any "H" sounds to occur between the notes.

RESOURCES

Intermediate Tenor/Bass Rehearsal/Performance CD

CD 1:13 Voices

CD 1:14 Accompaniment Only

CD 3:8 Vocal Practice Track—Tenor

CD 4:6 Vocal Practice Track—Bass

National Standards

1. Singing, alone and with others, a varied repertoire of music. **(a, b, c)**

6. Listening to, analyzing, and describing music. **(c)**

LINKS TO LEARNING

Vocal

The Vocal section is designed to prepare students to:

- Sing with appropriate breath support.
- Sing with pure vowel sounds.

Have students:

- Sing example incorrectly with two vowel sounds on eighth notes.
- Sing again correctly.
- Discuss what they had to do differently to sing correctly.

Theory

The Theory section is designed to prepare students to:

- Identify harmonic minor and relative minor.
- Describe falsetto voice.

Have students:

- Sing the B♭ major scale.
- Sing the G minor scale.
- Compare the two. What is different? What is the same?
- Demonstrate singing in falsetto.

LESSON PLAN

Suggested Teaching Sequence and Performance Tips

1. Introduce

Direct Students to:

- Read, discuss and complete the activities as outlined in the Getting Started section on page 48 ("America the Beautiful"—Memorial Day or The Fourth of July; "Auld Lang Syne"—New Years; "Deck The Halls"—Christmas; "Ma'oz Tzur"—Hanukkah). Discuss additional holidays that have specific music as part of their celebrations or observances. Ask students to share any other Hanukkah songs or customs they may know.

- Practice singing the exercise as shown in the Vocal section on page 49 to develop adequate breath support.

- Introduce the major scale and relative minor scale as outlined in the Theory section on page 49. Ask any student to sing *do*. Have the student sitting next to that singer sing *re*, and then the next singer sing *mi* and so forth. Continue going up and down the scale and around the room. Encourage singers to sing every scale pitch in their head while waiting to sing. Repeat exercise using a different *do*. Establish the relative minor scale and repeat the exercise with the relative minor scale beginning on *la*. Introduce the chromatic altered *si* for *sol*.

Light The Candles Of Hanukkah

For TB and Piano

Words by
MARY DONNELLY (ASCAP)

Music by
GEORGE L.O. STRID (ASCAP)

50   Intermediate Tenor/Bass

TEACHER 2 TEACHER

The students will enjoy the cheerful minor melody and lively rhythm patterns that "Light The Candles Of Hanukkah" shares with many traditional Hanukkah songs.

- Chant the solfège syllables for measures 5–12 at a steady tempo. Assign each student one pitch from *mi* to *mi* (*mi, fa, si, la, ti, do, re, mi*). Sing measures 5–12 again, this time with each student only singing the pitch for which he/she is responsible. Repeat several times, assigning a different pitch to each student.

- Sing measures 5–12 as a group a cappella using solfège syllables.

- Form groups of three to six students, and learn the solfège syllables for your voice part in measures 13–20 using the strategies from above. Perform this section for the class.

- Return to small groups and learn measures 21–28 in a similar manner.

Progress Checkpoints

Observe students' progress in:
- ✓ Relating music to corresponding holidays.
- ✓ Singing while using adequate breath support.
- ✓ Singing a major and relative minor scale in tune.
- ✓ Performing in large and small groups.

MORE ABOUT...

Composing Your Own Texts

Have students research the traditions and history of the Hanukkah story. Based on that infomation, have them write a new verse to the melody of measures 5–12, or the countermelody of measures 30–37. Incorporate the new verse into a performance of "Light The Candles Of Hanukkah."

2. Rehearse

Direct Students to:

- Work in Tenor/Baritone pairs to learn both parts in measures 30–37 using solfège syllables. Both singers should be able to sing either part. Allow each pair to perform twice for the class.

- As a class, sing the entire song using solfège syllables in parts.

- Recite the text and define all unfamiliar words (dreidel—a spinning top with the first letter of each word of the Hebrew phrase: "nes gadol hayah sham, (a great miracle happened there)" printed on each of the four sides; hora—a traditional Jewish closed circle dance).

- Learn the song with the text, accurate pitches and rhythm at a steady tempo. Rehearse each voice part separately. Allow each section to sing for the other.

- Once parts are secure, combine parts and sing the entire song with the text.

Progress Checkpoints

Observe students' progress in:

✓ Singing independently in two parts.

✓ Singing in tune.

✓ Singing with an understanding of the text.

52   Intermediate Tenor/Bass

CONNECTING THE ARTS

Dancing the Hora

The hora is an Israeli folk dance. Form a circle and join hands or hold onto each other's elbows or shoulders. Dance the following steps:

- Step to the left with left foot.
- Cross right foot behind left.
- Step to the left with left foot
- Hop on left foot and swing right foot across in front of left.
- Step in place with right foot
- Hop on right foot and swing left foot across in front of right.
- Repeat over and over until the end of the song.

young and old, for danc - ing in a___ ring.

young and old, for danc - ing in a___ ring.

'Round and 'round the ho - ra goes while mer - ri - ly we

'Round and 'round the ho - ra goes while mer - ri -

sing.   'Round and__ 'round the__ drei - dels__ turn; they

ly we sing.   'Round and__ 'round the__ drei - dels__ turn; they

Lesson 7 *Light The Candles Of Hanukkah*   **53**

3. Refine

Direct students to:

- Brainstorm as a class for ideas that will add stylistic variety and contrast to each of the six eight-measure sections.
- Form small groups of six to eight singers and work out a plan using dynamic contrasts, tempo changes, and/or stylistic variations for each phrase of "Light The Candles Of Hanukkah." Allow groups to sing for each other and critique each interpretation. As a class, decide on specific interpretation choices to incorporate in the final performance.
- Sing the entire song by memory using four-measure phrasing and the interpretation choices from the class.

Progress Checkpoints

Observe students' progress in:

- ✓ Determining various stylistic possibilities for performing the song.
- ✓ Singing with obvious observations of dynamics, tempos and styles.
- ✓ Performing expressively from memory.

CURRICULUM CONNECTIONS

Compare and Contrast

Research other winter holidays with traditional music from other cultures. Find differences and similarities in the celebrations (special songs, meals, dress, dances, games and family traditions).

ASSESSMENT

Informal Assessment

In this lesson, students showed the ability to:

- Use adequate breath support while singing slurred passages.
- Sing independently in a harmonic minor tonality.
- Identify and sing the major and relative minor tonalities.
- Make expressive decisions regarding variation and contrast in a song.
- Singing with an understanding of the text.

Student Self-Assessment

Have students evaluate their individual performances based on the following:

- Breath Management
- Phrasing
- Expressive Singing
- Accurate Pitches
- Correct Part-Singing

Have each student rate his/her performance of this song in the areas above on a scale of 1–5, 5 being the best.

MORE ABOUT...

Playing the Dreidel Game

Research how to make a dreidel. Work in groups of four. Each group should make a dreidel made of paper. On each side, write a one-measure pattern in G minor in 4/4 meter.

Exchange the paper dreidels and play the dreidel game. Spin the dreidel and then sing the pattern that appears on the side facing up. Spin and repeat singing several times. Set the dreidels side by side and sing the four-measure phrase that appears on the four topsides. Spin the dreidels and sing the new phrase.

spin.   We're so glad that it's Ha - nuk - kah.

spin.   We're so glad that it's Ha - nuk - kah.

Let the fun be - gin!   We're so glad that it's

Let the fun be - gin!   We're so glad that it's

Ha - nuk - kah.   Let the fun be - gin!

Ha - nuk - kah.   Let the fun be - gin!

Lesson 7 *Light The Candles Of Hanukkah* **55**

Individual and Group Performance Evaluation

To further measure growth of musical skills presented in this lesson, direct students to complete the Evaluation section on page 49.

- After singing either the B♭ major scale or G harmonic minor scale for a friend, evaluate the singing by asking, "How easily did he/she identify the type of scale sung?"
- After singing measures 38–45 as Tenor/Baritone duets, review each performance by asking, "Did this duet pair sing their parts with confidence using the correct rhythms, pitches and diction?"

EXTENSIONS

Exploring Other Songs of Hanukkah

Using solfège syllables, learn "Ma'oz Tzur," "Mi Y'maleil" or "S'vivon, sov, sov, sov." Look for similarities between these songs and "Light The Candles Of Hanukkah" (*tonality, text, rhythmic style and so on*). Add the text, sing for the class and incorporate the song into a performance with "Light The Candles Of Hanukkah."

Additional National Standards

The following National Standards are addressed through the Assessment, Extension, Enrichment and bottom-page activities:

4. Composing and arranging music within specific guidelines. **(a)**

5. Reading and notating music. **(c)**

7. Evaluating music and music performances. **(b)**

The Shepherd's Spiritual

OVERVIEW

Composer: American Spiritual, additional music by Donald Moore
Text: Traditional
Voicing: TB
Key: D major/E♭ major
Meter: 4/4
Form: IntroABABB'Coda
Style: Spiritual
Accompaniment: Piano, Tambourine
Programming: Seasonal Concert, Solo Feature, Contest

Vocal Ranges:

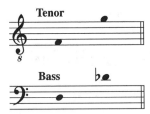

OBJECTIVES

After completing this lesson, students will be able to:

• Perform expressively from notation.
• Perform independently with accurate rhythm.
• Perform a varied repertoire representing styles from diverse cultures.

VOCABULARY

Have students review vocabulary in student lesson. Introduce terms found in the music. A complete glossary of terms is found on page 226 of the student book.

The Shepherd's Spiritual

Composer: American Spiritual, arranged by Donald Moore
Text: Traditional
Voicing: TB

VOCABULARY

spiritual
call and response
solo
altered pitch
quartet

🎲 **SKILL BUILDERS**

To learn more about syncopation, see Intermediate Sight-Singing, page 126.

Focus

• Perform expressively in both solo and ensemble singing.
• Read and perform rhythmic patterns that contain syncopation.
• Perform music representing the African American spiritual.

Getting Started

What makes a song fun to sing? Think of your favorite song. Why is the song appealing to you? On a sheet of paper, make a list of factors that contribute to making a song fun to sing. Share your list with the class.

As you learn "The Shepherd's Spiritual," look for features in the song that appear on your list. These might include (1) a singable melody, (2) catchy rhythms, (3) an inspirational text, (4) variety in texture (many voices versus a few voices), and (5) an opportunity to sing a solo. Among the many reasons to sing a song, having fun is one of the most important.

◆ History and Culture

"The Shepherd's Spiritual" is actually an arrangement of the holiday spiritual "Rise Up, Shepherd, and Follow." A part of the African American tradition, a **spiritual** is *a song that was first sung by slaves and is often based on a biblical theme or story.* Spirituals were probably sung while the slaves were working in the fields, engaging in social activities, or participating in worship. The use of syncopation and complex rhythms is very often found in spirituals.

This arrangement features **call and response,** *a technique in which a leader or group sings a phrase (call) followed by a response of the same phrase or a continuation of the phrase by another group.* This technique was often used in the creation and teaching of spirituals. It is found in the verses of this arrangement, and the call may be performed as a **solo** *(one person singing alone).*

56 Intermediate Tenor/Bass

RESOURCES

Intermediate Sight-Singing

Intermediate Sight-Singing
Sight-Singing in D Major, pages 99–102
Sight-Singing in E♭ Major, pages 141–143
Reading Rhythms in 4/4 Meter, pages 2–6
Reading Syncopation, pages 126–129

Teacher Resource Binder

Teaching Master 8, *Performing "The Shepherd's Spiritual" Musically*
Evaluation Master 3, *Assessing Performing Syncopated Rhythms*
Skill Builder 24, *Rhythm Challenge Using Syncopation*
Kodály 5, *Music Reading: Pitch*
For additional resources, see TRB Table of Contents.

Links to Learning

◆ Vocal

An **altered pitch** is the same as an accidental, or *any pitch that is changed by a sharp, flat or natural that is not included in the key signature of the piece.* Altered pitches are used in "The Shepherd's Spiritual" when F# (*mi*) changes to F♮ (*me*—pronounced "meh" or "mā"). Perform the following example to practice tuning altered pitches. Sing in the range that best fits your voice.

◆ Theory

Read and perform the following example to practice the syncopated rhythms used in this song. Divide into two groups. Chant and clap the lines separately and then together.

Evaluation

Demonstrate how well you have learned the skills and concepts featured in the lesson "The Shepherd's Spiritual" by completing the following:

- Form a **quartet** *(a group of four singers)*. Sing measures 4–12 taking turns singing the solo lines. Evaluate your performance based on in-tune singing, rhythmic accuracy and musical expression.

- With a partner, take turns singing measures 24–32 while the other claps or taps beats 2 and 4. Evaluate how well you were able to sing syncopation accurately and maintain the steady beat.

Lesson 8 *The Shepherd's Spiritual* **57**

RESOURCES

Intermediate Tenor/Bass Rehearsal/Performance CD

CD 1:15 Voices
CD 1:16 Accompaniment Only
CD 3:9 Vocal Practice Track—Tenor
CD 4:7 Vocal Practice Track—Bass

National Standards

1. Singing, alone and with others, a varied repertoire of music. **(b, c)**

LINKS TO LEARNING

Vocal

The Vocal section is designed to prepare students to:

- Recognize the difference between a major third and a minor third interval visually and aurally.
- Identify altered pitches.

Have students:

- Read and discuss Vocal section on page 57.
- Sing several altered pitches (*do* to *di*, *sol* to *si*, *mi* to *ma*)
- Sing examples on solfège syllables.
- Practice until all pitches are sung in tune.

Theory

The Theory section is designed to practice reading a two-part rhythmic exercise.

Have students:

- Learn each part separately.
- Chant, clap or tap the lines together.
- Switch roles.

The Shepherd's Spiritual

For TB and Piano

Arranged with additional music by
DONALD MOORE

Based on an American Spiritual

58   Intermediate Tenor/Bass

LESSON PLAN

Suggested Teaching Sequence and Performance Tips

1. Introduce

Direct students to:

- Read and discuss the information found in the Getting Started section on page 56.
- Practice singing the melodic pattern in the Vocal section on page 57. Relate to the melody in the score *(measures 9–12)*.
- Practice chanting the two-part exercise in the Theory section on page 57. Once students can chant the rhythms of each part, divide into two groups and chant the parts at the same time. Do the same procedure for clapping the exercise.

Progress Checkpoints

Observe students' progress in:

✓ Singing the correct pitches when switching from the minor third *(ma)* to major third *(mi)*.

✓ Chanting and clapping an exercise that contains syncopation.

TEACHER 2 TEACHER

"The Shepherd's Spiritual" is a lively spiritual that can showcase one or more soloists. Perform it with the tambourine part for added rhythmic excitement!

2. Rehearse

Direct students to:

- Begin chanting each eight-measure section observing the rhythm of each part. Use a metronome during the process of learning the piece. It will assist the students in developing an internal beat, help them with the syncopation that occurs throughout the piece.

- Practice chanting rhythmically with the articulation that will be used when singing on the words.

- Read the pitches that are in D major using solfège syllables. Ask students to write in the solfège syllables when accidentals occur. After this section is secure, move on to the E♭ major section and sing it using solfège syllables.

Progress Checkpoints

Observe students' progress in:

✓ Chanting the text using the correct rhythms.

✓ Singing the correct pitches in D major and E♭ major.

CULTURAL CONNECTIONS

Spirituals

The enslaved Africans brought music with the following elements to the New World: syncopation, polyrhythm, pentatonic and gap scales, and the idea of music combined with body movements.

From the suffering of the ocean crossing and a life of subjugation, they created a new genre, the "spiritual," or religious folk song of the slave. It revealed their unhappiness and suffering, taught facts, sent coded messages, provided a common language, and helped them share religious rituals and beliefs. In the spiritual, the singer must express a personal connection with a deity or god. The spiritual reflects a true historical picture of the lives of slaves as told by slaves themselves.

3. Refine

Direct students to:

- Pay particular attention to beginning consonants because they tend to add to the overall effectiveness in the style of a spiritual. It usually adds drive to the piece. In this piece, the "r" of "rise," the "sh" of "shepherd" and the "f" of "follow" strategically add the rhythmic drive. Stress these words and boost the consonant.

- In the Bass part, sing "ah" and "oo" during the solo line. Ask students to place a pulsated "d" before the vowel sound. The "d" should be made in the front of the mouth with a flat tongue. This will help keep the rhythmic drive in that part during the solo.

- In singing the word "follow" in measures 13–14, note the drastic dynamic change from measure 12 to 13. Have students circle that dynamic change. To add musical drive in those measures, stress the "fol," back off on the eighth note of "-low" and crescendo through the half note to the next "fol" and stress. Do this for both words, with the second "follow" leading to the word "rise." This same sequence happens again at measures 33–34 and measures 41–42.

60 Intermediate Tenor/Bass

TEACHING STRATEGY

Sight-Singing: Making Mistakes

The goal of sight-singing is to perform a piece of music at first sight, without studying it beforehand. At the beginning, students are likely to make a lot of mistakes. Help them understand that mistakes are how people learn, and that with practice they will get much better. Discuss how laughing at mistakes of others can be hurtful, but that if everyone laughs together during these first few attempts, it will reduce the pressure until everyone's sight-singing improves.

take good___ heed to the an-gel's words,

tutti
Rise up, shep-herd, and fol - low;___ You'll for-get your___ flocks, you'll for-
tutti
Rise up, shep-herd, and fol - low.___
Oo_____

get___ your herds,___ Rise up, shep-herd, and fol - low.
tutti f
Rise up, shep-herd, and fol - low.___

solo or unison

tutti f f

Lesson 8 *The Shepherd's Spiritual* **61**

- Note the sudden dynamic change between measures 47 and 49. Have the students circle those two dynamic changes to help during memorization. You may want to start softer than what is indicated in measure 52, for an even bigger dramatic affect on the word "follow." Whatever is done with the singers, remind the percussionist and the accompanist of the same dynamic changes with the tambourine part that is played throughout the piece. They will add much to the performance if they are sensitive to what you and the singers are doing musically.

Progress Checkpoints

Observe students' progress in:
- ✓ Singing initial consonants with rhythmic drive.
- ✓ Observing drastic dynamic changes in the vocals and accompaniment.

TEACHING STRATEGY

Extra Help: Clapping Off-Beats

If the students are having difficulty clapping the off-beats, have them do a step-clap pattern, with the step on the beat. Add the words "yes, sir," the word "yes" going with the steps, and "sir" with the claps. Eventually just whisper the words, then think them as they step-clap. Finally, remove the steps, leaving only the claps on the off-beats.

ASSESSMENT

Informal Assessment

In this lesson, students showed the ability to:

- Read and perform music representing the style of a spiritual in the keys of D major and E♭ major.
- Sing expressively with good intonation using rhythmic articulation when performing consonants.

Student Self-Assessment

Have students evaluate their individual performances based on the following:

- Diction
- Expressive Singing
- Accurate Pitches
- Accurate Rhythms
- Correct Part-Singing

Have each student rate his/her performance of this song in the areas above on a scale of 1–5, 5 being the best.

TEACHING STRATEGY

Interpreting the Piece Through Dynamics

Have students:

- Review the notation of "The Shepherd's Spiritual" for all dynamic markings.
- Identify the purpose behind each marking, such as phrasing, a certain meaning in the text, and so on.
- Sing the piece, attending to the dynamics and phrasing for more meaningful interpretation.

Individual and Group Performance Evaluation

To further measure growth of musical skills presented in this lesson, direct students to complete the Evaluation section on page 57.

- After singing measures 4–12 in quartets, evaluate the performance by asking, "How in tune were the singers? How accurate were their rhythms? Did they sing with the proper amount of expression?"

- After performing measures 24–32 in pairs, review each performance by asking, "Did this duet pair sing the correct rhythms while keeping beats 2 and 4 steady?"

MORE ABOUT...

Critiquing

Play a recording of a choir performing a song like "The Shepherd's Spiritual." The selection would need solo lines and various instruments. After the students have listened to the recording, ask them to comment on whether they enjoyed the piece, and what specifically did they enjoy about it. Ask for details concerning the instrumentalist, the soloist, and the choir. Ask them if they thought that all three worked as a team to make the performance great, or did any particular group stand out from the three. Ask them if there is anything about the recording that could be added to their performance to improve it or make it more exciting.

EXTENSION

Solo Opportunities

Since the solo lines in this piece are so short, you can provide an opportunity for several students to sing solos. Give the students the measure numbers for each solo *(8, 24, 28)*. Teach all of the students how you would like the solo to be sung. Tell them the number of solos on which they can audition. Also offer the freedom to audition on the solo of their choice. Audition during class, so that all students hear and can determine those soloists who are meeting the criteria set by you. Make a comment sheet that can be given to the soloist after the audition with your feedback on his or her performance. Consider a ballot-type vote from the students in selecting the soloist. The reward would be to perform the song on the concert with the soloist selected by you and the class.

Additional National Standards

2. Performing, alone and with others, a varied repertoire of music. **(b)**

5. Reading and notating music. **(a, b)**

7. Evaluating music and music performances. **(b)**

SPOTLIGHT

Vowels

The style of a given piece of music dictates how we should pronounce the words. If we are singing a more formal, classical piece, then we need to form taller vowels as in very proper English. If we are singing in a jazz or pop style, then we should pronounce the words in a more relaxed, conversational way. To get the feeling of taller vowels for classical singing, do the following:

- Let your jaw gently drop down and back as if it were on a hinge.
- Place your hands on your cheeks beside the corners of your mouth.
- Sigh on an *ah* [ɑ] vowel sound, but do not spread the corners of your mouth.
- Now sigh on other vowel sounds—*eh* [ɛ], *ee* [i], *oh* [o] and *oo* [u]—keeping the back of the tongue relaxed.
- As your voice goes from higher notes to lower notes, think of gently opening a tiny umbrella inside your mouth.

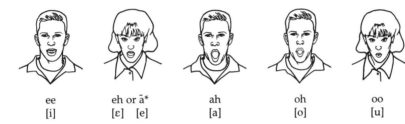

ee	eh or ā*	ah	oh	oo
[i]	[ɛ] [e]	[a]	[o]	[u]

Other vowel sounds used in singing are diphthongs. A **diphthong** is *a combination of two vowel sounds*. For example, the vowel *ay* consists of two sounds: *eh* [E] and *ee* [i]. To sing a diphthong correctly, stay on the first vowel sound for the entire length of the note, only lightly adding the second vowel sound as you move to another note or lift off the note.

I = *ah*_____(ee) [ɑi]

boy = *oh*_____(ee) [oi]

down = *ah*_____(oo) [ɑu]

*Note: This is an Italian "ā," which is one sound, and not an American "ā," which is a diphthong, or two sounds.

RESOURCES

Teacher Resource Binder
Vocal Development 15, *Vowels*
Reference 16, *My Music Dictionary*
Reference 29, *Zeroing in on IPA*

National Standards
1. Singing, alone and with others. **(b)**

VOWELS

Objectives
- Demonstrate basic performance techniques through proper use of vowels.

Suggested Teaching Sequence
Direct students to:
- Read the Spotlight On Vowels on student page 65 and identify the importance of uniform vowels in singing.
- Practice the exercise as presented on page 65.
- Identify the five basic vowels. Practice speaking and singing each.
- Define diphthong and demonstrate the proper and improper way to sing a diphthong.
- Find examples of each of the five basic vowels and diphthongs in music they are currently studying.
- Compare the concept of uniform vowels to appropriate large- and small-ensemble performance techniques.

Progress Checkpoints
Observe students' progress in:
- ✓ Their ability to speak the five basic vowels properly and uniformly.
- ✓ Their ability to define diphthong, find examples in the music and sing them properly.
- ✓ Their ability to relate the importance of uniform vowels in ensemble singing.

Now Is The Month of Maying

OVERVIEW

Composer: Thomas Morley (1557–1602), arranged by Sherri Porterfield

Text: Thomas Morley

Voicing: TTB

Key: A major

Meter: 4/4

Form: ABABAB

Style: British Renaissance Madrigal

Accompaniment: A cappella

Programming: Concert Opener, Contest

Vocal Ranges:

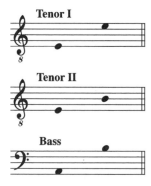

OBJECTIVES

After completing this lesson, students will be able to:

• Describe musical sound.

• Sing a varied repertoire of music.

• Perform a varied repertoire of music representing styles from diverse cultures.

VOCABULARY

Have students review vocabulary in student lesson. Introduce terms found in the music. A complete glossary of terms is found on page 226 of the student book.

Now Is The Month of Maying

Composer: Thomas Morley (1557–1602), arranged by Sherri Porterfield
Text: Thomas Morley
Voicing: TTB

VOCABULARY

Renaissance period
madrigal
homophony
polyphony
a cappella

MUSIC & HISTORY

To learn more about the Renaissance period, see page 98.

Focus

• Describe and perform homophony and polyphony.

• Sing music in a madrigal style.

• Perform music representing the Renaissance period.

Getting Started

Do you know any modern-day "Renaissance" men or women? Today we use that term for a person with a wide variety of interests and expertise. English composer Thomas Morley (1557–1602) could be considered an original Renaissance man. Not only did he live during the **Renaissance period** *(c. 1430–1600)*, he was a successful businessman, entrepreneur, organist, composer and teacher. Morley also wrote one of the most important instruction manuals of the time for vocal music and composition, "A Plaine and Easie Introduction to Practicall Musicke"(1597). He must have also been very wise and humble, because in the manual he wrote:

"…never think so well of yourself, but let other men praise you, if you are praiseworthy: then may you justly take it to yourself, so long as it is done with moderation and without arrogance."

That is still good advice for us to remember today.

◆ History and Culture

Thomas Morley is best known as a composer of **madrigals,** or *short secular choral pieces written in the common language, usually with themes of love.* During the Renaissance, **homophony** *(a type of music in which there are two or more parts with similar or identical rhythms being sung or played at the same time)* and **polyphony** *(a type of music in which there are two or more different melodic lines being sung at the same time)* were used in music to create harmony. Examples of both are found in "Now Is The Month Of Maying."

RESOURCES

Intermediate Sight-Singing

Sight-Singing in A Major, pages 152–163

Reading Rhythms in 4/4 Meter, pages 2–6

Reading Eighth Notes and Rests, pages 26–27

Reading Dotted Notes, pages 45, 46, 49

Teacher Resource Binder

Skill Builder 29, *Singing in Three Parts*

Skill Builder 30, *Solfège Hand Signs*

Music and History 1, *Characteristics of Renaissance Music: 1430–1600*

Music and History 3, *Thomas Morley, a "Renaissance" Composer*

Music and History 5, *Fine Art Teaching Strategy: Renaissance*

For additional resources, see TRB Table of Contents.

Links to Learning

◆ **Theory**

The following phrases are examples of homophony and polyphony. Read and perform each phrase using solfège syllables or a neutral syllable.

Homophony

Polyphony

◆ **Artistic Expression**

The term *madrigal style* now refers to the light, delicate and clearly articulated singing that is necessary for each independent **a cappella** *(singing without instrumental accompaniment)* vocal line to fit together. Work in small groups with other singers on your voice part until you can sing your part cleanly, expressively and as if you were singing a solo line.

Evaluation

Demonstrate how well you have learned the concepts and skills presented in "Now Is The Month Of Maying" by completing the following:

* Define *homophony* and *polyphony*. Locate examples of each in the music. Share your findings with a classmate and decide if your choices were correct.

* In a trio with one singer on a part, sing measures 1–8 to demonstrate "madrigal style" singing. This includes a light, delicate tone and clear articulation. Decide how well you did.

Lesson 9 *Now Is The Month Of Maying* **67**

RESOURCES

Intermediate Tenor/Bass Rehearsal/Performance CD

CD 1:17 Voices

CD 1:18 Accompaniment Only

CD 3:10 Vocal Practice Track—Tenor I

CD 3:11 Vocal Practice Track—Tenor II

CD 4:8 Vocal Practice Track—Bass

National Standards

1. Singing, alone and with others, a varied repertoire of music. **(c, e)**

6. Listening to, analyzing, and describing music. **(a)**

LINKS TO LEARNING

Theory

The Theory section is designed to prepare students to:

* Identify and perform homophony.
* Identify and perform polyphony.

Have students:

* Sing the homophony example on "loo."
* Discuss how the parts move together at the same time.
* Sing the polyphony example in solfège syllables.
* Discuss how the parts move independently.

Artistic Expression

The Artistic Expression section is designed to prepare students to sing in small groups without instrumental accompaniment.

Have students:

* Form trios and sing the previous exercises with one on a part.
* Define *a cappella* singing.
* Perform the examples in the Theory section with a small group.
* Practice until all parts are sung clearly and expressively.

LESSON PLAN

Suggested Teaching Sequence and Performance Tips

1. Introduce

Direct students to:

- Read and discuss the information found in the Getting Started section on page 66.
- Practice singing the homophonic and polyphonic exercises in the Theory section on page 67.
- Form trios and sing the exercises a cappella as described in the Artistic Expression section on page 67.

Progress Checkpoints

Observe students' progress in:

- ✓ Singing homophony and polyphony with confidence.
- ✓ Singing in a small ensemble a cappella.

Now Is The Month Of Maying

Arranged by
SHERRI PORTERFIELD

THOMAS MORLEY
(1557–1602)

TEACHER 2 TEACHER

"Now Is The Month Of Maying" is one of Thomas Morley's most accessible madrigals. The lively rhythmic exchanges between voices and repetitive harmonic structure make for a piece your chorister will enjoy singing.

2. Rehearse

Direct students to:

- Listen to measures 1–18. Locate and identify the homophonic and polyphonic sections that occur in these measures (*measures 1–4, 10–12 homophonic texture; measures 5–9 introduce slight polyphony in Tenor II; measures 13–18 clear use of polyphonic texture*).
- Sight-sing all parts using solfège syllables in measures 1–4.
- Repeat measures 1–4 on the syllable "doo" in a staccato style. Emphasize singing *forte*, but with lightness and buoyancy of feeling while using staccato articulation.
- Sing measures 1–4 *allegretto* and with a legato line this time. Do not let a legato line change the established buoyancy or rhythmic accuracy.
- Sight-sing measures 5–9.
- Have each student sing his/her part individually for measures 5–9 as if it were the main melody. Sing again with all parts emphasizing equal voicing by stressing the rhythmic differences of each line.
- Sight-sing and compare measures 10–18 to measures 1–9.

Progress Checkpoints

Observe students' progress in:

✓ Identifying uses of homophony and polyphony.

✓ Singing with various articulations.

✓ Their ability to sing parts with confidence.

MORE ABOUT...

The Madrigal Style

Madrigals, composed mostly in Italy and England, were secular vocal pieces, often with a theme of unrequited love. Many madrigals were polyphonic, with intricately interwoven melodic lines, which had many scalewise passages and fast-moving rhythms. The English madrigals often had couplets of rhymes, interspersed with refrains of *fa la* or the like. Madrigals were usually composed for individual voices on each part, to be sung with a light, quick style that enhanced the intricate weaving of the lines and quick rhythms. The dominant line was sung stronger, and each line came forward or receded to accommodate the most important melodic part. Help students identify characteristics of the madrigal in "Now Is The Month Of Maying."

3. Refine

Direct students to:

- Circle the notes you will sing in measure 15 to clarify voice crossing.

- Practice individual parts in measures 13–17. Work towards clarity of pitch, phrasing and rhythmic accuracy.

- Rehearse all parts together in measures 13–17.

- Isolate measures 10–12 and work to sing the accidentals in tune.

- Review measures 10–18 with all parts singing together.

- Listen to measures 19–end. Have students compare and contrast with measures 1–18 (*second portion of the piece is musically the same as first portion with the only difference in the text*).

- Work individual parts in measures 19–end for closer comparison with first portion of piece.

- Practice all parts together in measures 19–end, emphasizing changes in dynamics while maintaining a steady tempo.

- Review entire piece.

MORE ABOUT...

Celebrations During the Renaissance Period

The Elizabethans were very creative in their pursuit of leisure activities. All through the year they found special ways to keep themselves entertained. There were feasts and festivals for every season of the year. Many of the holiday celebrations begun in the Renaissance continue today.

During Lent, Shrove Tuesday was one of the festivals observed with feasts, carnivals, wearing masks and playing games. The May Day celebration, which is commemorated in the song "Now Is The Month Of Maying," consisted of the decorating of the Maypole and dancing around it. The year was finished out with All Hallow's Eve and Christmas.

- Review individual parts with an emphasis on singing accurate half-step leading tones and in the large leaps in the bass line. Have the non-singing students listen to determine if singers are "stepping up" or "sliding" into position.
- Bring out the text with clean and accurate articulation, clearly define when and where to take breaths.
- Work towards memorization of all verses.

Progress Checkpoints

Observe students' progress in:
- ✓ Identifying the similarities of the music.
- ✓ Bringing out the melody when singing the homophonic sections.
- ✓ Allowing for equal voices in the polyphonic sections
- ✓ Singing with energy throughout the piece, even in the soft sections.
- ✓ Singing leading tones in tune.
- ✓ Clean, clear attack of leaping intervals in the bass line.

MORE ABOUT...

Arranger Sherri Porterfield

Graduating with a B.S.E. in Music Education from the University of Memphis and a M.M. in choral conducting from the University of Missouri-Kansas City, Sherri Porterfield is currently a choral music director in the Olathe, KS School District. She has been selected twice to *Who's Who Among America's Teachers* and is a member of Music Educators National Conference, American Choral Directors Association, Pi Kappa Lambda National Music Honor Society and ASCAP.

ASSESSMENT

Informal Assessment

In this lesson, the students showed the ability to:

- Identify homophonic and polyphonic texture.
- Sing with good intonation and phrasing using dynamic markings as indicated in the score.
- Sing three-part a cappella repertoire.
- Sing a Renaissance madrigal in a stylistically appropriate manner.

Student Self-Assessment

Have students evaluate their individual performances based on the following:

- Diction
- Expressive Singing
- Accurate Pitches
- Accurate Rhythms
- Correct Part-Singing

Have each student rate his/her performance of this song in the areas above on a scale of 1–5, 5 being the best.

TEACHING STRATEGY

Dynamics

Have students identify the term dynamics as relating to the loudness or softness of a sound.

pp—*pianissimo*—very soft
p—*piano*—soft
mp—*mezzo piano*—medium soft
mf—*mezzo forte*—medium loud
f—*forte*—loud
ff—*fortissimo*—very loud
crescendo—gradually going from soft to loud
decrescendo—gradually going from loud to soft

grace - ful nymphs and speak, Shall we play bar - ley

break? Fa la la la la, Fa la la la, Fa la

Fa la la la la la la la la la la la la

Fa la la la la la la la la la la la la

Fa la la la la la la la. Say la.

la la la la. Say la.

la la la la

Additional National Standards

The following National Standards are addressed through the Assessment, Extension, Enrichment and bottom-page activities:

4. Composing and arranging music within specific guidelines. **(a)**

5. Reading and notating music. **(a)**

7. Evaluating music and music performances. **(a)**

Individual and Group Performance Evaluation

To further measure growth of musical skills presented in this lesson, direct students to complete the Evaluation section on page 67.

- After defining homophony and polyphony, find examples of both in the score *(homophony: measures 1–4, 10–12, 19–22, 28–30, 37–40, 46–48 and polyphony: measures 5–9, 13–18, 23–27, 31–36, 41–45, 49–54).*
- After singing measures 1–8 in trios with one on a part, review each performance by asking, "Did this trio sing their parts in tune using a light and delicate tone?"

EXTENSION

Writing in the Polyphonic Style

Try your hand at writing in the polyphonic style. Begin with a simple melody, such as "Row, Row, Row Your Boat." Sing through the melody and fill in the notes with scale-wise passages to create a more decorative, rhythmically active melody. Create a line above the melody that begins after the melody and has some different rhythms as well as the same rhythms as the melody. In the last two measures of your composition, use slower rhythms to prepare for the final cadence. Teach your composition to a friend and perform it for the class.

Der Herr segne euch

OVERVIEW

Composer: Johann Sebastian
Bach (1685–1750), arranged
by Barry Talley
Text: Psalm 115:14
Voicing: TB
Key: C major
Meter: 3/2
Form: IntroABCDEDEA'
Style: German Baroque
Anthem
Accompaniment: Piano
Programming: Contest,
Festival

Vocal Ranges:

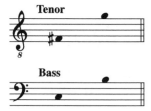

OBJECTIVES

After completing this lesson,
students will be able to:

• Identify music forms
presented through music
notation.

• Sing individually a varied
repertoire of music.

• Classify aurally presented
music representing diverse
periods.

Der Herr segne euch

Composer: Johann Sebastian Bach (1685–1750), arranged by Barry Talley
Text: Psalm 115:14
Voicing: TB

VOCABULARY

cantata
Baroque period
head voice
chest voice
counterpoint

MUSIC & HISTORY

*To learn more about the
Baroque period,
see page 102.*

Focus

• Identify and perform music written in counterpoint.

• Demonstrate musical artistry through the use of proper
German diction.

• Describe and perform music from the Baroque period.

Getting Started

Imagine having a piece of music composed specifically for
you! This is exactly what happened when German composer
Johann Sebastian Bach composed "Der Herr segne euch" as part
of a cantata to celebrate a wedding. A **cantata** is *a musical piece
made up of several movements for singers and instrumentalists.* "Der
Herr segne euch" is a blessing for the wedding couple.

◆ History and Culture

Genius can be defined as "extraordinary intellectual power,
especially as manifested in creative activity." German composer
Johann Sebastian Bach (1685–1750) was a musical genius. He is
considered by many to be the greatest composer who ever lived.
In addition to being tremendously gifted, Bach was a diligent
student who studied and practiced often.

Bach lived and composed during the **Baroque period**
(1600–1750). The music of the Baroque period used harmonic
structures differently, through the development of vertical
chords. This period also saw the development of new musical
forms, such as the cantata. Frequently, the music from this period
features a simple melody, supported by a fancy accompaniment
with a continuously moving bass line. Bach was such a
monumental composer of the Baroque style that the ending date
of the Baroque period is actually the year of his death.

74   **Intermediate Tenor/Bass**

RESOURCES

Intermediate Sight-Singing

Sight-Singing in C Major, pages 7–14,
  15–17, 28–30, 66–67, 110–111
Reading Dotted Notes, pages 45, 48, 49
2/2 Meter and Cut Time, page 140

Teacher Resource Binder

Teaching Master 9, *Pronunciation Guide
  for "Der Herr segne euch"*
Teaching Master 10, *Text Emphasis in
  "Der Herr segne euch"*
Music and History 6, *Characteristics of
  Baroque Music: 1600–1750*
Music and History 8, *Johann Sebastian
  Bach, a "Baroque" Composer*
For additional resources, see TRB Table
  of Contents.

Links to Learning

◆ Vocal

Perform the following example to increase ease in singing from your **head voice** *(the higher part of the singer's vocal range)* to your **chest voice** *(the lower part of the singer's vocal range)*. Begin in a light head voice and sing from high to low on "oo" while maintaining good breath support. Repeat the pattern a half step lower each time.

◆ Theory

Counterpoint is *the combination of two or more melodic lines.* The individual melodies constitute the horizontal line while the intervals occurring between them represent the vertical harmony. Bach was a master at composing contrapuntal music. Perform the following example to develop skill in singing two-part counterpoint.

Evaluation

Demonstrate how well you have learned the skills and concepts featured in the lesson "Der Herr segne euch" by completing the following:

• With two to four singers, sing the Theory section above in two parts. Evaluate how well your group was able to sing in two parts written in counterpoint.

• Write the text in German. Beneath the German, write the English translation. Underline the important words in the text. Read the text aloud, stressing the important words in the text. Transfer this word stress to your performance of the piece. Evaluate how well you were able to perform each appropriate word stress.

RESOURCES

Intermediate Tenor/Bass Rehearsal/Performance CD

CD 1:19 Voices

CD 1:20 Accompaniment Only

CD 3:12 Vocal Practice Track—Tenor

CD 4:9 Vocal Practice Track—Bass

National Standards

1. Singing, alone and with others, a varied repertoire of music. **(b)**

6. Listening to, analyzing, and describing music. **(b)**

9. Understanding music in relation to history and culture. **(a)**

LINKS TO LEARNING

Vocal

The Vocal section is designed to prepare students to:

• Develop breath support.

• Expand vocal range.

• Discover head and chest voice.

Have students:

• Demonstrate a "yawn-sigh" from very high to low.

• Sing each measure on an "oo" vowel. Start high and gradually slide down, making a smooth transition to the chest voice.

Theory

The Theory section is designed to prepare students to identify and develop skill in singing two-part counterpoint.

Have students:

• Learn both parts independently.

• Divide into two sections singing both parts at the same time.

• Perform counterpoint.

• Sing independently.

LESSON PLAN

Suggested Teaching Sequence and Performance Tips

1. Introduce

Direct students to:

- Read and discuss the information found in the Getting Started section on page 74.

- Practice singing the vocal exercise shown in the Vocal section on page 75 to develop breath support and extend the vocal range.

- Practice singing the two-part exercise in the Theory section on page 75 that demonstrates counterpoint. Sing the parts on a neutral syllable such as "loo" before singing it with the German text.

Der Herr segne euch
(May God Bless You)

For TB and Piano

Arranged by BARRY TALLEY
English translation by J. MARK BAKER

Text from Psalm 115:14
JOHANN SEBASTIAN BACH (1685–1750)

76   Intermediate Tenor/Bass

TEACHER2TEACHER

The imitative textures and beautiful legato phrases of Bach's "Der Herr segne euch" will challenge and inspire your students to their best singing. Give elegant shape to the two vocal lines, always listening for vowel purity.

Progress Checkpoints

Observe students' progress in:

✓ Their ability to sing in an extended range using appropriate breath support.

✓ Their ability to sing an exercise using counterpoint and a German text.

CURRICULUM CONNECTIONS

Time Line

Research the period from 1600–1750. Describe the lifestyle of the people who lived in the German cities. What forms of transportation did they have? Describe the schools and churches. What famous statesmen, scientist and writers lived during this time? What famous inventions or discoveries occurred? What was happening in America at this time?

2. Rehearse

Direct students to:

- Conduct in 3/2 *(three beats per measure with the half note receiving one beat)*. Chant the rhythms of each part in measures 7–15. When secure, combine parts.

- Apply this procedure to measures 19–27, noting the rhythm of the Tenor part in measures 7–15 is now in the Bass part.

- Establish the key and sing measures 7–27 using solfège syllables.

- Divide the piece into sections, paying particular attention to how the parts differ rhythmically. When the parts move together rhythmically, the music is described as *homophonic*. When the parts move with different rhythms, the music is *polyphonic*.

- Locate the piano interludes. Practice conducting and counting each interlude.

78   Intermediate Tenor/Bass

MORE ABOUT...

Composer Johann Sebastian Bach (1685–1750)

Bach created masterpieces of choral and instrumental music. He wrote both sacred and secular music. Bach's music is regarded as the high point of the Baroque era, which lasted from 1600 to 1750. Bach married twice and was the father of 20 children, several of whom became well-known composers. Johann Sebastian Bach died July 28, 1750.

Progress Checkpoints

Observe students' progress in:

✓ Performing with rhythmic accuracy while conducting in 3/2.

✓ Singing accurate pitches.

✓ Their ability to identify homophonic and polyphonic sections.

TEACHING STRATEGY

Performance Techniques

Have students:

1. Identify appropriate performance techniques to be used in the performance of this song.

2. Either in small ensembles or with the entire choir (large ensemble), perform the song exhibiting these performance techniques.

3. Describe the performance techniques experienced during the performance.

4. Critique the performance based on the observed performance techniques.

5. Repeat this process often in both informal and formal concert settings.

3. Refine

Direct students to:

- Sing sections on a neutral syllable, such as "loo." Strive to match voices for a vocal blend. Listen to both parts to achieve balance, while using energetic breath support.
- Apply the dynamic markings. Give particular attention to the sections marked with specific *crescendo/decrescendo (measures 51–52, 53–55, 71–72, 73–75 and 104–105).*
- Sing each section using the German text. Work to unify the sound and sing with expressive word stress.

TEACHING STRATEGY

Solo and Small Ensemble Performances

Have students:

1. Prepare solos and small ensembles for performance or competition.
2. Interpret music symbols and terms referring to dynamics, tempo and articulation during the performance.
3. Evaluate the quality of the performance using standard terminology.

Observe students' progress in:

✓ Singing phrases with energetic breath support.

✓ Listening within and outside the section to establish blend and balance.

✓ Dynamics performed as marked in the score.

✓ Proper word stress, precise diction and unified German text.

MUSIC LITERACY

When Does Polyphonic Texture Work?

To help students expand their music literacy, have them:

• Identify several familiar melodies and sing them as rounds, raising a hand when the melodies stop sounding good.

• Identify several familiar rounds, such as: "Frère Jacques" and "Row, Row, Row Your Boat."

• Discuss reasons some melodies work better than others as rounds. (*They are based on one chord, or a repeating chord sequence, that allows the harmony to remain consonant.*)

ASSESSMENT

Informal Assessment

In this lesson, students showed the ability to:

- Sing in two parts.
- Sing in an extended range, using appropriate breath support.
- Read and perform rhythms in 3/2 meter.
- Locate homophonic and polyphonic writing styles in the score.
- Apply dynamic markings as indicated in the score.
- Sing in German, using proper diction and word stress.

82   Intermediate Tenor/Bass

CURRICULUM CONNECTIONS

The Baroque Style

Have students:

- Research the social and musical characteristics of the Renaissance and Baroque periods.
- Identify characteristics of this piece that make it an example of Renaissance music.
- Identify the characteristics of this piece that make it an example of Baroque music.

Find examples of art, architecture, poetry, drama, or dance that reflect any or all of the characteristics identified in the piece.

Student Self-Assessment

Have students evaluate their individual performances based on the following:

- Breath Management
- Phrasing
- Diction
- Foreign Language
- Correct Part-Singing

Have each student rate his/her performance of this song in the areas above on a scale of 1–5, 5 being the best.

ASSESSMENT

Evaluating the Quality of a Performance

Have students:

1. Watch a video or listen to an audio recording of this piece as performed by the choir.
2. Compare this performance to exemplary models such as other recordings or other live performances of the piece.
3. Develop constructive suggestions for improvement based on the comparison.

Individual and Group Performance Evaluation

To further measure growth of musical skills presented in this lesson, direct students to complete the Evaluation section on page 75.

- After singing the exercise from the Theory section in groups of two or four singers, evaluate the performance by asking, "How confident were the singers on their parts? Were the correct rhythms, pitches and lyrics used?"

- After writing the English translation below the German text, speak the text to a friend and then switch roles. After speaking the text using word stress, sing the piece with the same emphasis. Review each performance by asking, "Was the proper word stress used when the text was spoken and then sung?"

84   Intermediate Tenor/Bass

TEACHING STRATEGY

Performing from Memory

Have students:

1. Memorize this piece by learning shorter phrases at a time.

2. Perform it from memory on a program or in competition.

3. Further develop memorization skills by memorizing other songs and solos to perform for the class informally or at formal concerts.

EXTENSION

Translating from German

After studying the German text of "Der Herr segne euch" create an English text for the song. Keep the main idea of the song and strive to divide the words in a way that fits the rhythm and the style of the piece. Pay careful attention to syllabic stress. After creating a text, practice refining it through performance and evaluation. Experiment by replacing certain words and working until you have created a meaningful English translation.

MUSIC, SOCIETY AND CULTURE

Have students perform additional songs representing diverse cultures, including American and Texas heritage. Go to **music.glencoe.com**, the Web site for Glencoe's choral music programs, for additional music selections students can perform.

Additional National Standards

The following National Standards are addressed through the Assessment, Extension, Enrichment and bottom-page activities:

1. Singing, alone and with others, a varied repertoire of music. **(d)**

7. Evaluating music and music performances. **(b)**

8. Understanding relationships between music, the other arts, and disciplines outside the arts. **(b)**

Ave Verum Corpus

OVERVIEW

Composer: Wolfgang Amadeus Mozart (1756–1791), arranged by Joyce Eilers

Text: Eucharistic Hymn

Voicing: TTB

Key: F major

Meter: 2/2

Form: Through-composed

Style: German Classical Anthem

Accompaniment: Piano or A cappella

Programming: Festival, Special Services, Honor Choir

Vocal Ranges:

Tenor I

Tenor II

Bass

OBJECTIVES

After completing this lesson, students will be able to:

- Demonstrate characteristic vocal timbre individually.
- Sing a varied repertoire of music.
- Classify aurally presented music representing diverse periods.

VOCABULARY

Have students review vocabulary in student lesson. Introduce terms found in the music. A complete glossary of terms is found on page 226 of the student book.

Ave Verum Corpus

Composer: Wolfgang Amadeus Mozart (1756–1791), arranged by Joyce Eilers

Text: Eucharist hymn

Voicing: TTB

VOCABULARY

Classical period

legato

International Phonetic Alphabet

Focus

- Sing with legato phrasing and proper breath support.
- Sing a Latin text with comprehension and expression.
- Describe and perform music from the Renaissance period.

Getting Started

A personalized gift from a friend is a joy to receive. People with special talents have the ability to give unique and creative gifts to their family and friends. Match the following people with the gift they might give.

MUSIC & HISTORY

To learn more about the Classical period, see page 106.

1. Julia Child	**a.** an evening gown
2. Walt Whitman	**b.** a gold bracelet
3. Coco Chanel	**c.** a nature poem
4. Mickey Mantle	**d.** a French dessert
5. Charles Tiffany	**e.** an autographed baseball

And, of course, if you were a friend of Wolfgang Amadeus Mozart, you might receive a song.

◆ History and Culture

Wolfgang Amadeus Mozart (1756–1791), one of the most famous composers in Western music, lived and worked in Vienna, Austria, during the **Classical period** *(1750–1820).*

In the 1780s, the picturesque village of Baden, Austria, was a one-day carriage ride from Vienna. Mozart and his wife, Constanza, enjoyed frequent trips to Baden. The small parish church in Baden offered comfort and solace to the Mozart family. In appreciation, Mozart wrote the beautiful "Ave Verum Corpus" as a gift for the church chorus master, Anton Stoll. The compact and simple 46 measure song was probably first performed by Stoll's amateur church choir. It is often described as a masterpiece of calm repose and dignity. What a gift it has proven to be!

RESOURCES

Intermediate Sight-Singing

Sight-Singing in F Major, pages 39–41, 76–77, 112–116

Reading Dotted Notes, pages 45, 48, 49

Reading Rhythms in 2/2 Meter and Cut Time, page 140

Teacher Resource Binder

Teaching Master 11, *Pronunciation Guide for "Ave Verum Corpus"*

Teaching Master 12, *Pronunciation Checkup for "Ave Verum Corpus"*

Music and History 11, *Characteristics of Classical Music: 1750–1820*

Music and History 13, *Wolfgang Amadeus Mozart, a "Classical" Composer*

For additional resources, see TRB Table of Contents.

Links to Learning

◆ Vocal

The long **legato** *(a style of singing that is connected and sustained)* phrases in "Ave Verum Corpus" give singers the opportunity to develop proper breath support. One technique for good breath support is to breathe slowly and breathe early. As the introduction is played, begin a slow, deep breath at the indicated places and sing the first phrase softly on "doo" in a comfortable octave. Practice singing the entire phrase in one breath.

*Good place to start your breath

*Best place to start your breath

doo   doo_   doo_   doo   doo_   doo_   doo_ doo

◆ Artistic Expression

The **International Phonetic Alphabet** (IPA), developed in Paris, France, in 1886, is *a phonetic alphabet that provides a notational standard for all languages.* The following chart shows the IPA symbols for the Latin vowels. Recite the text of "Ave Verum Corpus" using only the following sounds for the vowels.

Written	Pronounced	IPA	Transliterated
a	f_a_ther	[ɑ]	ah
e	f_e_d	[ɛ]	eh
i	f_ee_t	[i]	ee
o	f_ou_ght	[ɔ]	aw
u	f_oo_d	[u]	oo

Evaluation

Demonstrate how well you have learned the skills and concepts presented in the lesson "Ave Verum Corpus" by completing the following:

- Find two 4-measure phrases in "Ave Verum Corpus" that you are able to sing in one breath, and perform these phrases for a friend. How did you do?

- With a friend, recite the text of "Ave Verum Corpus," alternately speaking every four measures. Listen to each other and check for correct pronunciation. Decide which words of the text need more practice.

LINKS TO LEARNING

Vocal

The Vocal section is designed to prepare students to:

- Sing *legato* phrases.
- Plan breaths for singing long phrases.

Have students:

- Practice taking a 4-count, then 8-count prepartory breath.
- Sing example in one breath.
- Sing in a smooth, *legato* style.

Artistic Expression

The Artistic Expression section is designed to:

- Introduce IPA.
- Establish correct Latin vowel pronunciations.

Have students:

- Practice speaking the vowels listing on page 87.
- Pronounce the text of "Ave Verum Corpus" using uniform vowel sounds.

RESOURCES

Intermediate Tenor/Bass Rehearsal/Performance CD

CD 1:21 Voices

CD 1:22 Accompaniment Only

CD 3:13 Vocal Practice Track—Tenor I

CD 3:14 Vocal Practice Track—Tenor II

CD 4:10 Vocal Practice Track—Bass

National Standards

1. Singing, alone and with others, a varied repertoire of music. **(b, e)**

6. Listening to, analyzing, and describing music. **(b)**

LESSON PLAN

Suggested Teaching Sequence and Performance Tips

1. Introduce

Direct students to:

- Read and discuss the information presented in the Getting Started section on page 86. Complete and discuss the multiple choice gift quiz (*1. Julia Child = d. a French dessert; 2. Walt Whitman = c. a nature poem; 3. Coco Chanel = a. an evening gown; 4. Mickey Mantle = e. an autographed baseball; 5. Charles Tiffany = b. a gold bracelet*). Discuss what qualities would make a piece of music perfect, and start a list of pieces on the board that fit the criteria according to the students.

- Complete the breathing activities as outlined in Vocal section on page 87. Experiment with different tempos for the first phrase after taking a slow, early breath.

- Write out the Latin text indicating the stressed syllables with a (') marking. Write the English translation directly under the Latin word. Working in partners, have students practice reciting the Latin text as outlined in the Artistic Expression section on page 87.

Ave Verum Corpus

For TTB and Piano (may be sung a cappella)

Arranged by
JOYCE EILERS

WOLFGANG AMADEUS MOZART
(1756–1791)

* If performed a cappella, omit bracketed measures
** Tempo is suggested by arranger

 **TEACHER 2 TEACHER**

It does not take long for young singers to appreciate Latin texts. The pure and unchanging vowels make a beautiful tone quality and vocal blend instantly attainable.

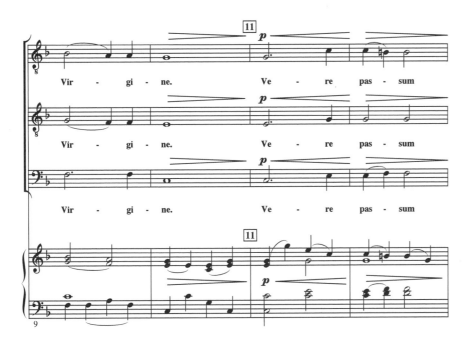

- Sing an F major scale and an F chromatic scale to establish tonality. Working in voice-part sections, go through the piece and only sing the half notes and longer using solfège syllables. Repeat until pitches and rhythms are confident.

- In sectionals, sit or stand in a circle. Assign one singer measure 3, the next singer measure 4, the next measure 5 and so forth. Working around the circle, have each student sing his/her measure at the correct time. Repeat, starting with a different student singing measure 3. Repeat until all measures are correct.

- Sing the entire piece at a steady tempo using solfège syllables.

Progress Checkpoints

Observe students' progress in:

✓ Using proper breath support throughout the phrase.

✓ Reading pitches and rhythm correctly.

CULTURAL CONNECTIONS

Recordings

Listen to a recording of "Ave Verum Corpus" and analyze and critique the phrasing, dynamics and Latin pronunciation (e.g., Mozart: *Requiem*; "Ave Verum Corpus").

2. Rehearse

Direct students to:

- Return to sectional circles and add the Latin text. Have each student sing one measure again. Repeat and start with a different student.

- Sing the entire piece at a steady tempo with the Latin text. Have each voice-part section perform for the class. Allow students to compliment and critique the intonation, rhythm and Latin pronunciation.

- Draw *crescendo* and *decrescendo* markings on the board and discuss the basic idea of musical phrasing. Ask students to choose a four-measure phrase from "Ave Verum Corpus" with which they can successfully demonstrate the phrasing. Allow students to perform for the class and compliment and critique the results. Students will discover that when starting a phrase softly after preparing with a slow, deep breath, their air supply will be more focused and last longer.

- In sectionals, have each voice part decide on an arm/hand movement or simple choreography that shows *crescendo/decrescendo* while they sing each phrase. Allow sections to perform for each other. Then sing the entire piece while each section does their phrase movements together.

Progress Checkpoints

Observe students' progress in:

✓ Singing proper Latin vowel sounds.

✓ Their ability to express the mood of the piece physically.

90

CONNECTING THE ARTS

Program Notes and Visual Art

Have students:

- Research the background of "Ave Verum Corpus" and the life of Wolfgang Amadeus Mozart. Write program notes for a performance of "Ave Verum Corpus."

- Design and draw a stained-glass window that visually portrays the grace, style and phrasing of "Ave Verum Corpus."

ra - tum un - da flu - xit et san - gui -

ne. Es - to no - bis prae - gus -

ne. Es - to no - bis prae - gus -

ne. Es - to no - bis

3. Refine

Direct students to:

Practice the 4/4 conducting pattern. Assign each student one of the following sections: measures 3–10, 11–18, 22–29, 30–46. Then divide the class into two or three small ensembles and have the students conduct their phrase, showing a steady tempo and the phrasing. Come back together as one choir and choose four students to conduct the class.

Progress Checkpoints

Observe students' progress in:

✓ Their ability to stay in character while performing.

✓ Keeping a steady beat and using proper hand gestures while conducting.

MORE ABOUT...

Performing Opportunities

Since the melody of "Ave Verum Corpus" should be a staple in every singer's repertoire, give all students the opportunity to sing the melody in any comfortable octave or key. Perhaps every rehearsal could begin with a small "Ave Verum Corpus" recital by several singers. In this arrangement the Bass part has some very large and difficult skips. Do not hesitate to rearrange parts, alter notes (substitute another note from the chord and so forth) or change octaves to keep each phrase in a comfortable and accessible tessitura for your singers.

ASSESSMENT

Informal Assessment

In this lesson, students showed the ability to:

- Explain and demonstrate musical phrasing matching their singing with movement.
- Perform independently in small groups while singing sections of the piece.

Student Self-Assessment

Have students evaluate their individual performances based on the following:

- Breath Management
- Phrasing
- Foreign Language
- Intonation
- Correct Part-Singing

Have each student rate his/her performance of this song in the areas above on a scale of 1–5, 5 being the best.

MORE ABOUT...

Wolfgang Amadeus Mozart (1756–1791)

As a representative composer of the Classical period (1750–1820), Mozart embodied the spirit of the classical style: crisp harmonies, exuberant melodies, formal balance and symmetry. He composed in virtually all forms of the time, including symphonies, operas, string quartets, art songs and masses. A household word, due to the immense popularity of the movie *Amadeus*, Mozart died at the early age of 35, cutting short the career of one of the most prolific composers of all times.

Individual and Group Performance Evaluation

To further measure growth of musical skills presented in this lesson, direct students to complete the Evaluation section on page 87.

- After singing two four-measure phrases for a friend, evaluate the performance by asking, "Did he/she sing each phrase in one breath? If not, how long did one breath last?"

- After pronouncing the text of "Ave Verum Corpus" with a friend, review each four-measure phrase by asking, "Which phrases need more work for a uniform vowel sound with the correct pronunciation?"

EXTENSION

Dramatic Scene

Work with a partner to improvise a scene between Mozart and Stoll. The setting could be the church after a choir rehearsal, at the coffee house right around the corner, or another location in Baden. What conversation might transpire between these two friends about the beginnings of "Ave Verum Corpus"? Perform the scenes for the class.

Additional National Standards

The following National Standards are addressed through the Assessment, Extension, Enrichment and bottom-page activities:

1. Singing, alone and with others, a varied repertoire of music. **(a)**

7. Evaluating music and music performances. **(a)**

8. Understanding relationships between music, the other arts, and disciplines outside the arts. **(a)**

Da unten im Tale

OVERVIEW

Composer: German Folk Song, arranged by Johannes Brahms (1833–1897), adapted by Barry Talley
Text: Barry Talley
Voicing: TB
Key: F major
Meter: 3/4
Form: Strophic
Style: German Folk Song
Accompaniment: Piano
Programming: Large or Small Ensembles, Contest, Festival

Vocal Ranges:

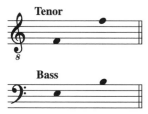

OBJECTIVES

After completing this lesson, students will be able to:

• Perform independently with accurate intonation.

• Perform independently with accurate rhythms.

• Classify aurally presented music representing diverse periods.

Da unten im Tale

Composer: German Folk Song, arranged by Johannes Brahms (1833–1897)
Text: Barry Talley
Voicing: TB

VOCABULARY

lied
Romantic period
unison
interval
third

Focus

• Perform harmony with intervals of a third.

• Read and perform dotted quarter notes.

• Describe and perform music from the Romantic period.

Getting Started

…The joys of love and the sorrows of love…

There are a lot of songs about love—some are happy and some are sad. Whether of joy or sorrow, the songs of love frequently have captivating melodies and poignant words. As for the sad love songs, have you ever heard of these classic break-up songs?

"In My Life" by The Beatles

"Fifty Ways To Leave Your Lover" by Paul Simon

"Don't It Make My Brown Eyes Blue" by Crystal Gayle

"Loving Arms" by The Dixie Chicks

If there were a classic break-up song list from the nineteenth century, "Da unten im Tale" by Johannes Brahms would certainly be on it.

MUSIC & HISTORY

To learn more about the Romantic period, see page 110.

◆ History and Culture

"Da unten im Tale" ("Below in the Valley") is a German **lied,** or *a song in the German language, generally with a secular text.* It is based on a traditional folk song. Born in Hamburg, Germany, Johannes Brahms (1833–1897) was a prominent composer of the **Romantic period** *(1820–1900).* The lyrical, uncluttered and rich style that Brahms used in his instrumental and choral pieces also enhanced his settings of folk songs. These songs often dealt with the joys and sorrows of love. It is interesting to note that although Brahms was an expert at writing love songs, he remained a bachelor his entire life.

VOCABULARY

Have students review vocabulary in student lesson. Introduce terms found in the music. A complete glossary of terms is found on page 226 of the student book.

RESOURCES

Intermediate Sight-Singing

Sight-Singing in F Major, pages 39–41, 76–77, 112–116

Reading Rhythms in 3/4 Meter, pages 17–22

Reading Dotted Notes, pages 45, 48, 49

Teacher Resource Binder

Teaching Master 13, *Pronunciation Guide for "Da unten im Tale"*

Music and History 16, *Characteristics of Romantic Music: 1820–1900*

Music and History 18, *Johannes Brahms, a "Romantic" Composer*

Music and History 20, *Fine Art Teaching Strategy: Romantic*

For additional resources, see TRB Table of Contents.

Links to Learning

◆ Vocal

Read and perform the following example in **unison** (*all parts singing the same notes at the same time*) and then as a round. Sing only those pitches that are within your range. When you sing in a round, listen to the **interval** (*the distance between two notes*) formed between the scale pitches. This interval is a **third** (*an interval of two pitches that are three notes apart on the staff*) and is found often in "Da unten im Tale."

◆ Theory

In music notation, the dot next to a note increases the length of that note by half its value. Therefore, a dotted quarter note is one and a half beats long. Read and perform the following rhythmic patterns while keeping a steady tempo. When singing, sustain the dotted quarter notes for their full value.

Evaluation

Demonstrate how well you have learned the skills and concepts presented in "Da unten im Tale" by completing the following:

- In a tenor-bass duet consisting of yourself and one other singer, sing measures 4–8 to show that you can sing harmony with intervals of a third. Discuss how well you did.

- Alone or in a small group, sing measures 4–12 to show the difference in the rhythmic patterns of measures 5–7 and measures 9–10. How well were you able to show a distinction between the two patterns?

- Compose a four-measure melodic phrase in $\frac{3}{4}$ meter. Use some dotted quarter notes and vary your rhythmic patterns. Begin and end your melody on *do*, as seen in the Vocal section above. Share your melodic phrase with a classmate and check for rhythmic and melodic accuracy.

Vocal

The Vocal section is designed to prepare students to develop listening and singing skills necessary to perform harmony in thirds.

Have students:

- Sing the exercise in unison.
- Divide into three sections and perform it as a three-part round.
- Describe the musical terms *interval, unison* and *third*.
- Develop listening and singing skills necessary to perform harmony in thirds.

Theory

The Theory section is designed to prepare students to sing a rhythm pattern that includes a dotted quarter note.

Have students sing the exercise on the neutral syllable "doo."

RESOURCES

Intermediate Tenor/Bass Rehearsal/Performance CD

CD 1:23 Voices

CD 1:24 Accompaniment Only

CD 3:15 Vocal Practice Track—Tenor

CD 4:11 Vocal Practice Track—Bass

National Standards

1. Singing, alone and with others, a varied repertoire of music. **(b)**

6. Listening to, analyzing, and describing music. **(b)**

LESSON PLAN

Suggested Teaching Sequence and Performance Tips

Direct students to:

- Read and discuss the information presented in the Getting Started section on page 94.

- Clap or tap the rhythm in measures 4–12. Chant the solfège syllables of the Tenor part in unison while clapping or tapping the rhythm. Repeat while chanting the solfège syllables of the Bass part.

- Work in sectional groups. Each section will stand in a circle. One student sings measure 4 using solfège syllables. Then the student standing next to him sings measure 5. The next student sings measure 6 and so on. Make the measures connect without a break. Rehearse several times, starting with a different student each time.

- Sing the entire song together using solfège syllables.

- Repeat each word of the German text after spoken by the teacher or a fluent student. Repeat until comfortable with the words.

- Chant the German words to the rhythm of the song.

- Return to sectional circles (see activity above) and repeat the activity of singing one measure/one student, but this time sing with the German words.

- Sing the entire song together with the German words.

- German nouns are always capitalized (*Tale = valley; Wasser = water; Lieb = love; Treu = fidelity; Falscheit = falsehood*).

Da unten im Tale
(Down There in the Valley)

For TB and Piano

Choral arrangement by BARRY TALLEY
English translation by J. MARK BAKER

German Folk Song arranged by
JOHANNES BRAHMS (1833–1897)

96   Intermediate Tenor/Bass

TEACHER 2 TEACHER

This German text is very accessible for young singers because of its straightforward, syllabic setting. Although there are only two verses in this arrangement, Brahms originally set four verses. Challenge your singers to develop more proficiency with German by learning all four verses.

- In small groups, decide on three or four elements of choral singing that would improve the performance of blend, dynamics, clear diction, phrase shaping, breath support, stress syllables.

- Write each element in large letters on an 11x17 sheet of paper. Put each musical element "flashcard" on a music stand in the front of the room. Have the class sing, focusing on the one element. Discuss the effectiveness of the performance. Repeat process with a different element.

- Perform from memory at a formal concert, demonstrating the performance elements discussed above.

Progress Checkpoints

Observe students' progress in:

✓ Their ability to work independently in small groups.

✓ Using correct pronunciation of the German vowel combinations.

ASSESSMENT

Informal Assessment

In this lesson, students showed the ability to:

- Rehearse in sectional groups with specified guidelines.

- Sing a German text with comprehension.

- Produce a more sophisticated musical performance by focusing on certain musical elements.

MORE ABOUT...

Johannes Brahms

Johannes Brahms (1833–1897) grew up in a poor family in Hamburg, Germany. As a young man he was exposed to both classical and popular music, and served as an arranger for his father's dance hall orchestra. He spent many years working as a conductor and pianist. He began composing rather late in life, but wrote for every genre except opera, which like marriage, he constantly avoided. His music portrays the best of nineteenth-century musical traditions. His attention to classical forms and structure is a strong contrast to the progressive style championed by Wagner, Liszt and others.

Student Self-Assessment

Have students evaluate their individual performances based on the following:

- Breath Management
- Phrasing
- Diction
- Foreign Language
- Correct Part-Singing

Have each student rate his/her performance of this song in the areas above on a scale of 1–5, 5 being the best.

Individual and Group Performance Evaluation

To further measure growth of musical skills presented in this lesson, direct students to complete the Evaluation section on page 95.

- After singing measures 4–8 in Tenor/Bass duets, evaluate the performance by asking, "How in tune were the thirds?"

- After singing measures 4–12 alone or in small groups, review each performance by asking, "Were the rhythmic patterns accurate? Were they distinctly different?"

- After composing a four-measure melodic phrase in 3/4 meter, perform it for the class. Evaluate each phrase by asking, "Was the phrase rhythmically correct? Did it begin and end on *do*?"

98 Intermediate Tenor/Bass

Additional National Standards

The following National Standards are addressed through the Assessment, Extension, Enrichment and bottom-page activities:

4. Composing and arranging music within specific guidelines. **(a)**

5. Reading and notating music. **(a)**

7. Evaluating music and music performances. **(a)**

Music & History

Links to Music

Renaissance Period **100**

 Now Is The Month Of Maying **66**

Baroque Period **104**

 Der Herr segne euch **74**

Classical Period **108**

 Ave Verum Corpus **86**

Romantic Period **112**

 Da unten im Tale **94**

Contemporary Period **116**

 Be Cool **14**

RENAISSANCE

OVERVIEW

Objectives

After completing this lesson, students will be able to:

- Describe the Renaissance period, including important developments.
- Describe characteristics of Renaissance music.

Introduce the Renaissance period through visual art. Analyze the painting by Sandro Botticelli on page 100. Direct students to discuss Renaissance interest in religious subjects, as depicted in *The Adoration of the Magi*.

Sandro Botticelli (1445–1510) was an Italian painter who lived and worked in Florence, Italy, during the Renaissance. *The Adoration of the Magi* reflects the Renaissance interest in religious subjects. Framing the central figures within the strong geometric pillars emphasized those figures over others. Botticelli was also commissioned by the Pope to paint frescoes in the Sistine Chapel in the Vatican.

Sandro Botticelli. *The Adoration of the Magi.* c. 1480. Tempera and oil on panel. 70.2 x 104.2 cm (27 5/8 x 41"). National Gallery of Art, Washington, D. C. Andrew W. Mellon Collection.

RESOURCES

Teacher Resource Binder

Music and History 1, *Renaissance Music*

Music and History 3, *Thomas Morley*

Transparency 1, *The Adoration of the Magi*, Sandro Botticelli

Music and History 5, *Fine Art Teaching Strategy*

For additional resources, see Music and History section.

Listening Selections CD

(found in the Teacher Resource Binder)

Track 1 "As Vesta Was Descending"

Track 2 "Three Voltas" from *Terpsichore*

Focus

- Describe the Renaissance period, including important developments.
- Describe characteristics of Renaissance music.

The Renaissance— A Time of Exploration

The **Renaissance period** *(1430–1600)* was a time during the fifteenth and sixteenth centuries of rapid development in exploration, science, art and music. This period could be called the beginning of modern history and the beginning of Western civilization as we know it now.

The development and use of the compass as a navigational aid in China made it possible for explorers to travel to new continents and to discover other cultures. Renaissance sailors first took to the seas to supply Europeans with Asian spices such as peppercorns, nutmeg and cinnamon. Also from the East came precious jewels and fine silk, a fabric especially valued for women's clothing.

Sailors also brought back information and customs from other cultures. This new information, along with a revived interest in writings from the ancient Greek and Roman cultures, was quickly spread across Europe, thanks to the invention of the printing press and mass-produced books. The invention of the printing press, credited to Johann Gutenberg, was one of the most significant developments of the Renaissance. As books became more available and less expensive, more people learned to read and began to consider new ideas.

A major change in the Christian religion occurred at this time. During the Protestant Reformation, various groups of Christians left the Catholic Church and formed some of the present-day Protestant denominations. Many Protestant groups translated Bibles from the Catholic Church's language of Latin to the language spoken by the people.

Remarkable advances were made in the arts and sciences by:

- Thomas Weelkes—English composer
- Gerardus Mercator—German mapmaker
- Vasco da Gama—Portuguese explorer who rounded the Horn of Africa and went on to India

COMPOSERS

Josquin des Prez
(c. 1450–1521)

Andrea Gabrieli
(c. 1510–1586)

Michael Praetorius
(1571–1621)

Thomas Weelkes
(c. 1576–1623)

ARTISTS

Gentile Bellini
(1429–1507)

Sandro Botticelli
(1445–1510)

Leonardo da Vinci
(1452–1519)

Michelangelo
(1475–1564)

Raphael
(1483–1520)

AUTHORS

Martin Luther
(1483–1546)

William Shakespeare
(1565–1616)

VOCABULARY

Renaissance period

sacred music

mass

motet

secular music

lute

polyphony

a cappella

madrigal

word painting

Music History *Renaissance*   **101**

LESSON PLAN
Suggested Teaching Sequence

1. Examine the Renaissance period in a historical perspective.

Direct students to:

- Read and discuss the information found on student page 101.
- Turn to the time line on pages 102–103 and read the citations.
- Discuss why these are considered important dates during the Renaissance period.
- Identify specific accomplishments that were made during the Renaissance period and the people associated with those accomplishments.
- Compare each of these events to what occurred after the Renaissance period.

2. Define the musical aspects of Renaissance music.

Direct students to:

- Read and discuss information on Renaissance music found on student page 102.
- Describe the difference between sacred and secular music.
- Define *polyphony*, *mass* and *motet*.

3. Discuss the performance guidelines of Renaissance music.

Direct students to:

- Read the Performance Links found on student page 110.
- Discuss the performance guidelines.

National Standards

6. Listening to, analyzing, and describing music. **(a, b, c, e, f)**
8. Understanding relationships between music, the other arts, and disciplines outside the arts. **(a, b, c, d, e)**
9. Understanding music in relation to history and culture. **(a, c, d, e)**

This feature is designed to expand students' appreciation of choral and instrumental music of the Renaissance period.

1. Choral Selection:

"As Vesta Was Descending" by Thomas Weelkes

Direct students to:

- Read the information on student page 103 to learn more about Thomas Weelkes and "As Vesta Was Descending."
- Review the meaning of the musical style of the madrigal.
- Define *word painting*.
- After listening to the recorded performance, identify the word painting techniques used (*descending*—all the voices move downward, *ascending*—all the voices move upward, *running down amain*—the voices vigorously "run" downward separately, *two by two*—groups of two voices sing together, *three by three*—groups of three voices sing together, *all alone*—one solo voice). At the end of the piece, "Long live fair Oriana" is repeated over and over (52 times) to honor and gain the favor of Oriana, a common nickname for Queen Elizabeth I of England.

2. Instrumental Selection:

"Three Voltas" from *Terpsichore* by Michael Praetorius

Direct students to:

- Read the information on student page 103 to learn more about Michael Praetorius and "Three Voltas" from *Terpsichore*.
- After the first listening, discuss the ancient instruments that are heard.

102

Renaissance Music

During the Renaissance, the Catholic Church gradually lost some of its influence over the daily lives of people. Much of the important music of the period, however, was still **sacred music**, or *music associated with religious services and themes*. In music, a **mass** is *a religious service of prayers and ceremonies*. A **motet** is *a shorter choral work, also set to a Latin text and used in religious services, but not part of the regular mass*. These two types of compositions were the most important forms of sacred Renaissance music. In Protestant churches, sacred music was composed and sung in the languages of the worshippers.

Like sacred music, **secular music**, or *music not associated with religious services or themes*, flourished during the Renaissance period. The center of musical activity gradually began to shift from churches to castles and towns. Music became an important form of entertainment for members of the emerging middle class. Social dancing became more widespread. Dance music of this period was written for **lute**, *an early form of the guitar*, and other instruments.

The Renaissance period is often referred to as the "golden age of polyphony." **Polyphony**, which literally means "many-sounding," is *a type of music in which there are two or more different melodic lines being sung or played at the same time*. Much of the choral music of the time was polyphonic, with as many as sixteen different vocal parts. Instruments were sometimes used to accompany and echo the voices.

Performance Links

When performing music of the Renaissance period, it is important to apply the following guidelines:

- Sing with clarity and purity of tone.
- Balance the vocal lines with equal importance.
- In polyphonic music, sing the rhythms accurately and with precision.
- When designated by the composer, sing **a cappella** (*unaccompanied or without instruments*).

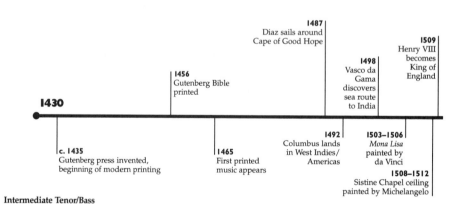

1487
Diaz sails around
Cape of Good Hope

1509
Henry VIII
becomes
King of
England

1456
Gutenberg Bible
printed

1498
Vasco da
Gama
discovers
sea route
to India

1430

1492
Columbus lands
in West Indies/
Americas

1503–1506
Mona Lisa
painted by
da Vinci

c. 1435
Gutenberg press invented,
beginning of modern printing

1465
First printed
music appears

1508–1512
Sistine Chapel ceiling
painted by Michelangelo

102   Intermediate Tenor/Bass

MORE ABOUT

Renaissance Painting

During the Renaissance, the styles, subjects and even art materials of painters changed. Painting became more realistic; human figures appeared more lifelike. Painters were able to use perspective and to give three-dimensional quality. Many paintings still depicted religious subjects, especially scenes from the Bible. Other artists began to show nonreligious subjects in their works. Oil paints, which were first used during the early 1400s, made it possible for painters to revise and refine their ideas as they worked.

Listening Links

CHORAL SELECTION

"As Vesta Was Descending" by Thomas Weelkes (c.1576–1623)

Thomas Weelkes was an important English composer and organist. "As Vesta Was Descending" is an outstanding example of a **madrigal**, *a musical setting of a poem in three or more parts*. Generally, a madrigal has a secular text and is sung a cappella. This madrigal was written in honor of Queen Elizabeth I of England. This piece is an excellent example of **word painting**, *a technique in which the music reflects the meaning of the words*. Listen carefully to discover what occurs in the music on the following words: "descending," "ascending," "running down amain," "two by two," "three by three," and "all alone." Why do you think Weelkes chose to use the repeated text at the end?

INSTRUMENTAL SELECTION

"Three Voltas" from *Terpsichore* by Michael Praetorius (1571–1621)

During the Renaissance, a favorite type of composition involved a combination of dances in changing tempos and meters. Some of the dance music developed into stylized pieces for listening, which were not intended for actual dancing. *Terpsichore*, by German composer Michael Praetorius, is a collection of 312 short dance pieces, written in four, five or six parts, with no particular instrumentation specified.

You will hear authentic early instruments in this recording. By listening carefully, guess which modern-day instruments are descended from these early ones.

Check Your Understanding

1. List three major nonmusical changes that took place during the Renaissance period.
2. Describe polyphony as heard in "As Vesta Was Descending."
3. Describe how music from the Renaissance is different from music of today.

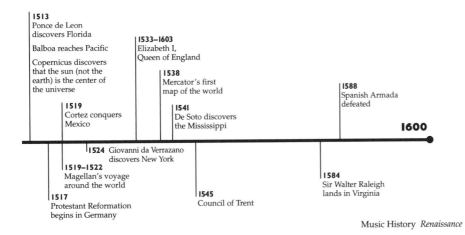

1513
Ponce de Leon
discovers Florida

Balboa reaches Pacific

Copernicus discovers
that the sun (not the
earth) is the center of
the universe

1519
Cortez conquers
Mexico

1519–1522
Magellan's voyage
around the world

1517
Protestant Reformation
begins in Germany

1524 Giovanni da Verrazano
discovers New York

1533–1603
Elizabeth I,
Queen of England

1538
Mercator's first
map of the world

1541
De Soto discovers
the Mississippi

1545
Council of Trent

1588
Spanish Armada
defeated

1584
Sir Walter Raleigh
lands in Virginia

1600

Music History *Renaissance* **103**

Answers to Check Your Understanding

1. Answers will vary. For example, the use of the compass made it possible to explore new continents. The invention of the printing press and mass-produced books helped information spread rapidly. The Protestant Reformation led to the formation of many of the world's present-day Protestant denominations.

2. Polyphony is when two or more melodic lines begin at different places and act independently of each other. In "As Vesta Was Descending," polyphony can be heard throughout the piece, in contrast to the sections sung all together.

3. Answers will vary. For example, now we use many different instruments to provide interesting accompaniments for songs—then, they were sung a cappella or with simple instruments that echoed the voice lines. One thing the two styles have in common is a frequent use of dissonance.

- After the second listening, discuss which modern day instruments are descended from these early ones. *(The first Volta features a cornett, three sackbuts, drum and tabor. The second Volta is performed on pommer, three sackbuts and tabor. The third Volta features three recorders, pommer, three sackbuts, two violins, viola, violoncello, lute, drum and tabor. The cornett was the most highly prized instrument of the sixteenth century, but has no modern descendent. It was made of wood and had finger holes like a recorder, but was played with a mouthpiece similar to a trumpet's. A sackbut is the ancestor of the modern trombone. The tabor is a type of drum. The pommer, or shawm, was the double-reed forefather of the oboe.)*

ASSESSMENT

Informal Assessment

In this lesson, students showed the ability to:

- Share what they know about the Renaissance period.
- Describe musical characteristics, styles and forms found in Renaissance music.
- Describe some characteristics of Renaissance art.

Student Self-Assessment

Direct students to:

- Review the questions in Check Your Understanding on page 111.
- Write a paragraph answering each of the three questions about music during the Renaissance period.

BAROQUE

OVERVIEW

Objectives

After completing this lesson, students will be able to:

- Describe the Baroque period including, important developments.
- Describe characteristics of Baroque music.

Introduce the Baroque period through visual art. Analyze the painting by Orazio Gentileschi on student page 104. Direct students to discuss the technique of placing the subjects in sharp relief before a dark background. Note the small table pipe organ.

The work of the Italian painter Orazio Gentileschi (1563–1639) was influenced by the innovative style of Caravaggio. In later years, Orazio's works tend to place a single figure or a restricted figure group in sharp relief before a dark background. The subject of this painting, St. Cecilia, is often referred to as the patron saint of music. She is playing a small table pipe organ.

Orazio Gentileschi. *Saint Cecilia and an Angel.* c. 1610. Oil on canvas. 87.8 x 108.1 cm (34 5/8 x 42 1/2"). National Gallery of Art, Washington, D. C. Samuel H. Kress Collection.

104   Intermediate Tenor/Bass

RESOURCES

Teacher Resource Binder

Music and History 6, *Baroque Music*

Music and History 8, *Johann Sebastian Bach*

Transparency 3, *Saint Cecilia and an Angel*, Orazio Gentileschi

Music and History 10, *Fine Art Teaching Strategy*

For additional resources, see Music and History section.

Listening Selections CD

(found in the Teacher Resource Binder)

Track 3 "Gloria in excelsis Deo" from *Gloria in D Major*

Track 4 "The Arrival of the Queen of Sheba" from *Solomon*

Focus

- Describe the Baroque period, including important developments.
- Describe characteristics of Baroque music.

The Baroque Period— A Time of Elaboration

The **Baroque period** *(1600–1750)* was a time of powerful kings and their courts. In Europe, elaborate clothing, hats and hairstyles for the wealthy men and women matched the decorated buildings, gardens, furniture and paintings of this period. The term *baroque* comes from a French word for "imperfect or irregular pearls." Often, pearls were used as decorations on clothing.

There was a great interest in science and exploration. During the Baroque period, Galileo perfected the telescope by 1610, providing the means for greater exploration of the universe. Sir Isaac Newton identified gravity and formulated principles of physics and mathematics. Bartolomeo Cristofori developed the modern pianoforte in which hammers strike the strings. Exploration of new worlds continued, and colonization of places discovered during the Renaissance increased.

Most paintings and sculptures of the time were characterized by their large scale and dramatic details. Artwork celebrated the splendor of royal rulers. For example, the Palace at Versailles near Paris, was built and decorated as a magnificent setting for King Louis XIV of France. It features notably elaborate architecture, paintings, sculptures and gardens.

The Baroque period was a time of great changes brought about through the work of extraordinary people such as:

- Johann Sebastian Bach—German composer
- Orazio Gentileschi—Italian painter
- Alexander Pope—English poet
- Galileo Galilei—Italian mathematician who used his new telescope to prove that the Milky Way is made up of individual stars

COMPOSERS

Johann Pachelbel
(1653–1706)

Antonio Vivaldi
(1678–1741)

Johann Sebastian Bach
(1685–1750)

George Frideric Handel
(1685–1759)

ARTISTS

El Greco
(1541–1614)

Orazio Gentileschi
(1563–1639)

Peter Paul Rubens
(1577–1640)

Rembrandt van Rijn
(1606–1669)

Jan Steen
(1626–1679)

Jan Vermeer
(1632–1675)

AUTHORS

Ben Jonson
(1572–1637)

René Descartes
(1596–1650)

John Milton
(1608–1674)

Molière
(1622–1673)

Alexander Pope
(1688–1744)

Samuel Johnson
(1709–1784)

VOCABULARY

Baroque period

basso continuo

opera

oratorio

concerto grosso

Music History *Baroque*   **105**

National Standards

6. Listening to, analyzing, and describing music. **(a, b, c, e, f)**

8. Understanding relationships between music, the other arts, and disciplines outside the arts. **(a, b, c, d, e)**

9. Understanding music in relation to history and culture. **(a, c, d, e)**

LESSON PLAN

Suggested Teaching Sequence

1. Examine the Baroque period in a historical perspective.

Direct students to:

- Read and discuss the information found on student page 105.
- Turn to the time line on pages 106–107 and read the citations.
- Discuss why these are considered important dates during the Baroque period.
- Identify specific accomplishments that were made during the Baroque period and the people associated with those accomplishments.
- Compare each of these events to what occurred before and after the Baroque period.

2. Define the musical aspects of Baroque music.

Direct students to:

- Read and discuss information on Baroque music found on student page 106.
- Discuss instruments used during this period.
- Define *basso continuo, oratorio, opera* and *concerto grosso.*

3. Discuss the performance guidelines of Baroque music.

Direct students to:

- Read the Performance Links found on student page 106.
- Discuss the performance guidelines.

This feature is designed to expand students' appreciation of choral and instrumental music of the Baroque period.

1. Choral Selection:

"Gloria in excelsis Deo" from *Gloria in D Major* **by Antonio Vivaldi**

Direct students to:

- Read the information on student page 107 to learn more about Antonio Vivaldi and "Gloria in excelsis Deo" from *Gloria in D Major.*

- Listen to the recorded performance to enjoy the energy and emotion of this piece.

- After listening again, discuss the use of ornamentation. (*A great amount of ornamentation is used in the accompaniment. The vocal line fits with this elaborate accompaniment by providing contrast with long tones and silences that allow the accompaniment to be heard.*)

2. Instrumental Selection:

"The Arrival of the Queen of Sheba" from *Solomon* **by George Frideric Handel**

Direct students to:

- Read the information on student page 107 to learn more about George Frideric Handel and "The Arrival of the Queen of Sheba" from *Solomon.*

- Review the meaning of *oratorio.*

- Listen to the recorded performance to identify the two instruments that perform a duet. (*Oboes*)

- Identify the instrument family to which they belong. (*Woodwind*)

106

Baroque Music

The music of the Baroque period shows the same kind of dramatic flair that characterized the clothing, architecture and art of the time. Most of the compositions of that period have a strong sense of movement, often including a **basso continuo**, or *a continually moving bass line.*

The Baroque period brought about a great interest in instrumental music. Keyboard instruments were refined, including the clavichord, harpsichord and organ. The modern string family of instruments were now used, and the trumpet became a favorite melody instrument in orchestras.

During the Baroque period, a number of new forms of music were developed. **Opera**, *a combination of singing, instrumental music, dancing and drama that tells a story,* was created beginning with *Orfeo*, by Claudio Monteverdi (1567–1643). The **oratorio**, *a large-scale work for solo voices, chorus and orchestra based on a literary or religious theme,* was also developed. In 1741, George Frideric Handel (1685–1759) composed the *Messiah*, one of the most famous oratorios still performed today. The **concerto grosso** (*a multi-movement Baroque piece for a group of soloists and an orchestra*) was also made popular with Antonio Vivaldi's (1678–1741) *The Four Seasons* and Johann Sebastian Bach's (1685–1750) *Brandenberg Concertos.*

Performance Links

When performing music of the Baroque period, it is important to apply the following guidelines:

- Sing with accurate pitch.
- Be conscious of who has the dominant theme and make sure the accompanying part or parts do not overshadow the melody.
- Keep a steady, unrelenting pulse in most pieces. Precision of dotted rhythms is especially important.
- When dynamic level changes occur, all vocal lines need to change together.

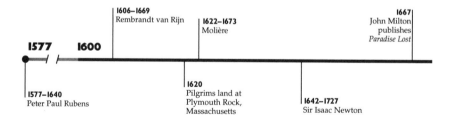

106   Intermediate Tenor/Bass

MORE ABOUT

Baroque Painting

The Baroque period was a time of reaction to the reserved, restrained attitudes of the Renaissance. Baroque art became more and more emotional and excessive, with an emphasis on opulence, ornamentation and gaudy elegance. The aristocracy was still in power and commissioned even grander art to impress themselves and others.

Listening Links

CHORAL SELECTION

"Gloria in excelsis Deo" from *Gloria in D Major* by Antonio Vivaldi (1678–1741)

Antonio Vivaldi was one of the greatest composers and violinists of his time. He wrote operas and concertos, as well as sacred works (oratorios, motets and masses) for chorus, soloists and orchestra. One of his most popular choral works is the *Gloria in D Major* mass. "Gloria in excelsis Deo" is a magnificent choral piece. It is full of energy and emotion that is expressed with great drama. It was composed for three solo voices and chorus, and is accompanied by a variety of instruments. Does ornamentation occur in the vocal parts, in the accompaniment, or both?

INSTRUMENTAL SELECTION

"The Arrival of the Queen of Sheba" from *Solomon* by George Frideric Handel (1685–1759)

George Frideric Handel was a German-born composer who lived in England for most of his life. The oratorio *Solomon* tells the story of King Solomon, of tenth-century Israel. Solomon was known for his great wisdom. Sheba, the Queen of Ethiopia, came to visit and challenge Solomon, but he wisely answered all her questions, and she left as an ally. *Solomon* was written for two choruses, five soloists, a chamber orchestra and a harpsichord. Two instruments are featured playing a duet in this piece. What is the name of these instruments, and to what instrument family do they belong?

Check Your Understanding

1. List three major nonmusical developments that took place during the Baroque period.

2. How would the performance of the oratorio *Solomon* differ from the performance of an opera?

3. Describe how music from the Baroque period is different from music of the Renaissance.

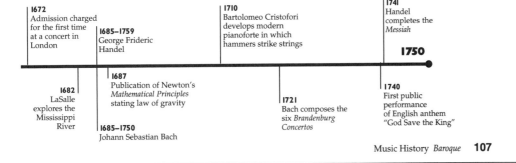

Music History *Baroque* **107**

Answers to Check Your Understanding

1. Answers will vary. For example, invention of the telescope, discovery of the law of gravity, exploration and colonization, pilgrims land at Plymouth Rock.

2. Opera and oratorios are both written for solo voices, chorus and orchestra. They both tell a story. Operas, however, are designed to be performed on stage with dancing, costuming and scenery. Oratorios like *Solomon* are composed to be sung in a church or concert setting.

3. Music in the Baroque period can be described as large scale with complex details and dramatic elaborations. In contrast, music of the Renaissance period emphasized smaller groups performing, often unaccompanied, with an emphasis on polyphony.

ASSESSMENT

Informal Assessment

In this lesson, students showed the ability to:

- Share what they know about the Baroque period.
- Describe musical characteristics, styles and forms found in Baroque music.
- Describe some characteristics of Baroque art.

Student Self-Assessment

Direct students to:

- Review the questions in Check Your Understanding on page 107.
- Write a paragraph answering each of the three questions about the Baroque period.

ENRICHMENT

Research Project

As a small group activity, assign each group one of the following important figures of the Baroque period: J. S. Bach, George Frideric Handel, Antonio Vivaldi, Orazio Gentileschi, Alexander Pope, Galileo Galilei, Sir Isaac Newton, and Bartolomeo Cristofori. Have each group do research on the contributions of each, and then present findings to the rest of the class.

CLASSICAL

OVERVIEW

Objectives

After completing this lesson, students will be able to:

- Describe the Classical period, including important developments.
- Describe characteristics of Classical music.

VOCABULARY

Have students review vocabulary in student lesson. A complete glossary of terms is found on page 226 of the student book.

Introduce the Classical period through visual art. Analyze the painting by Elisabeth Vigeé-LeBrun on student page 114. Direct students to discuss how this painting expresses friendship and maternal love. Review background information of Vigeé-LeBrun's *The Marquise de Pezé and the Marquise de Rouget with Her Two Children* on page 114.

 French artist Elisabeth Vigée-LeBrun (1755–1842) lived and worked in Paris during the time of the French Revolution and was forced to flee the city in disguise in 1789. A majority of Vigeé-LeBrun paintings are portraits of women and children. This painting expresses friendship and maternal love.

Elisabeth Vigée-LeBrun. *The Marquise de Pezé and the Marquise de Rouget with Her Two Children.* 1787. Oil on canvas, 123.4 x 155.9 cm (48 5/8 x 61 3/8"). National Gallery of Art, Washington, D. C. Gift of the Bay Foundation in memory of Josephine Bay and Ambassador Charles Ulrick Bay.

RESOURCES

Teacher Resource Binder

Music and History 11, *Classical Music*

Music and History 13, *Wolfgang Amadeus Mozart*

Transparency 5, *The Marquise de Pezé and the Marquise de Rouget with Her Two Children*, Elisabeth Vigeé-LeBrun

Music and History 15, *Fine Art Teaching Strategy*

For additional resources, see Music and History section.

Listening Selections CD

(found in the Teacher Resource Binder)

Track 5 "The Heavens Are Telling" from *Creation*

Track 6 *Eine Kleine Nachtmusik*, First Movement

Focus

- Describe the Classical period, including important developments.
- Describe characteristics of Classical music.

The Classical Period— A Time of Balance, Clarity and Simplicity

The **Classical period** *(1750–1820)* was a time when people became influenced by the early Greeks and Romans for examples of order and ways of living life. Travelers of the period visited the ruins of ancient Egypt, Rome and Greece and brought the ideas of the ancients to the art and architecture of the time. As a result, the calm beauty and simplicity of this classical art from the past inspired artists and musicians to move away from the overly decorated styles of the Baroque period. The music, art and architecture reflected a new emphasis on emotional restraint and simplicity.

In the intellectual world, there was increasing emphasis on individual reason and enlightenment. Writers such as Voltaire and Thomas Jefferson suggested that through science and democracy, rather than mystery and monarchy, people could choose their own fate. Such thinking, brought on by the enlarging middle class and the excesses of the wealthy royal class, was the beginning of important political changes in society. In many parts of Europe, the power and authority of royalty were attacked, and members of the middle class struggled for their rights. There was a revolution against England by the American colonies, which resulted in the establishment of the United States. In France, the monarchy was overthrown, and the king and most of his court were beheaded.

Some of the most important contributors of the time were:

- Wolfgang Amadeus Mozart—Austrian composer
- Elisabeth Vigée-Lebrun—French painter
- Ben Franklin—American writer, inventor, diplomat
- Joseph Priestley—English chemist who discovered oxygen
- Robert Fulton—American inventor who produced the first submarine, "Nautilus"

Music History *Classical* **109**

COMPOSERS

Carl Philipp Emanuel Bach
(1714–1788)

Johann Christian Bach
(1735–1762)

Franz Joseph Haydn
(1732–1809)

Wolfgang Amadeus Mozart
(1756–1791)

Ludwig van Beethoven
(1770–1827)

ARTISTS

Louis de Carmontelle
(1717–1806)

Thomas Gainsborough
(1727–1788)

Francisco Göya
(1746–1828)

Jacques-Louis David
(1748–1825)

Elisabeth Vigée-Lebrun
(1755–1842)

AUTHORS

Voltaire
(1694–1778)

Benjamin Franklin
(1706–1790)

William Wordsworth
(1770–1850)

Jane Austen
(1775–1817)

VOCABULARY

Classical period

chamber music

symphony

crescendo

decrescendo

sonata-allegro form

LESSON PLAN

Suggested Teaching Sequence

1. Examine the Classical period in a historical perspective

Direct students to:

- Read and discuss the information found on student page 109.
- Turn to the time line on pages 110–111 and read the citations.
- Discuss why these are considered important dates during the Classical period.
- Identify specific accomplishments that were made during the Classical period and the people associated with those accomplishments.
- Compare each of these events to what occurred before and after the Classical period.

2. Define the musical aspects of Classical music.

Direct students to:

- Read and discuss information on Classical music found on student page 110.
- Define *chamber music* and *symphony*.
- Identify two major composers of the Classical period.

3. Discuss the performance guidelines of Classical music.

Direct students to:

- Read the Performance Links found on student page 110.
- Discuss the performance guidelines.

National Standards

6. Listening to, analyzing, and describing music. **(a, b, c, e, f)**
8. Understanding relationships between music, the other arts, and disciplines outside the arts. **(a, b, c, d, e)**
9. Understanding music in relation to history and culture. **(a, c, d, e)**

This feature is designed to expand students' appreciation of choral and instrumental music of the Classical period.

Choral Selection:

"The Heavens Are Telling" from _Creation_ by Franz Joseph Haydn

Direct students to:

- Read the information on student page 111 to learn more about Franz Joseph Haydn and "The Heavens Are Telling" from _Creation_.

- Listen to the recorded performance to identify the sections sung by the full chorus and those sung by the trio of soloists.

- While listening again, identify the imitative section, and list the order of the voice parts as they enter with the words "With wonders of His work." _(Bass, Tenor, Soprano, Alto)_

Instrumental Selection:

Eine Kleine Nachtmusik, **First Movement by Wolfgang Amadeus Mozart**

Direct students to:

- Read the information on student page 111 to learn more about Wolfgang Amadeus Mozart and _Eine Kleine Nachtmusik,_ First Movement.

- Read the definition of _sonata-allegro form._

- Listen to the recorded performance to identify the three large sections.

- While listening again, write down Exposition, Development and Recapitulation as each section begins.

Music of the Classical Period

The music of the Classical period was based on balance, clarity and simplicity. Like the architecture of ancient Greece, music was fit together in "building blocks" by balancing one four-bar phrase against another. Classical music was more restrained than the music of the Baroque period, when flamboyant embellishments were common.

The piano replaced the harpsichord and became a favorite instrument of composers. Many concertos were written for the piano. The string quartet was a popular form of **chamber music** _(music performed by a small instrumental ensemble, generally with one instrument per part)._ The **symphony** _(a large-scale work for orchestra)_ was also a common type of music during this period. Orchestras continued to develop and expand into four families: brass, percussion, strings and woodwinds. Other forms, such as the opera, mass and oratorio, continued to develop as well.

Two major composers associated with the Classical period are Franz Joseph Haydn (1732–1809) and Wolfgang Amadeus Mozart (1756–1791). A third major composer, Ludwig van Beethoven (1770–1827), began composing during this period. Beethoven's works bridge the gap between the Classical and Romantic periods, and are discussed in the next period.

Performance Links

When performing music of the Classical period, it is important to apply the following guidelines:

- Listen for the melody line so the accompaniment parts do not overshadow it.
- Sing chords in tune.
- Make dynamic level changes that move smoothly through each **crescendo** _(a dynamic marking that indicates to gradually sing or play louder)_ and **decrescendo** _(a dynamic marking that indicates to gradually sing or play softer)._
- Keep phrases flowing and connected.

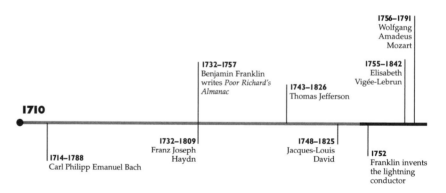

110   Intermediate Tenor/Bass

MORE ABOUT

Classical Painting

The styles developed by painters, sculptors and architects during the Classical period were largely a reaction against the excessive detail and embellishment of artworks produced during the late Baroque period. A prominent art historian of the time, Johann Wienckelmann, urged artists to imitate "the noble simplicity and calm grandeur" of the Greeks. Structures such as the Brandenburg Gate in Berlin and Jefferson's home, Monticello, are clear indications that artists responded. Painters and sculptors also worked toward balance, simplicity and clarity.

Listening Links

CHORAL SELECTION

"The Heavens Are Telling" from *Creation* by Franz Joseph Haydn (1732–1809)

Franz Joseph Haydn was an Austrian composer who was Beethoven's teacher, and Mozart's friend. The *Creation* is an oratorio based on a poem from John Milton's *Paradise Lost* and the first chapters of the book of Genesis from the Bible. The angels Gabriel, Uriel and Raphael are portrayed by three soloists, and they describe events of each day of the creation. "The Heavens Are Telling" is a grand celebration of praise that alternates between the full chorus and the trio of soloists. List the order of the choral voice parts in the imitative section as they enter with the words, "With wonders of His work."

INSTRUMENTAL SELECTION

Eine Kleine Nachtmusik, First Movement by Wolfgang Amadeus Mozart (1756–1791)

Wolfgang Amadeus Mozart, another Austrian composer, began his musical career at an extremely early age. By the time he was four years old, Mozart had already mastered the keyboard, and by age five, he had written his first composition. Considered one of the greatest composers of all time, he composed 600 musical works.

The first movement of *Eine Kleine Nachtmusik* is written in **sonata-allegro form**, *a large ABA form consisting of three sections: exposition, development and recapitulation.* The Exposition (section A) presents two themes: (a) and (b). Next comes the Development section (section B). The Recapitulation is a return to the original theme (a). Listen to this selection and write down the name for each section of the sonata-allegro form as you hear it.

Check Your Understanding

1. List three major nonmusical changes that took place during the Classical period.

2. Describe the characteristics of Classical music heard in *Eine Kleine Nachtmusik*.

3. Describe how music from the Classical period is different from music of the Baroque period.

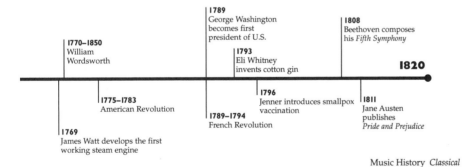

1770–1850
William
Wordsworth

1789
George Washington
becomes first
president of U.S.

1793
Eli Whitney
invents cotton gin

1808
Beethoven composes
his *Fifth Symphony*

1820

1775–1783
American Revolution

1796
Jenner introduces smallpox
vaccination

1811
Jane Austen
publishes
Pride and Prejudice

1789–1794
French Revolution

1769
James Watt develops the first
working steam engine

Music History *Classical* **111**

Answers to Check Your Understanding

1. Answers will vary. Revolutions in the American colonies and in France that produced new governments and new social structures; oxygen was discovered; the first submarine was produced.

2. The classical musical characteristics found in *Eine Kleine Nachtmusik*, First Movement are: the music is based on balance, clarity and simplicity; it is written in *sonata-allegro* form.

3. Answers will vary. The music of the Classical period left the exaggerated embellishments and the use of improvisation behind; it emphasized precision and balance.

ROMANTIC

OVERVIEW

Objectives

After completing this lesson, students will be able to:

• Describe the Romantic period, including important developments.

• Describe characteristics of Romantic music.

VOCABULARY

Have students review vocabulary in student lesson. A complete glossary of terms is found on page 226 of the student book.

Introduce the Romantic period through visual art. Analyze the painting by George Caleb Bingham on student page 118. Direct students to discuss the instruments being played. What kind of music might have been performed? Is there a story in the picture? Review background information on Bingham's *The Jolly Flatboatmen* on page 112.

 The American artist George Caleb Bingham (1811–1879) was born in Virginia and raised in Missouri. He became known for his river scenes, often of boatmen bringing cargo to the American West along the Missouri and Mississippi rivers. The scene here is a group of boatmen on a flatboat amusing themselves with their own music and dancing.

George Caleb Bingham. *The Jolly Flatboatmen*. 1846. Oil on canvas. 96.9 x 123.2 cm (38 1/8 x 48 1/2"). National Gallery of Art, Washington, D. C. Private Collection.

112   Intermediate Tenor/Bass

RESOURCES

Teacher Resource Binder

Music and History 16, *Romantic Music*

Music and History 18, *Johannes Brahms*

Transparency 7, *The Jolly Flatboatmen*, George Caleb Bingham

Music and History 20, *Fine Art Teaching Strategy*

For additional resources, see Music and History section.

Listening Selections CD

(found in the Teacher Resource Binder)

Track 7 "Toreador Chorus" from *Carmen*

Track 8 "The Moldau"

Focus

- Describe the Romantic period, including important developments.
- Describe characteristics of Romantic music.

The Romantic Period— A Time of Drama

A new sense of political and artistic freedom emerged during the **Romantic period** *(1820–1900)*. The period began in the middle of the Industrial Revolution, a time when manufacturing became mechanized and many people left farm life to work and live in cities where the manufacturing plants were located. Scientific and mechanical achievements were made in the development of railroads, steamboats, the telegraph and telephone, photography, and sound recordings.

The Industrial Revolution caused a major change in the economic and social life of the common people and also produced a wealthy middle class. More people were able to take part in cultural activities, such as attending music performances and going to art museums. Musicians and artists experienced greater freedom to express their individual creative ideas. This was because they were able to support themselves by ticket sales or sales of their art, instead of relying on the patronage of royalty or the church.

As people moved into the cities, nature and life in the country became the inspiration for many artists. The paintings of William Turner expressed the feelings suggested by nature. Later, French Impressionistic painters, including Claude Monet and Pierre-Auguste Renoir, developed new techniques bringing nature and natural light alive for the viewer.

Some of the most prominent thinkers and creators of this period were:

- Georges Bizet—French composer
- George Caleb Bingham—American painter
- Charles Dickens—English author
- Samuel F. B. Morse—American inventor who developed the telegraph

COMPOSERS

Ludwig van Beethoven (1770–1827)
Franz Schubert (1797–1828)
Felix Mendelssohn (1809–1847)
Frédéric Chopin (1810–1849)
Franz Liszt (1811–1886)
Richard Wagner (1813–1883)
Giuseppe Verdi (1813–1901)
Bedrich Smetana (1824–1884)
Johannes Brahms (1833–1897)
Georges Bizet (1838–1875)
Peter Ilyich Tchaikovsky (1840–1893)
Antonín Dvořák (1841–1904)
Claude Debussy (1862–1918)

ARTISTS

George Caleb Bingham (1811–1879)
Edgar Degas (1834–1917)
Paul Cezanne (1839–1906)
Auguste Rodin (1840–1917)
Claude Monet (1840–1926)
Pierre-Auguste Renoir (1841–1919)
Mary Cassatt (1845–1926)
Paul Gauguin (1848–1903)
Vincent van Gogh (1853–1890)

AUTHORS

Alexandre Dumas (1802–1870)
Henry Wadsworth Longfellow (1807–1882)
Charles Dickens (1812–1870)
Jules Verne (1828–1905)
Louisa May Alcott (1832–1884)
Mark Twain (1835–1910)
Rudyard Kipling (1865–1905)

VOCABULARY

Romantic period
music critic
overture
symphonic poem

Music History *Romantic*   **113**

National Standards

6. Listening to, analyzing, and describing music. **(a, b, c, e, f)**
8. Understanding relationships between music, the other arts, and disciplines outside the arts. **(a, b, c, d, e)**
9. Understanding music in relation to history and culture. **(a, c, d, e)**

LESSON PLAN

Suggested Teaching Sequence

1. Examine the Romantic period in a historical perspective

Direct students to:

- Read and discuss the information found on student page 113.
- Share what they know about the composers, artists and authors listed on this page.
- Turn to the time line on pages 114–115 and read the citations.
- Discuss why these are considered important dates during the Romantic period.
- Identify specific accomplishments that were made during the Romantic period and the people associated with those accomplishments.
- Compare each of these events to what occurred before and after the Romantic period.

2. Define the musical aspects of Romantic music.

Direct students to:

- Read and discuss information on Romantic music found on student page 114.
- Name several important Romantic composers.
- Define *music critic, overture* and *symphonic poem.*

3. Discuss the performance guidelines of Romantic music.

Direct students to:

- Read the Performance Links found on student page 114.
- Discuss the performance guidelines.

This feature is designed to expand students' appreciation of choral and instrumental music of the Romantic period.

Choral Selection:

"Toreador Chorus" from *Carmen* **by Georges Bizet**

Direct students to:

- Read the information on student page 115 to learn more about Georges Bizet and "Toreador Chorus" from *Carmen*.

- Review the definition of *opera*.

- Listen to the recorded performance to identify the mood created by this chorus.

- After listening again, write two or three sentences to describe this Procession of the Bullfighters scene from *Carmen*.

Instrumental Selection:

"The Moldau" by Bedrich Smetana

Direct students to:

- Read the information on student page 115 to learn more about Bedrich Smetana and "The Moldau."

- Review the definition of *symphonic poem*.

- Listen to the recorded performance to identify the story being told in the music about the Moldau River. *(For example, its beginning as a stream in the mountains, becoming a wide river, passing by hunters in the forest, etc.)*

Music of the Romantic Period

Music of the Romantic period focused on both the heights and depths of human emotion. The new musical ideas were expressed through larger works with complex vocal melodies and colorful harmonies. During this time, most of the brass and woodwind instruments developed into what they are today, and these instruments were used to add more tone and depth to the music.

Composers began to think about selling their music to the new audiences of middle-class people. Two types of music that appealed to these audiences were the extravagant spectacles of opera and the boldness of grand symphonic music. As music became public, it became subject to public scrutiny, particularly by music critics. A **music critic** is *a writer who gives an evaluation of a musical performance*.

Much of the music of the time was related to literature, such as Felix Mendelssohn's (1809–1847) *A Midsummer Night's Dream*, which was based on the play by William Shakespeare. A well-known section of this work is the **overture**, or *a piece for orchestra that serves as an introduction to an opera or other dramatic work*. The **symphonic poem** is *a single-movement work for orchestra, inspired by a painting, play or other literary or visual work*. Franz Liszt (1811–1886) was a prominent composer of this style of music. The Romantic period was also a time of nationalism, which was reflected in works such as Liszt's *Hungarian Dances*, Richard Wagner's focus on Germanic music, and the tributes to Italy found in Giuseppe Verdi's operas.

Performance Links

When performing music of the Romantic period, it is important to apply the following guidelines:

- Understand the relation of the text to the melody and harmony.
- Concentrate on phrasing, and maintain a clear, beautiful melodic line.
- Perform accurately the wide range of dynamics and tempos.
- Sing confidently in foreign languages to reflect nationalism in music.

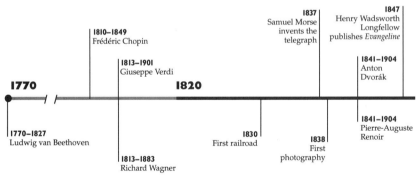

1810–1849 Frédéric Chopin

1837 Samuel Morse invents the telegraph

1847 Henry Wadsworth Longfellow publishes *Evangeline*

1813–1901 Giuseppe Verdi

1841–1904 Anton Dvořák

1770

1820

1770–1827 Ludwig van Beethoven

1830 First railroad

1838 First photography

1841–1904 Pierre-Auguste Renoir

1813–1883 Richard Wagner

114 Intermediate Tenor/Bass

MORE ABOUT

Romantic Painting

Emotional response is the significant feature of many Romantic paintings. Interest in exploring feelings and reaction, rather than formal structure, is typical of visual arts and music during the Romantic period.

Point out the details in *The Jolly Flatboatmen*. Ask: In which ways does this painter use the elements and principals of art differently than artists of other periods studied?

Listening Links

CHORAL SELECTION

"Toreador Chorus" from *Carmen* by Georges Bizet (1838–1875)

Carmen, by French composer Georges Bizet, is considered to be one of the most popular operas ever written. The opera tells the story of a gypsy girl who is arrested when she gets into a fight. Placed in the custody of the soldier Don Jose, Carmen soon entices him into a love affair. She then meets Escamilio, a toreador (bullfighter), and tries to get rid of Don Jose. Jilted, Don Jose stabs Carmen and kills himself. The "Toreador Chorus" is heard during the Procession of the Bullfighters. As you listen to the music, write two or three sentences to describe this procession scene in the opera as you think it would look.

INSTRUMENTAL SELECTION

"The Moldau" by Bedrich Smetana (1824–1884)

Bedrich Smetana was a prominent Czech composer. Smetana had a passion for music and composed in spite of his father's desire for him to become a lawyer. His musical efforts were focused mainly on trying to produce Czech national music based on the folk songs and dances that already existed. Smetana awoke one morning to find himself totally deaf. This created a depression that stayed with him through the remainder of his life. "The Moldau" represents Smetana's deep feeling about the beauty and significance of the river that flows through the city of Prague.

Check Your Understanding

1. List three major nonmusical changes that took place during the Romantic period.

2. Describe how "The Moldau" reflects nationalism in music of the Romantic period.

3. Describe how music of the Romantic period is different from music of another period.

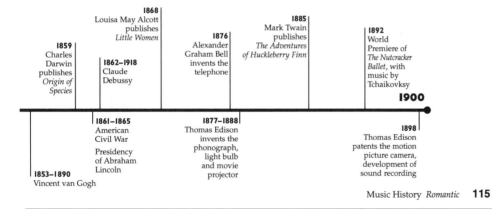

Music History *Romantic* **115**

Answers to Check Your Understanding

1. Answers will vary. For example, Industrial Revolution, development of railroads, steamboats, the telegraph and telephone, photography and sound recordings are a few choices they might use.

2. Smetana focused this composition on the major river that runs through his country of Czechoslovakia (now the Czech Republic), the Moldau River. He uses Czech folk songs and dance music in the piece to show his patriotism and pride in his country.

3. Answers will vary. For example, music of the Classical period was structured, less emotional, and emphasized clarity, repose and balance. Music of the Romantic period was full of emotion and less structured than music of the Classical period. Nationalism was an important element in Romantic music.

ASSESSMENT

Informal Assessment

In this lesson, students showed the ability to:

- Share what they know about the Romantic period.
- Describe musical characteristics, styles and forms found in Romantic music.
- Describe some characteristics of Romantic art.

Student Self-Assessment

Direct students to:

- Review the questions in Check Your Understanding on page 115.
- Write a paragraph answering each of the three questions about the Romantic period.

ENRICHMENT

Research Project

Have students:

- Write a paragraph that describes the Romantic period, based on research of one of the events in the time line. (*For example, the inventions of the telegraph and motion pictures were a result of the Industrial Revolution. New musical instruments were made as well.*)
- Write an additional paragraph that tells how this Romantic period time line event is related to the students' world. (*For example, how new electronic sound devices, such as synthesizers, influence the sound of pop music today.*)

CONTEMPORARY

OVERVIEW

Objectives

After completing this lesson, students will be able to:

- Describe the Contemporary period, including important developments.
- Describe characteristics of Contemporary music.

VOCABULARY

Have students review vocabulary in student lesson. A complete glossary of terms is found on page 226 of the student book.

Introduce the Contemporary period through art. Analyze the painting by Romare Howard Bearden on student page 116. Direct students to discuss the art form of collage. Review background information on Bearden's *The Piano Lesson (Homage to Mary Lou)* on page 116.

African American artist Romare Howard Bearden (1911–1988) is recognized as one of the most creative visual artists of the twentieth century. He experimented with many different styles and mediums but found a unique form of expression in collage. He had a great interest in literature, history, music, mathematics and the performing arts.

Romare Bearden. *The Piano Lesson (Homage to Mary Lou)*. 1983. Color lithograph on paper. 75.2 x 52.3 cm (29 1/2 x 20 1/2"). The Pennsylvania Academy of the Fine Arts, Philadelphia, Pennsylvania. The Harold A. and Ann R. Sorgenti Collection of Contemporary African American Art.

116 Intermediate Tenor/Bass

RESOURCES

Teacher Resource Binder

Music and History 21, *Contemporary Music*

Music and History 23, *Bob Chilcott*

Transparency 9, *The Piano Lesson (Homage to Mary Lou)*, Romare Howard Bearden

Music and History 25, *Fine Art Teaching Strategy*

For additional resources, see Music and History section.

Listening Selections CD

(found in the Teacher Resource Binder)

Track 9 "The Battle of Jericho"

Track 10 "Infernal Dance of King Kaschei" from *The Firebird*

Focus

- Describe the Contemporary period, including important developments.
- Describe characteristics of Contemporary music.

The Contemporary Period— The Search for Originality

Nothing characterizes the **Contemporary period** *(1900–present)* better than technology. Many technological advances began on October 4, 1957, when the Soviet Union successfully launched *Sputnik I*, the world's first artificial satellite. While the Sputnik launch was a single event, it marked the start of the Space Age and began many new political, military, technological and scientific developments.

Isolation was greatly reduced worldwide by developments in travel (rail, sea and air) and communication (telephone, radio, television and the Internet). It was also reduced as countries came together during World War I and World War II. Elements of cultures merged as people moved from their countries to various parts of the world for economic, political or social reasons. It no longer seems strange, for example, to see Chinese or Mexican restaurants in most communities in the United States or McDonald's® restaurants in Europe and Asia.

Some of the noteworthy leaders of this period have been:

- Igor Stravinsky—Russian/American composer
- Romare Bearden—American artist
- Robert Frost—American poet
- Wilbur and Orville Wright—American inventors who designed and flew the first airplane
- Albert Einstein—German/American scientist who formulated theories of relativity

COMPOSERS

Sergei Rachmaninoff (1873–1943)
Arnold Schoenberg (1874–1951)
Béla Bartók (1881–1945)
Igor Stravinsky (1882–1971)
Sergey Prokofiev (1891–1953)
Carl Orff (1895–1982)
Aaron Copland (1900–1990)
Benjamin Britten (1913–1976)
Leonard Bernstein (1918–1990)
Moses Hogan (1957–2003)

ARTISTS

Henri Matisse (1869–1954)
Pablo Picasso (1881–1973)
Wassily Kandinsky (1866–1944)
Marc Chagall (1887–1985)
Georgia O'Keeffe (1887–1986)
Romare Howard Bearden (1911–1988)
Andy Warhol (1930–1987)

AUTHORS

Robert Frost (1874–1963)
Virginia Woolf (1882–1941)
Ernest Hemingway (1899–1961)
Rachel Carson (1907–1964)
James Baldwin (1924–1997)
JK Rowling (b. 1965)

VOCABULARY

Contemporary period
synthesizer
twelve-tone music
aleatory music
fusion

Music History *Contemporary* **117**

National Standards

6. Listening to, analyzing, and describing music. **(a, b, c, e, f)**
8. Understanding relationships between music, the other arts, and disciplines outside the arts. **(a, b, c, d, e)**
9. Understanding music in relation to history and culture. **(a, c, d, e)**

LESSON PLAN
Suggested Teaching Sequence

1. Examine the Contemporary period in a historical perspective.

Direct students to:

- Read and discuss the information found on student page 117.
- Share what they know about the composers, artists and authors listed on this page.
- Turn to the time line on pages 120-121 and read the citations.
- Discuss why these are considered important dates during the Contemporary period.
- Identify specific accomplishments that were made during the Contemporary period and the people associated with those accomplishments.
- Compare each of these events to what occurred before the Contemporary period.

2. Define the musical aspects of Contemporary music.

Direct students to:

- Read and discuss information on Contemporary music found on student page 118.
- Name several important Contemporary composers.
- Identify the influences of technology on music of the Contemporary period.
- Define *synthesizer, twelve-tone music, aleatory music* and *fusion*.

3. Discuss the performance guidelines of Contemporary music.

Direct students to:

- Read the Performance Links found on student page 118.
- Discuss the performance guidelines.

117

This feature is designed to expand students' appreciation of choral and instrumental music of the Contemporary period.

Choral Selection:

"The Battle of Jericho," Traditional Spiritual, arranged by Moses George Hogan

Direct students to:

- Read the information on student page 119 to learn more about Moses George Hogan and "The Battle of Jericho."
- Listen to the recorded performance to identify specific musical effects added by the arranger, Moses Hogan.
- List these musical effects. *(The men's voices add energetic rhythmic effects to the harmonized melody in the women's voices. Word painting is used several times, especially at the end, for the words "come a tumbalin' down.")*

Instrumental Selection:

"Infernal Dance of King Kaschei" from *The Firebird* by Igor Stravinsky

Direct students to:

- Read the information on student page 119 to learn more about Igor Stravinsky and "Infernal Dance of King Kaschei" from *The Firebird*.
- Listen to the recorded performance to enjoy the energy and drama of this ballet selection.
- Listen again to the first section of the piece to count the loud shrieks of the firebird in that section. *(7)*

Music of the Contemporary Period

Technology has had a large influence on Contemporary music. Most people have access to music via radio, television and recordings. Technology has also influenced the music itself. The invention of electrified and electronic instruments led many composers to experiment with the new sounds. One of the most important new instruments was the **synthesizer**, *a musical instrument that produces sounds electronically, rather than by the physical vibrations of an acoustic instrument.*

The Contemporary period has witnessed a number of musical styles. Maurice Ravel (1875–1937) and Claude Debussy (1862–1918), for example, wrote music in the Impressionist style, often describing an impression of nature. Some of the music of Igor Stravinsky (1882–1971) and others was written in a neo-Classical (or "new" classical) style. Other music was considered avant-garde (or unorthodox or experimental); this included Arnold Schoenberg's (1874–1951) **twelve-tone music**, *a type of music that uses all twelve tones of the scale equally.* Composers experimented with **aleatory music**, or *a type of music in which certain aspects are performed randomly and left to chance.*

In addition, composers began using the rhythms, melodies and texts of other cultures in their compositions in a trend called **fusion**, or *the act of combining various types and cultural influences of music into a new style.*

Performance Links

When performing music of the Contemporary period, it is important to apply the following guidelines:

- Sing on pitch, even in extreme parts of your range.
- Tune intervals carefully in the skips found in many melodic lines.
- Sing changing meters and unusual rhythm patterns precisely.
- Perform accurately the wide range of dynamics and tempos.

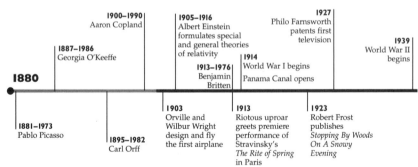

MORE ABOUT

Contemporary Art

The word that best describes the art of the Contemporary period is *diversity.* Today's artists make even greater use of new materials and techniques to express their ideas, beliefs and feelings. Many of these artists are moving away from traditional styles of art. Art movements of the past have given way to an astonishing array of individual art styles. Some of these styles reflect the influence of earlier artists while others reject entirely any reference to historical models.

Listening Links

CHORAL SELECTION

"The Battle of Jericho," Traditional Spiritual, arranged by Moses George Hogan (1957–2003)

Moses Hogan, born in New Orleans, Louisiana, was a pianist, conductor and arranger. He has been one of the most influential arrangers of our time in the revitalization of the songs of our forebearer. His contemporary settings of African American spirituals have been revered by audiences and praised by critics. He had a unique talent for expanding the harmonies and rhythms while preserving the traditional essence of these spirituals. Hogan's arrangements have become staples in the repertoires of choirs worldwide. What specific musical effects did Hogan add in his arrangement of "The Battle of Jericho"?

INSTRUMENTAL SELECTION

"Infernal Dance of King Kaschei" from *The Firebird* by Igor Stravinsky (1882–1971)

Igor Stravinsky was born in Russia, but lived the last twenty-five years of his life in California. *The Firebird* is a ballet that begins when Prince Ivan gives a magical golden bird with wings of fire its freedom in return for a feather. With the help of the magic feather, Ivan conquers an evil king and frees the princesses and prisoners that the king had held captive. Prince Ivan falls in love with a princess and they live happily ever after.

In the first section of this piece, you can hear the loud shrieks of the firebird. How many times did you hear this sudden loud sound?

Check Your Understanding

1. List three major nonmusical changes that took place during the Contemporary period.

2. Discuss the differences between a composer and an arranger.

3. Describe how music of the Contemporary period is different from music of the Romantic period.

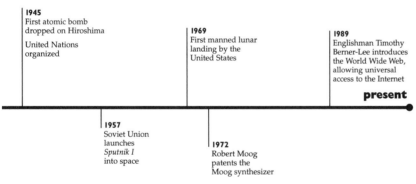

1945
First atomic bomb dropped on Hiroshima

United Nations organized

1957
Soviet Union launches *Sputnik I* into space

1969
First manned lunar landing by the United States

1972
Robert Moog patents the Moog synthesizer

1989
Englishman Timothy Berner-Lee introduces the World Wide Web, allowing universal access to the Internet

present

Music History *Contemporary* **119**

Answers to Check Your Understanding

1. Answers will vary. For example, Space Age/Sputnik; developments in travel and communication; WWI and WWII; theory of relativity

2. An arranger is a musician who adapts a composition or folk music for particular voices or instruments, or for another style of performance. A composer creates a piece of music as an original work.

3. Answers will vary. Music of the Romantic period focuses on the heights and depths of human emotion. Nationalism is reflected in many musical works. Music of the Contemporary period is marked by change and experimentation—new forms, new instruments, music written with no tonal center, music featuring a fusion of musical styles, and so forth.

ASSESSMENT

Informal Assessment

In this lesson, students showed the ability to:

- Share what they know about the Contemporary period.
- Describe musical characteristics, styles and forms found in Contemporary music.
- Describe some characteristics of Contemporary art.

Student Self-Assessment

Direct students to:

- Review the questions in Check Your Understanding on page 119.
- Write a paragraph answering each of the three questions about the Contemporary period.

ENRICHMENT

Research Project

The technology boom of the 1990s has brought so many possibilities for expansion of the arts. However, some people feel that there is a danger that the standards for excellence in the arts will be lost because now everyone is capable of making it. At the same time, each field of art may be taken to a level never imagined before.

Direct students to:

- Discuss the advantages and disadvantages of technology as it applies to art and music.
- Have small groups do research on the specifics of each, and then present findings to the rest of the class.

DICTION

OBJECTIVES

- Demonstrate basic performance techniques using proper diction.

Suggested Teaching Sequence

Direct students to:

- Read the Spotlight On Diction on student page 120 and identify the importance of diction in singing.
- Define *articulators*.
- Describe the difference between voiced and unvoiced consonants.
- Speak the voiced and unvoiced consonants out loud and find examples in music they are currently studying.
- Compare the concept of proper diction to effective performance practices.
- Discuss on the proper use of the "r" consonant when singing.

Progress Checkpoints

Observe students' progress in:

- ✓ Their ability to speak voiced and unvoiced consonants properly.
- ✓ Their ability to name the parts of the body that are the articulators.
- ✓ Their ability to recognize voiced and unvoiced consonants in other music they are studying.
- ✓ Their ability to relate the importance of proper diction in other areas such as drama, speech and public speaking.

SPOTLIGHT

Diction

Singing is a form of communication. To communicate well while singing, you must not only form your vowels correctly, but also say your consonants as clearly and cleanly as possible.

There are two kinds of consonants: voiced and unvoiced. Consonants that require the use of the voice along with the **articulators** *(lips, teeth, tongue, and other parts of the mouth and throat)* are called voiced consonants. If you place your hand on your throat, you can actually feel your voice box vibrate while producing them. Unvoiced consonant sounds are made with the articulators only.

In each pair below, the first word contains a voiced consonant while the second word contains an unvoiced consonant. Speak the following word pairs, then sing them on any pitch. When singing, make sure the voiced consonant is on the same pitch as the vowel.

Voiced:	Unvoiced Consonants:	More Voiced Consonants:
[b] bay	[p] pay	[l] lip
[d] den	[t] ten	[m] mice
[g] goat	[k] coat	[n] nice
[dʒ] jeer	[tʃ] cheer	[j] yell
[z] zero	[s] scenic	[r] red
[ʒ] fusion	[ʃ] shun	
[ð] there	[ө] therapy	More Unvoiced Consonants:
[v] vine	[f] fine	[h] have
[w] wince	[hw] whim	

The American "r" requires special treatment in classical choral singing. To sing an American "r" at the end of a syllable following a vowel, sing the vowel with your teeth apart and jaw open. In some formal sacred music and English texts, you may need to flip or roll the "r." For most other instances, sing the "r" on pitch, then open to the following vowel quickly.

RESOURCES

Teacher Resource Binder

Evaluation Master 6, *Diction Checkup*
Vocal Development 9, *Diction*
Vocal Development 13, *Posture & Breathing*

National Standards

1. Singing, alone and with others, a varied repertoire of music. **(b)**
8. Understanding relationships between music, the other arts, and disciplines outside the arts. **(b)**

Choral Library

The Battle Cry Of Freedom 122

Come Travel With Me 128

Frog Went A-Courtin' 140

Guantanamera 152

Joshua! 158

Leave Her, Johnny 170

New River Train 174

On The Deep, Blue Sea 184

Pretty Saro 198

Santa Lucia 206

Sing To The Lord 212

You Gentlemen Of England 218

The Battle Cry Of Freedom

OVERVIEW

Composer: George Frederick Root (1825–1895), arranged by Patti DeWitt

Text: George Frederick Root

Voicing: TB

Key: D major/G major

Meter: 4/4

Form: ABAA'B'A'

Style: Patriotic

Accompaniment: None

Programming: Thematic programming, Festival, Patriotic

Vocal Ranges:

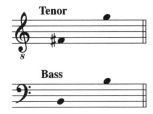

Objectives

After completing this lesson, students will be able to:

- Use standard terminology to describe intervals in detail.
- Read and perform independently with accurate rhythm and intonation.
- Perform music representative of diverse cultures, including American heritage.

VOCABULARY

Have students review vocabulary in student lesson. Introduce terms found in the music. A complete glossary of terms is found on page 226 of the student book.

The Battle Cry Of Freedom

Composer: George Frederick Root (1825–1895), arranged by Patti DeWitt
Text: George Frederick Root
Voicing: TB

VOCABULARY

stepwise motion
skipwise motion
fermata

Focus

- Identify and perform melodies with stepwise and skipwise motion.
- Read and perform dotted eighth and sixteenth note rhythmic patterns.
- Sing music representing American heritage.

Getting Started

Military historians know that certain songs are associated with particular wars. Sing any of these war favorites that you know.

a. "Yankee Doodle"	from the American Revolutionary War
b. "Over There"	from World War I
c. "God Bless America"	from World War II
d. "Blowin' In The Wind"	from the Vietnam War
e. "From A Distance"	from the 1990 Persian Gulf War

After you learn "The Battle Cry Of Freedom," you can add it to your list as a favorite song from the American Civil War.

◆ History and Culture

American composer George Frederick Root (1825–1895) wrote sacred and patriotic songs. "The Battle Cry Of Freedom" is the most famous of his 28 Civil War songs. Written after Root had read President Lincoln's proclamation calling for troops, the song was published in 1862. It became a favorite with the civilian population as well as the troops. "The Battle Cry Of Freedom" was played at Fort Sumter on April 14, 1865, when Brigadier General Robert Anderson raised the Union flag over the recaptured fort. The song remained popular with Union as well as Confederate troops.

🎲 SKILL BUILDERS

To learn more about dotted rhythms, see Intermediate Sight-Singing, *page 89.*

RESOURCES

Intermediate Sight-Singing

Sight-Singing in D Major, pages 99–102

Sight-Singing in G Major, pages 82–85, 89–90

Reading Dotted Notes, pages 45, 48, 49

Reading Sixteenth Notes, pages 57–60, 89–90

Teacher Resource Binder

Teaching Master 14, *Creating Melodic Patterns in D Major*

Evaluation Master 2, *Analyzing Pitch Accuracy*

Evaluation Master 8, *Evaluating Rhythmic Accuracy*

Skill Builder 12, *Constructing Major Scales*

Skill Builder 30, *Solfège Hand Signs*

For additional resources, see TRB Table of Contents.

Links to Learning

◆ **Vocal**

When Root wrote "The Battle Cry Of Freedom," he used a melody that has **stepwise motion** (*melodic movement from a given note to another note that is directly above or below it on the staff*) and **skipwise motion** (*melodic movement from a given note to another note that is two or more notes above or below it on the staff*). In a comfortable octave, perform the following example to practice singing stepwise and skipwise motion. Which do you think is easier to sing?

Yes, we'll ral - ly 'round the flag, boys, we'll ral - ly once a - gain.

Shout - ing the bat - tle cry of free - dom.

◆ **Theory**

Read and perform the following example to practice rhythmic patterns that contain dotted rhythms. Observe the fermata sign over the last note. A **fermata** (⌢) is *a symbol that indicates to hold a note longer than its given value.*

ti ti ta   ti ti ta   tim ka ta   tim ka ta   ta   tim ka ti ti ti ti   ta–a   ta

Evaluation

Demonstrate how well you have learned the skills and concepts featured in the lesson "The Battle Cry Of Freedom" by completing the following:

- Locate in the music two examples of melodic stepwise motion and two examples of skipwise motion. Support your answers by explaining why you made the choices you did.

- Record yourself singing measures 12–22. Play it back and indicate in your music or on a sheet of paper any rhythmic or melodic mistakes. Evaluate how well you were able to perform dotted rhythms correctly.

RESOURCES

Intermediate Tenor/Bass Rehearsal/Performance CD

CD 2:1 Voices
CD 2:2 Accompaniment Only
CD 3:16 Vocal Practice Track—Tenor
CD 4:12 Vocal Practice Track—Bass

National Standards

1. Singing, alone and with others, a varied repertoire of music. **(a, b, c, d, e)**
5. Reading and notating music. **(a, b, c)**
9. Understanding music in relation to history and culture. **(a, b)**

LESSON PLAN

Suggested Teaching Sequence and Performance Tips

1. Introduce

Direct students to:

- Read and discuss the information found in the Getting Started section on student page 122.
- Practice the exercises in the Vocal and Theory sections on page 123.
- Mark the breath marks in their choral score and breath rhythmically.
- Circle the two fermatas in the music.
- Mark in their music when their part has the melody. Note how the melody goes back and forth between parts.

Progress Checkpoints

Observe students' progress in:

✓ Clearly marking their score with the breath marks.

✓ Counting and performing the dotted eighth- and sixteenth-note rhythms with accuracy.

✓ Identifying which part has the melody.

The Battle Cry Of Freedom

For TB a cappella

Arranged by
PATTI DeWITT

GEORGE FREDERICK ROOT
(1825–1895)

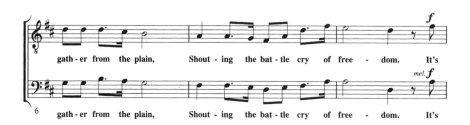

124   Intermediate Tenor/Bass

TEACHER 2 TEACHER

Nothing makes a male chorus sing out more than a rousing, robust patriotic number such as "The Battle Cry Of Freedom." With its easy intervals and march-like rhythms, your Tenor/Bass chorus will join forces to create a concert opener or closer that will bring your audience to their feet and salute!

up with the star. While we ral - ly 'round the flag, boys, We'll
up with the star. While we ral - ly 'round the flag, boys, We'll

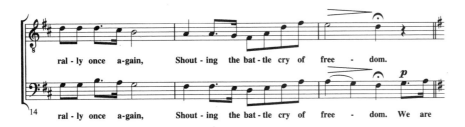

ral - ly once a - gain, Shout - ing the bat - tle cry of free - dom.
ral - ly once a - gain, Shout - ing the bat - tle cry of free - dom. We are

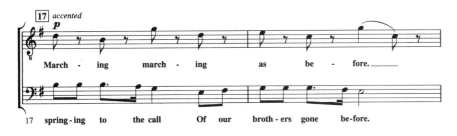

March - ing march - ing as be - fore. _____
spring - ing to the call Of our broth - ers gone be - fore.

Shout - ing that bat - tle cry of free - dom; March - ing with a
Shout - ing the bat - tle cry of free - dom; And we'll fill the va - cant ranks With a

mil - lion more, _____ Shout - ing the bat - tle cry of free - dom; It's
mil - lion free - men more. Shout - ing the bat - tle cry of free - dom;

ENRICHMENT

Concert Staging

Staging this song with your Tenor/Bass choir can make this an audience favorite. Use a "school assembly" size flag with a long pole. Ask two of your boys to hold the flagpole, one on each side. Arrange the remaining boys in various levels—kneeling, standing and so forth—around the two boys holding the flag. Have them sing the song in this formation. After rehearsing in this formation, get feedback from the boys if this made a difference in how the choir expressed the text. Did they like singing in the formation instead of standard risers?

2. Rehearse

Direct students to:

- Chant the rhythm to measures 1–34. Avoid rushing.
- Watch you for the cutoff every time a *fermata* occurs.
- Sing on solfège syllables once the chanting is comfortable.

Progress Checkpoints

Observe students' progress in:

- ✓ Breathing rhythmically where marked.
- ✓ Singing correct pitches and accurate rhythms in each section.
- ✓ Holding the fermata as directed and watching you for the cutoff.

3 Refine

Direct students to:

- Speak through the text as you model the desired vowel sounds. Avoid rushing.
- Transfer the solfège syllables to text phrase by phrase.
- Model the phrases musically as you want them to be sung. Ask them to repeat as modeled.

Progress Checkpoints

Observe students' progress in:

- ✓ Their accuracy in speaking and singing through text with all parts.
- ✓ Uniformity of vowel sounds as a section and as a choir.
- ✓ Singing musically and with good intonation in individual parts and as a choir.
- ✓ Breathing rhythmically.

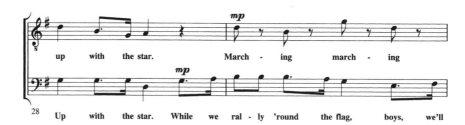

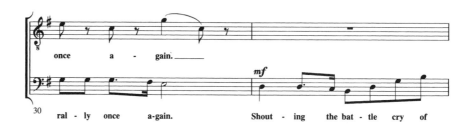

ASSESSMENT

Informal Assessment

In this lesson, students showed the ability to:

- Read and perform music with complex rhythmic patterns.
- Sing expressively with good intonation using consonants, uniform vowel sounds and musical phrasing.

Student Self-Assessment

Have students evaluate their individual performances based on the following:

- Breath Management
- Diction
- Tall Vowels
- Accurate Pitches
- Accurate Rhythms

Have each student rate his/her performance of this song in the areas above on a scale of 1–5, 5 being the best.

Individual and Group Performance Evaluation

To further measure growth of musical skills presented in this lesson, direct students to complete the Evaluation section on page 123.

- After all students have found two examples of step-wise motion and two examples of skip-wise motion in their music, ask for volunteers to share their answers with supporting reasons for their choices.
- Have students record themselves singing measures 12–22. Have students listen to their recordings and evaluate how well they were able to sing with accurate rhythms and pitches.

Additional National Standards

The following National Standards are addressed through the Assessment, Extension, Enrichment and bottom-page activities:

6. Listening to, analyzing, and describing music. **(c)**

7. Evaluating music and music performances. **(b)**

SPOTLIGHT

Careers In Music

Teacher

Music teachers share their love of music with their students. To teach music in a public school, you must have a bachelor's degree in music education. That will require at least four years of college, including one semester of student teaching. High school and junior high music teachers usually specialize in one performance area such as choir, band or orchestra. They may also teach general music, music theory, music appreciation, keyboard and guitar. Elementary music teachers enjoy working with young children. Their job is varied in that they teach singing, dancing, how to play instruments, listening, world music and much more.

At the college level, a music professor must have additional training. Although the minimum requirement is to have a master's degree in music, most colleges require you to have a doctorate as well. College professors teach students how to become professional musicians and professional teachers.

Some musicians choose to teach music through their church or synagogue. Church musicians may be full-time or part-time employees. They might serve as singers, choir directors, organists, instrumentalists or **cantors** *(people who sing and teach music in temples or synagogues).* Some of these positions require a college degree in music.

Private studio teachers enjoy working with students on a one-on-one basis. They teach from their homes, from private studios, or sometimes at schools. Private instructors teach voice, piano/keyboard, or any of the musical instruments. Their hours are flexible, but they often work in the evenings or weekends because that is when their students are not in school.

Spotlight *Careers In Music* **127**

RESOURCES

Teacher Resource Binder

Reference 5, *Careers in Music*

National Standards

9. Understanding music in relation to history and culture. **(c)**

CAREERS IN MUSIC

Objective

• Describe music-related vocations and avocations.

Suggested Teaching Sequence

Direct students to:

• Read the Spotlight On Careers in Music on page 127 and identify the many teaching opportunities in music.

• Divide into small groups and brainstorm on the many different teaching careers available in music. Make a list and share findings with the class. Why are these jobs important?

• Share personal experiences of music teachers that have influenced their lives in positive ways. If possible, invite those teachers to speak to the class about their careers.

• Search the Internet or local library for other career opportunities in music.

Progress Checkpoints

Observe students' progress in:

✓ Their ability to identify teaching careers in music.

✓ Their ability to describe the importance of the role of a music teacher.

✓ Their ability to discover other career opportunities in music.

Come Travel With Me

Come Travel With Me

OVERVIEW

Composer: Scott Farthing
Text: Walt Whitman
Voicing: TTB
Key: C major
Meter: 4/4
Form: ABACA
Style: Contemporary American Song
Accompaniment: Piano
Programming: Concert, Contest, Festival

Vocal Ranges:

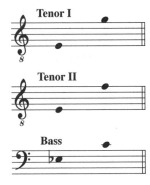

Tenor I

Tenor II

Bass

Objectives

After completing this lesson, students will be able to:

• Interpret music terms and symbols referring to dynamics when performing.

• Read and perform independently with accurate rhythm, including triplet patterns.

• Identify the relationships between the processes and concepts of other subjects and those of music.

VOCABULARY

Have students review vocabulary in student lesson. Introduce terms found in the music. A complete glossary of terms is found on page 226 of the student book.

128

Composer: Scott Farthing
Text: Walt Whitman
Voicing: TTB

VOCABULARY

dynamics

triplet

ritardando

a tempo

trio

Focus

• Identify dynamic markings in music.

• Read and perform rhythmic patterns that contain triplets.

• Relate music to other subjects (poetry).

Getting Started

Lets go! Wherever you are, let's go!

Come travel with me.

Let's go! We must not stop here, let's go!

We will not fear!

The words in a song often create an image in the singer's mind. The text or poetry plays a very important role in making the song come alive. Read the words above. Who do you think is telling the story, and to whom is he speaking? The traveler encourages the reader to explore, travel and face the journey of life not with fear, but with a sense of joyful abandon.

◆ **SPOTLIGHT**

To learn more about posture, see page 13.

◆ History and Culture

American poet Walt Whitman (1819–1892) is considered one of the world's major literary leaders. "Leaves of Grass," published in 1892, contains over 300 poems. It is interesting to note that many of Whitman's poems contain musical references of some type and that he felt music was an inspiration to his writing.

The text of "Come Travel With Me" is loosely based on Walt Whitman's famous poem "Song of the Open Road." In this poem, Whitman shares with the readers his overwhelming zest for life and his appreciation for the world around him. The music and adaptation of words to "Come Travel With Me" were written in 2001 by Scott Farthing, who at the time was a high school choral director in the Kansas City, Missouri, area.

128   Intermediate Tenor/Bass

RESOURCES

Intermediate Sight-Singing

Sight-Singing in C Major, pages 7–14, 15–17, 28–30, 66–67, 110–111

Reading Triplet Rhythms, pages 135–136

Teacher Resource Binder

Teaching Master 15, *Images Create Sounds*

Teaching Master 16, *How High Can I Sing?*

Evaluation Master 8, *Evaluating Rhythmic Accuracy*

Vocal Development 11, *Flexibility and Range*

Interdisciplinary 21-22, *Language Arts*

For additional resources, see TRB Table of Contents.

Links to Learning

◆ Vocal

The **dynamics** *(the symbols in music that indicate how loud or soft to sing)* used in "Come Travel with Me" add expression and interest to the song. Perform the following example with the indicated dynamic markings.

◆ Theory

A **triplet** is *a group of notes in which three notes of equal duration are sung in the time normally given to two notes of equal duration.* A quarter note triplet consists of three quarter notes performed in two beats. Practice the following example to learn how to perform quarter note triplets.

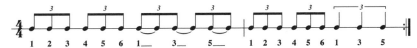

◆ Artistic Expression

In music, tempo markings are used to tell a singer how fast or slow to sing. **Ritardando** *(rit.)* is *a term used to indicate gradually slowing down.* Sometimes following the ritardando is **a tempo,** or *a term used to indicate the return to the original tempo.* Sing measures 10–13 and apply these tempo markings.

Evaluation

Demonstrate how well you have learned the skills and concepts featured in the lesson "Come Travel With Me" by completing the following:

- Make a chart that represents the dynamic markings in this song. In one column, list the boxed measure numbers; in the other column, list the dynamic markings for that section. Check your work with a classmate.
- As a **trio** *(a group of three singers with usually one on a part)*, perform measures 21–36 to show that you can read and sing triplets correctly. How well did you do?

Choral Library Come Travel With Me **129**

RESOURCES

Intermediate Tenor/Bass Rehearsal/Performance CD

CD 2:3 Voices
CD 2:4 Accompaniment Only
CD 3:17 Vocal Practice Track—Tenor I
CD 3:18 Vocal Practice Track—Tenor II
CD 4:13 Vocal Practice Track—Bass

National Standards

1. Singing, alone and with others, a varied repertoire of music. **(a, b, d, e,)**
5. Reading and notating music. **(a, b, c)**
8. Understanding relationships between music, the other arts, and disciplines outside the arts. **(b)**

LINKS TO LEARNING

Vocal

The Vocal section is designed to prepare students to:

- Understand dynamics.
- Perform expressively following dynamic markings.

Have students:

- Read the definition of dynamics.
- Perform the example following the dynamic markings indicated in the music.

Theory

The Theory section is designed to prepare students to understand and perform triplets.

Have students:

- Read the definition of triplets.
- Tap or clap the quarter note pulse.
- Speak the exercise on numbers, while tapping the quarter note pulse.
- Speak the exercise on numbers, while watching the director conduct, feeling the quarter note pulse inside.

Artistic Expression

The Artistic Expression section is designed to prepare students to understand *ritard* and *a tempo* and apply these markings to their performances.

Have students:

- Read the definitions of *ritard* and *a tempo*.
- Sing measures 10–13 and apply these tempo markings to their performance.

LESSON PLAN

Suggested Teaching Sequence and Performance Tips

1. Introduce

Direct students to:

- Read and discuss the information found in the Getting Started section on page 128.
- Practice the exercise shown in the Vocal section on page 129 to demonstrate the use of dynamics.
- Practice the rhythm exercises as shown in the Theory section on page 129 to increase ability to read and perform the triplet patterns in the song.

For the 2001 National ACDA Junior High Honor Choir
Dr. Lynne Gackle, Conductor

Come Travel With Me

TTB and Piano

Inspired by Walt Whitman's
Song of the Open Road

Words and Music by
SCOTT FARTHING

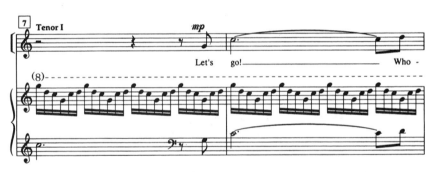

130   Intermediate Tenor/Bass

TEACHER 2 TEACHER

With its limited ranges and piano accompaniment, this is the ideal work for the middle and high school male choir. The text encourages the young spirit to explore the journey of life.

Progress Checkpoints

Observe students' progress in:

✓ Their ability to sing with the indicated dynamic markings.

✓ Their ability to perform triplet patterns accurately with clear articulation.

TEACHING STRATEGY

Performance Techniques for Large-Ensembles

Have students:

• Identify appropriate performance techniques to be used with "Come Travel With Me" (phrasing, articulation, intonation, diction, tempo, dynamic contrast, interpretation, tone, blend, balance, and so forth).

• Explain/describe these performance techniques in relationship to this song.

• Perform this piece for memory at a formal concert.

• Critique the performance techniques observed at the formal concert.

2. Rehearse

Direct students to:

- Listen to the recorded performance of "Come Travel With Me." Discuss the piece in terms of importance and emphasis of text.
- Locate triplet passages *(measures 17, 23, 25, 27, 32, 47, 51, 52)* and chant for rhythmic accuracy.
- Chant the rhythms in measures 15–36.
- Practice measures 15–36 (the A section) on solfège syllables and check for accuracy, paying particular attention to the accidentals in measures 20, 28, 35, and 36.
- Change to a neutral *too* syllable, when pitches and rhythms are accurate.
- Sing the repeat of the A section at measures 45–50 and secure pitches, rhythms and accents.
- Repeat the same procedure for the B section in measures 36–45. Measures 36–45 are sung in a contrasting legato style.

MORE ABOUT...

Careers in Music: Performance

Many people make a living through professions associated with music. Some are teachers, composers, conductors, managers, salespersons, technicians and more. One of the more visible careers in music is that of a professional performer. As a performer, one may become a solo artist, a member of an ensemble (band, orchestra or vocal group), or a member of a troupe (opera, Broadway). There are many career opportunities in the field of music performance.

- Chant rhythmic entrances for the last section measures 50–61. When rhythms are accurate, add pitches and text.
- Add text throughout when pitches and rhythms are secure. Strive for clear and clean articulation of all the text.

Progress Checkpoints

Observe students' progress in:

✓ Performing triplets and rhythmic passages accurately.

✓ Enunciating with clear and clean articulation.

✓ Their ability to maintain three-part harmony with proper vocal production.

EXTENSION

Walt Whitman

Have students find the text of other Walt Whitman poems. (For example, "O Captain, My Captain" or a poem from *Leaves of Grass*.) Compare and contrast those poems to the text of "Come Travel With Me." Describe the kind of music best suited to the text of each poem.

3. Refine

Direct the students to:

- Sing the entire song with emphasis on exploded and tall vowel sounds.
- Refine the *legato* section in measures 36–45 using breath and energy to connect the phrases.
- Practice to secure the staggered entrances at the end of the song.
- Emphasize the composer's dynamic markings throughout. Associate singing *forte* with fullness rather than just singing loudly. Associate singing *piano* with singing energetically.

ENRICHMENT

Express Yourself

Read the text of "Come Travel with Me." Write your interpretation of the text and relate it to experiences in your own life.

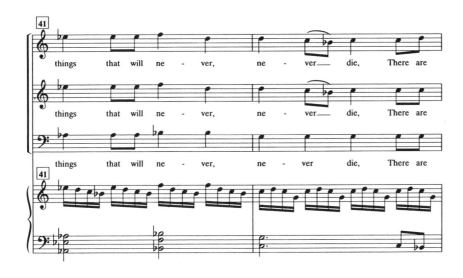

- Maintain rhythmic vitality throughout to lend excitement and energy to the text.
- Add facial expression to portray the meaning of text and enhance the performance.

Progress Checkpoints

Observe students' progress in:

✓ Performing with accurate pitches and rhythm.

✓ Singing with energy and clear, crisp diction.

✓ Performing contrasting dynamic levels.

TEACHING STRATEGY

Solo and Small Ensemble Performances

Have students:

1. Prepare solos and small ensembles for performance or competition.

2. Interpret music symbols and terms referring to dynamics, tempo and articulation during the performance.

3. Evaluate the quality of the performance using standard terminology.

ASSESSMENT

Informal Assessment

In this lesson, students showed the ability to:

- Sing with the dynamic marking indicated in the music.
- Accurately sing a triplet rhythmic pattern.
- Articulate text clearly and understandably.

TEACHING STRATEGY

Concert Etiquette

Have students:

1. Identify appropriate concert etiquette in a variety of settings (formal concerts, informal concerts, large concert halls, small concert halls, and so forth).
2. Attend a variety of live performances.
3. Discuss the appropriate and inappropriate concert behaviors observed.
4. Write a short analysis of appropriate concert etiquette for each setting.

Student Self-Assessment

Have students evaluate their individual performances based on the following:

- Diction
- Tall Vowels
- Expressive Singing
- Performance of Dynamics
- Accurate Rhythms

Have each student rate his/her performance of this song in the areas above on a scale of 1–5, 5 being the best.

CURRICULUM CONNECTIONS

English and American Literature

Walt Whitman (1819–1892) is considered by many to be the greatest of all American poets. Whitman celebrated the freedom and dignity of the individual and sang the praises of democracy and the brotherhood of man. His *Leaves of Grass*, unconventional in both content and technique, is probably one of the most influential volume of poems in the history of American literature.

Individual and Group Performance Evaluation

To further measure growth of musical skills presented in this lesson, direct students to complete the Evaluation section on page 129.

- After making a chart that represents the dynamic markings in this song as indicated, have each student exchange charts with a classmate. The students should evaluate each other's work.
- Divide into trios with one singer on each part. Have each trio perform measures 21–36 for the rest of the class. The class should evaluate. Did this trio sing triplets correctly?

MUSIC, SOCIETY AND CULTURE

Have students perform additional songs representing diverse cultures, including American and Texas heritage. Go to **music.glencoe.com**, the Web site for Glencoe's choral music programs, for additional music selections students can perform.

138 Intermediate Tenor/Bass

Additional National Standards

The following National Standards are addressed through the Assessment, Extension, Enrichment and bottom-page activities:

6. Listening to, analyzing, and describing music. **(c)**

7. Evaluating music and music performances. **(b)**

SPOTLIGHT

Concert Etiquette

The term **concert etiquette** describes *how we are expected to behave in formal musical performances.* Understanding appropriate concert etiquette allows you to be considerate of others, including audience members and performers. It also helps everyone attending to enjoy the performance.

Different types of musical performances dictate certain behavior guidelines. How one shows excitement at a rock concert is certainly worlds apart from the appropriate behavior at a formal concert or theatre production. Understanding these differences allows audience members to behave in a manner that shows consideration and respect for everyone involved.

What are the expectations of a good audience member at a formal musical presentation?

- Arrive on time. If you arrive after the performance has begun, wait outside the auditorium until a break in the music to enter the hall.
- Remain quiet and still during the performance. Talking and moving around prevents others from hearing and enjoying the performance.
- Leave the auditorium only in case of an emergency. Try to leave during a break in the musical selections.
- Sing or clap along only when invited to do so by the performers or the conductor.
- Applaud at the end of a composition or when the conductor lowers his arms at the conclusion of the performance. It is customary to not applaud between movements or sections of a major work.
- Save shouting, whistling and dancing for rock concerts or athletic events. These are never appropriate at formal musical performances.

Remembering these important behavior guidelines will ensure that everyone enjoys the show!

Spotlight *Concert Etiquette*   **139**

RESOURCES

Teacher Resource Binder
Evaluation Master 5, *Concert Etiquette Quiz*

National Standards
7. Evaluating music and musical performances. **(a, b)**

Objective
- Apply concert etiquette in a variety of settings.

Suggested Teaching Sequence
Direct students to:
- Read the Spotlight On Concert Etiquette on student page 139 and discuss the importance of concert etiquette in respecting the efforts of others.
- Identify the six elements that constitute proper concert etiquette.
- Compare the elements of concert etiquette to appropriate performance practices. In what ways are they related to one another?
- Apply concert etiquette during live performances in a variety of settings such as school concerts and assemblies, professional symphony and/or opera performances and solo recitals.
- Divide the class into small groups and assign each group one concert venue. Ask each group to make a list of five appropriate and five inappropriate behavior expectations for the assigned venue. Share findings with the class.

Progress Checkpoints
Observe students' progress in:
- ✓ Their ability to identify the elements of concert etiquette.
- ✓ Their ability to understand the importance of concert etiquette.
- ✓ Their ability to apply concert etiquette in a variety of settings.

Frog Went A-Courtin'

OVERVIEW

Composer: Traditional Folk Song, arranged by Audrey Snyder

Text: Traditional

Voicing: TB

Key: G Major, A♭ Major, A Major

Meter: Cut Time

Form: Verse

Style: American Folk Song

Accompaniment: Piano

Programming: Light Concert

Vocal Ranges:

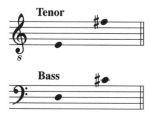

Objectives

After completing this lesson, students will be able to:

• Perform independently with accurate intonation.

• Use standard terminology to describe intervals in detail, including octave and unison.

• Perform music representative of diverse cultures, including American heritage.

Frog Went A-Courtin'

Composer: Traditional Folk Song, arranged by Audrey Snyder

Text: Traditional

Voicing: TB

VOCABULARY

narrative song

modulation

pentatonic scale

octave

SPOTLIGHT

To learn more about diction, see page 119.

Focus

• Perform music based on the pentatonic scale.

• Use standard terminology to describe octave and unison.

• Perform music that represents an American narrative folk song.

Getting Started

Mickey Mouse®, Donald Duck®, Scooby Doo®, Tom and Jerry®…

Who is your favorite cartoon animal? If the American folk song "Frog Went A-Courtin'" were a cartoon, Frog, Miss Mouse and Uncle Rat would certainly be unforgettable characters. In this story, Frog is courtin' (going out with) Miss Mouse and asks her to marry him. She asks permission from Uncle Rat, who replies, "Marry whom you please." That is a fitting answer for a perfectly silly cartoon story.

◆ History and Culture

"Frog Went A-Courtin'" is a **narrative song,** or *a song that tells a story.* Since the melody remains the same for all eight verses, arranger Audrey Snyder uses **modulation,** or *a change in the key or tonal center of a piece of music within a song,* to create variety. The tonal center or key at the beginning of the song is G major. As the song progresses, it modulates to the key of Ab major and then to A major.

Although this arrangement contains eight verses, other versions have many more verses. In one version, numerous wedding guests are introduced, including a flyin' moth, a juney bug, a bumbley bee, a broken back flea, Mrs. Cow, a little black tick and the old gray cat.

Audrey Snyder has also included several opportunities for you to develop the characters using spoken dialogue and dramatic effects. Have fun singing this well-known narrative folk song.

RESOURCES

Intermediate Sight-Singing

Sight-Singing in G Major, pages 82–85, 89–90

Sight-Singing in A♭ Major, pages 176–177

Sight-Singing in A Major, pages 152–163

Reading Rhythms in Cut Time, page 140

Teacher Resource Binder

Teaching Master 17, *Developing Stage Presence*

Evaluation Master 6, *Diction Checkup*

Evaluation Master 10, *Ensemble Performance Evaluation*

Skill Builder 20, *Naming Intervals*

Interdisciplinary 24–25, *Theatre*

For additional resources, see TRB Table of Contents.

Links to Learning

◆ **Vocal**

"Frog Went A-Courtin'" is based on the **pentatonic scale,** *a five-tone scale that contains the pitches* do re, mi, sol, *and* la *of a corresponding major scale.* In a comfortable range for your voice, sing the pentatonic scales as shown for the three key signatures used in this

song.

◆ **Theory**

An **octave** is *an interval of two pitches that are eight notes apart on a staff.* For example, if you were to sing low "G" and someone else were to sing high "G" at the same time, then you would be singing in octaves. On the other hand, if you both were to sing the same note at the same time, then you would be singing in unison. Find examples of singing in octaves and singing in unison in the music.

◆ **Artistic Expression**

As you sing "Frog Went A-Courtin'," it becomes apparent that the three characters are very animated and full of personality. Using the text and style of the song as your guide, draw Frog, Miss Mouse, and Uncle Rat as cartoon characters.

Evaluation

Demonstrate how well you have learned the skills and concepts featured in the lesson "Frog Went A-Courtin'" by completing the following:

- On a sheet of staff paper, write the notes for a pentatonic scale in three different keys. Sing or play each pattern to check that the notes are correct.

- With a small group, sing verse 7 (measures 104–118) to demonstrate your ability to sing unisons and octaves with clear diction. Ask a classmate to evaluate your performance.

- Make a program cover for "Frog Went A-Courtin'" using your cartoon drawings of the characters. Critique the artwork based on how well it conveys the character and spirit of the song.

RESOURCES

Intermediate Tenor/Bass Rehearsal/Performance CD

CD 2:5 Voices

CD 2:6 Accompaniment Only

CD 3:19 Vocal Practice Track—Tenor

CD 4:14 Vocal Practice Track—Bass

National Standards

1. Singing, alone and with others, a varied repertoire of music. **(a, b, c, d)**

6. Listening to, analyzing, and describing music. **(c)**

9. Understanding music in relation to history and culture. **(b)**

LINKS TO LEARNING

Vocal

The Vocal section is designed to prepare students to understand and sing the pentatonic scale in various keys.

Have students:

- Read the definition of pentatonic scale.
- Listen as you play a pentatonic scale in G major.
- Sing the pentatonic scale in G major, A♭ major and A major as notated in the examples.

Theory

The Theory section is designed to prepare students to understand and sing the interval of an octave and unison.

Have students:

- Read the definition of octave and unison.
- Find examples of octave intervals and unison notes in their choral scores.
- Sing an octave interval by having one section sing a low "G" and another section sing a high "G."
- Sing in unison by having one section sing the same low "G" and the other section match that low "G."

Progress Checkpoints

Observe students' progress in:

✓ Singing the pentatonic scale in various keys with good intonation.

✓ Singing octaves and unisons with good intonation.

*The sound of horse hooves; use temple blocks or coconut shells.
**Knock on a piece of wood, or use whatever sounds like a knock on a door.
***May be sung as a solo or by a small group.

Choral Library *Frog Went A-Courtin'* **143**

CAREERS IN MUSIC

Music as an Avocation

One school activity that helps develop students' stage presence is participation in musical theater. If your school periodically stages plays or musicals (or if there is a community theater that accepts volunteers), this might be an avocation of interest to some students. Explain that a role in the musical theatre or a play can be varied. It can be as simple as being a member of the background chorus or "crowd scene" to playing the lead role and learning numerous lines and solo numbers. Have students compare and contrast this avocations opportunity with other they might have already pursued.

2. Rehearse

Direct students to:

- Count verse 1 in measures 5–19 and then chant the text to the correct rhythm. Chant the text of verse 2, noticing where syllabification alters the rhythms.
- Learn the pitches in measures 5–19 and transfer to the text.
- Read the remaining verses, pointing out differences between verse 1 and each new verse. For example, verse 3 introduces spoken text; verse 4 features the melody with a harmony part; verses 5 and 6 are like verse 1; verses 7 and 8 begin in unison before dividing into parts.
- Locate unisons and octaves in the score.

*May be sung as a solo or by a small group (sung or spoken in a high voice).

144   Intermediate Tenor/Bass

CURRICULUM CONNECTIONS

Technology in Music

Have students:

1. Identify technology used in music (computer, midi, mp3, CD, audio/video recordings, synthesizer, sound equipment, electronic sounds, and so forth).
2. Discuss what effect technology has on music.
3. Create a musical composition using a form of technology.
4. Perform a solo or small ensemble for the class incorporating technology.

*Pat lap with both hands.

Progress Checkpoints

Observe students' progress in:
- ✓ Their ability to count simple rhythms correctly.
- ✓ Their ability to sing correct pitches in tune.
- ✓ Their ability to compare and contrast each verse for its specific content.
- ✓ Their ability to locate octaves and unisons in the score.

EXTENSION

Pantomime Presentations

Divide the choir into small groups. Ask each to actively portray the story told in "Frog Went A-Courtin'." To begin, list the active character(s) in each verse. Create a pantomime with the character(s) that depicts the action in that verse. Allow each group to present their pantomime of the story for the whole choir. Select the best features of all the pantomimes to create one to perform in concert when singing "Frog Went A-Courtin'."

3. Refine

Direct students to:

- Mark in their scores which part is singing the melody.
- Work to make the process of transferring the melody from the tenors to the basses and vice versa as seamless as possible, as if being sung by only one voice.
- Add the dynamic markings that provide further artistic shape after the rhythms, pitches and lyrics are secure.
- Incorporate the recommended percussion instruments.
- Perform from memory for a formal concert.

ENRICHMENT

Animal Sociology

The animals in "Frog Went A-Courtin'" are depicted as having a well-organized social structure. Ask the students to recall other examples from literature and movies they've encountered that portray animals living in a community. Contrast these fictionalized versions with documented scientific knowledge. For example, researchers have determined that elephants have an extremely complex and tightly woven family structure, and are known to mourn over the corpse of a deceased family member.

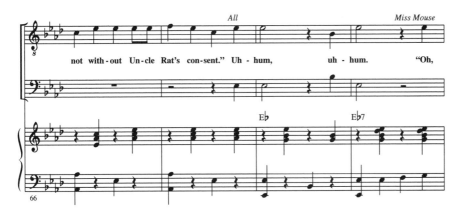

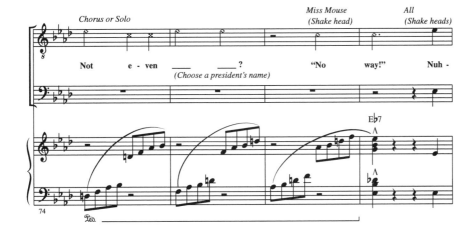

Progress Checkpoints

Observe students' progress in:

✓ Their ability to sing a line connected to another part.

✓ Their ability to produce audible differences in dynamic levels.

ASSESSMENT

Creating an Assessment Rubric

Have students:

1. Discuss the characteristics of a desirable performance of this piece, using all their knowledge of performance techniques.
2. Identify the criteria by which they think an adjudicator might assess the performance of this piece.
3. For each criterion, decide what characteristics will comprise an adequate, good, very good and excellent performance.
4. Design a rubric chart.
5. Apply the rubric to assess quartets or small ensembles performing all or part of this song.

ASSESSMENT

Informal Assessment

In this lesson, students showed the ability to:

- Sing music based on the pentatonic scale in three difference keys.

- Compare and contrast the settings of eight identical verses.

- Sing octaves and unisons with good intonation.

Have students evaluate their individual performances based on the following:

- Posture
- Expressive Singing
- Accurate Pitches
- Accurate Rhythms
- Correct Part-Singing

Have each student rate his/her performance of this song in the areas above on a scale of 1–5, 5 being the best.

*May be sung as a solo or by a small group.

MORE ABOUT...

Folk Music

Folk music is music that has been passed on from generation to generation, often in the oral tradition. Typically, folk song composers are unknown, and a song may change slightly when one person learns it then shares it with someone else. Folk songs exist in "tune families," which include all songs that originated from a specific tune. Any related song in a tune family can be shorter or longer than the original, or the rhythm, melody, scale or form can be altered. For this reason, students may, at one time or another, have heard the song "Frog Went A-Courtin'" but with slightly different rhythm patterns, melody or text.

Individual and Group Performance Evaluation

To further measure growth of musical skills presented in this lesson, direct students to complete the Evaluation section on page 141.

- After each student has written the notes for a pentatonic scale in three different keys, select several students to come forward and play their scales on the keyboard. The teacher may also collect them and evaluate. Did they succeed in this assignment?

MUSIC, SOCIETY AND CULTURE

Have students perform additional songs representing diverse cultures, including American and Texas heritage. Go to **music.glencoe.com**, the Web site for Glencoe's choral music programs, for additional music selections students can perform.

Additional National Standards

The following National Standards are addressed through the Assessment, Extension, Enrichment and bottom-page activities:

5. Reading and notating music. **(d)**

7. Evaluating music and music performances. **(b)**

8. Understanding relationships between music, the other arts, and disciplines outside the arts. **(a, b)**

- Have students divide into small groups and perform measures 104–118 for the rest of the class. The class should evaluate by asking, "Did this group sing unisons and octaves in tune and with clear diction?"
- Display the cartoon drawings created in the Artistic Expression activity. Have the class critique the artwork and choose the best characters for your next program cover.

Choral Library *Frog Went A-Courtin'* **151**

Guantanamera

OVERVIEW

Composer: Cuban Folk Song, arranged by John Higgins

Text: Based on the poem "Simple Verses" by José Martí (1835–1895), with English lyrics by John Higgins

Voicing: TB

Key: E♭ major

Meter: 4/4

Form: Verse/Refrain

Style: Cuban Folk Song

Accompaniment: Piano

Programming: Concert, Multicultural

Vocal Ranges:

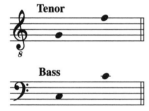

Objectives

After completing this lesson, students will be able to:

- Perform a varied repertoire of music representing styles from diverse cultures.
- Relate music to history and culture.
- Identify the relationships between the processes of other subjects and those of music.

Guantanamera

Composer: Cuban Folk Song, arranged by John Higgins

Text: Based on the poem "Simple Verses" by José Martí (1853–1895), with English lyrics by John Higgins

Voicing: TB

VOCABULARY

refrain

syllabic stress

SPOTLIGHT

To learn more about vowels, see page 65.

Focus

- Perform Spanish diction with clarity and proper syllabic stress.
- Perform music that represents the Cuban heritage.
- Relate music to history, culture and literature.

Getting Started

Did you know that some songs begin as poems before they are set to music? It is possible that your favorite song started out as a set of written words that did not have a specific melody connected to it. Often, composers will start with an existing poem or text and then set it to music. Such is the case with "Guantanamera."

◆ History and Culture

"Guantanamera" is based on a poem entitled "Simple Verses," written by Cuban writer José Martí. Martí was born in Cuba in 1853. While growing up, Martí had a strong desire that his country would gain its independence. His poetry was inspirational and promoted virtues such as equality among all men, compassion, integrity, love and freedom. Ralph Waldo Emerson and Walt Whitman, famous American poets, admired Martí's writings. After years of exile in New York City, Martí returned to his native Cuba in 1895 and was killed while taking part in the struggle for independence against the Spanish army.

The term *Guantanamera* refers to a girl from the city of Guantanamo, Cuba. The term *guajira* is a colloquial (slang) term for a country girl. Both of these terms are found in the **refrain** (*a repeated section at the end of a verse in a song*). These terms could actually refer to a girl or to the city of Guantanamo itself.

RESOURCES

Intermediate Sight-Singing

Sight-Singing in E♭ Major, pages 141–143

Reading Rhythms in 4/4 Meter, pages 2–6

Teacher Resource Binder

Teaching Master 18, *Pronunciation Guide for "Guantanamera"*

Teaching Master 19, *Text Emphasis in "Guantanamera"*

Teaching Master 20, *José Martí: Cuban Poet*

Evaluation Master 7, *Evaluating Musical Expression*

For additional resources, see TRB Table of Contents.

Links to Learning

◆ Vocal

Perform the following example to practice singing with tall uniform vowels and tuning the harmonies found in "Guantanamera."

◆ Theory

Perform the following example by clapping the eighth note pulse at a slow tempo and chanting the rhythmic pattern on the neutral syllable "da."

◆ Artistic Expression

Speak the Spanish text of the piece using proper **syllabic stress,** or *the stressing of one syllable over another.* Stress the syllables that are underlined.

guan-ta-na-me-ra! gua-ji-ra guan-ta-na-me-ra

Yo soy un hom-bre sin-ce-ro de don-de cre-ce la pal-ma

Y an-tes de mor-rir-me quie-ro, e-char mis ver-sos del al-ma

Evaluation

Demonstrate how well you have learned the skills and concepts featured in the lesson "Guantanamera" by completing the following:

- With a partner, take turns chanting the text of "Guantanamera" in Spanish. Evaluate how well you were able to use correct syllabic stress.
- Sing the refrain in Spanish, accurately performing all pitches and rhythms. How well did you do?
- Using the Internet or the library, learn more about José Martí. Write a short introduction about him to be read at a performance of "Guantanamera." What did you learn? How might your introduction enhance the performance of this song?

Choral Library Guantanamera **153**

RESOURCES

Intermediate Tenor/Bass Rehearsal/Performance CD

CD 2:7 Voices

CD 2:8 Accompaniment Only

CD 3:20 Vocal Practice Track—Tenor

CD 4:15 Vocal Practice Track—Bass

National Standards

1. Singing, alone and with others, a varied repertoire of music. **(a, b, c, d)**
8. Understanding the relationships between music, the other arts, and disciplines outside the arts. **(b)**
9. Understanding music in relation to history and culture. **(a)**

LINKS TO LEARNING

Vocal

The Vocal section is designed to prepare students to:

- Sing with tall uniform vowels.
- Tune the harmonies found in "Guantanamera."

Have students:

- Listen and watch as you demonstrate proper mouth shape for tall vowels and sing each one.
- Sing the example focusing on tall vowels and making them uniform with their neighbor.

Theory

The Theory section is designed to prepare students to sing the rhythms found in "Guantanamera."

Have students:

- Tap or clap the eighth note pulse indicated by stems down in the example.
- Speak the rhythms indicated by stems up on a neutral syllable, while continuing to clap the eighth note pulse.
- Locate these rhythms in their choral score.

Artistic Expression

The Artistic Expression section is designed to prepare students to articulate the Spanish diction with proper syllabic stress.

Have students:

- Learn the Spanish pronunciation by echoing the teacher or a Spanish-speaking student. A pronunciation can be found in the Teacher Resource Binder, Teaching Master 18.
- Speak the Spanish text with proper syllabic stress as indicated by the underscored syllables.

LESSON PLAN

Suggested Teaching Sequence and Performance Tips

1. Introduce

Direct students to:

- Read and discuss the information found in the Getting Started section on page 152.
- Practice singing the harmonic progressions as shown in the Vocal section on page 153.
- Practice performing the rhythm patterns found in the piece as shown in the Theory section on page 153.
- Practice pronouncing the Spanish text with appropriate syllabic stress as found in the Artistic Expression section on page 153.
- Sight-sing the pitches in measures 5–12 on solfège syllables or a neutral syllable. When pitches are secure, add text.

Progress Checkpoints

Observe students' progress in:

- ✓ Their ability to sing all rhythms with accuracy.
- ✓ Their ability to sing the Spanish diction with proper pronunciation and syllabic stress.

Guantanamera

For TB and Piano

Cuban Folk Song
Arranged by JOHN HIGGINS

English lyrics by JOHN HIGGINS
Piano Arrangement by DEAN CROCKER

TEACHER 2 TEACHER

"Guantanamera" is a Cuban folk song that is based upon a poem entitled "Simple Verses" by Cuban writer José Martí. In addition to developing two-part singing in the male chorus, this song can be used as a tool to teach students about various aspects of Cuban history and culture, including language (diction), prominent writers from the country, as well as its political history.

ENRICHMENT

Cuban History and Writer José Martí

Research the life of writer José Martí (1853–1895). Learn about his background and career. Examine some of his poetry to find out his ideas. Also, explore what was going on in Cuba during his lifetime and discuss the possible connections between the political climate of the country and his writings. Discuss how both poetry and music can be used to express ideas.

2. Rehearse

Direct students to:

- Review the Refrain (measures 5–12). Check again to make sure that pitches, rhythms and diction are accurate.

- Clap the rhythm of the bass part in measures 14–26. Be sure to maintain a steady quarter note pulse by tapping the feet.

- Clap the rhythm of the tenor part in measures 14–26. Again, keep a steady quarter note pulse. Separate the parts and have each section clap its own line.

- Rehearse the Spanish diction as a class for the section beginning at measure 14. A pronunciation guide can be found in the Teacher Resource Binder, Teaching Master 18. When the text is secure, chant the text in rhythm as outlined in measures 14–26.

- Sight-sing the pitches of both parts beginning at measure 14, using a neutral syllable and the piano for support. If necessary, separate the parts by having one section sing as the other section claps its rhythmic patterns. When pitches are secure, add text and perform.

- Sight-sing the contents of measure 29. Notice that it is identical to measure 5.

Progress Checkpoints

Observe students' progress in:

✓ Their ability to sing all rhythms and pitches correctly.

✓ Their ability to articulate the Spanish diction with proper pronunciation and syllabic stress.

3. Refine

Direct students to:

- Return to the beginning of the piece. Discuss the English lyrics of the piece and decide what kind of mood is presented. Sing the piece again with a tone and style that is appropriate for the lyrics.
- Continue refining the piece by rehearsing the diction (chanting) and singing the piece at a consistently faster tempo until the suggested metronome marking is achieved.

Progress Checkpoints

Observe students' progress in:

✓ Their performance of the score in a way that is appropriate for the style and mood.

✓ Their performance of the piece at the desired tempo while maintaining accuracy of pitches and diction.

ASSESSMENT

Informal Assessment

In this lesson, students showed the ability to:

- Sing Spanish diction with proper articulation and syllabic stress.
- Understand and sing a folk song of Cuban heritage.
- Relate a Cuban folk song to Cuban history and culture.

TEACHING STRATEGY

Constructing a Rubric for Assessment

Have students:

- Choose three criteria for the rubric to be used for "Guantanamera."
- Discuss performance characteristics that would constitute an adequate, good and excellent performance.
- Make a grid with the criteria across the top, and the categories of achievement (adequate, good and excellent) down the right column.
- Fill in the characteristics appropriate to each box.
- Listen to a performance of the piece and use the rubric to assess the quality of performance.

Student Self-Assessment

Have students evaluate their individual performances based on the following:

- Posture
- Spanish Language
- Tall Vowels
- Expressive Singing
- Accurate Rhythms

Have each student rate his/her performance of this song in the areas above on a scale of 1–5, 5 being the best.

Individual and Group Performance Evaluation

To further measure growth of musical skills presented in this lesson, direct students to complete the Evaluation section on page 153.

- Divide into pairs, each student chanting the Spanish text to "Guantanamera" for his partner. The partner should evaluate the use of correct syllable stress and offer suggestions for improvement.

- Have each student, or if time does not allow, selected students or volunteers to come forward and perform the refrain in Spanish for the rest of the class. The class should evaluate the accuracy of pitches and rhythms and offer suggestions for improvement.

- After students have researched and written about José Martí, open a class discussion about what the students have learned. Choose the best paragraph and use as an introduction to this piece at your next concert.

Additional National Standards

The following National Standards are addressed through the Assessment, Extension, Enrichment and bottom-page activities:

6. Listening to, analyzing, and describing music. **(a, b, c)**

7. Evaluating music and music performances. **(a, b)**

Joshua! (Fit The Battle Of Jericho)

OVERVIEW

Composer: Traditional Spiritual, adapted and arranged by Kirby Shaw

Text: Traditional

Voicing: TTB

Key: F minor

Meter: 4/4

Form: ABAC

Style: Spiritual

Accompaniment: Piano

Programming: Concert, Festival, Multicultural

Vocal Ranges:

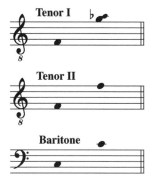

Objectives

After completing this lesson, students will be able to:

• Use standard terminology to describe music notation and the techniques used in creating an arrangement.

• Perform a varied repertoire of music representing styles from diverse cultures, including the African American spiritual.

Have students review vocabulary in student lesson. Introduce terms found in the music. A complete glossary of terms is found on page 226 of the student book.

158

Joshua!
(Fit The Battle Of Jericho)

Composer: Traditional Spiritual, adapted and arranged by Kirby Shaw

Text: Traditional

Voicing: TTB

VOCABULARY

arrangement

imitation

descant

syncopation

improvisation

◯ SPOTLIGHT

To learn more about improvisation, see page 181.

Focus

• Describe techniques used in creating an arrangement.

• Perform music representing the African American spiritual.

Getting Started

Think of a short simple song from childhood that you know very well. Sing through the song in your head. Once you have done this, add a driving rock beat to the piece and sing the new arrangement in your head. Now add a bass guitar, a lead guitar and a synthesizer to your piece. What does the piece sound like now? If you are amazed by the way you have arranged the piece that is now in your head, wait until you sing Kirby Shaw's arrangement of "Joshua! (Fit The Battle Of Jericho)."

◆ History and Culture

"Joshua! (Fit The Battle Of Jericho)" is a traditional African American spiritual. Taken from Old Testament scripture, the text tells the story of Joshua, an experienced military leader who conquered the city of Jericho. The ancient city of Jericho is considered the oldest known inhabited city in the world.

An **arrangement** is *a song in which a composer takes an existing song and adds extra features.* In this arrangement of "Joshua!," Kirby Shaw has added syncopated rock rhythms, as well as using **imitation** *(the act of one part copying what another part has already sung).* He has also added a **descant** *(a special part that is usually sung higher than the other parts)* and occasional jazz-style harmonies.

RESOURCES

Intermediate Sight-Singing

Sight-Singing in F Minor, pages 178–179

Reading Rhythms in 4/4 meter, pages 2–6

Reading Syncopation, pages 126–129

Teacher Resource Binder

Teaching Master 21, *All About Arranging "Joshua! (Fit the Battle of Jericho)"*

Evaluation Master 6, *Diction Checkup*

Skill Builder 24, *Rhythm Challenge Using Syncopation*

Interdisciplinary 21–22, *Language Arts*

For additional resources, see TRB Table of Contents.

Links to Learning

◆ Vocal

Read and perform the following example to become familiar with the harmonies and rhythms found in "Joshua! (Fit The Battle Of Jericho)."

Doo doot doo,___ doo doot doo,___ doo doot doo.___

◆ Theory

Some of the syncopated rhythms in this piece are quite interesting. **Syncopation** is *the placement of accents on a weak beat or a weak portion of the beat.* Clap, chant and step the following rhythmic patterns. Repeat as desired.

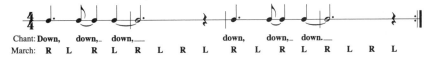

Chant: **Down, down,_ down,___ down,_ down,_ down.___**
March: **R L R L R L R L R L R L R L**

◆ Artistic Expression

Improvisation is *the art of singing or playing music, making it up as you go.* It is often used in the performance of spirituals. After you know the song well, try singing an improvisational descant in measures 59–67.

Evaluation

Demonstrate how well you have learned the skills and concepts featured in the lesson "Joshua! (Fit The Battle Of Jericho)" by completing the following:

- Define and locate in the music examples of descant, imitation and syncopation. Describe how they were used to create this arrangement.

- Perform an improvised descant in measures 59–67 in the style of the piece. Critique your improvisation based on your ability to keep in the style of the piece and how well your improvisation complemented the other parts.

Choral Library *Joshua! (Fit The Battle Of Jericho)* **159**

RESOURCES

Intermediate Tenor/Bass Rehearsal/Performance CD

CD 2:9 Voices
CD 2:10 Accompaniment Only
CD 3:21 Vocal Practice Track—Tenor I
CD 3:22 Vocal Practice Track—Tenor II
CD 4:16 Vocal Practice Track—Bass

National Standards

1. Singing, alone and with others, a varied repertoire of music. **(a, b, c, d)**
9. Understanding music in relation to history and culture. **(a)**

LINKS TO LEARNING

Vocal

The Vocal section is designed to prepare students to become familiar with the harmonies and rhythms found in the music.

Have students:

- Divide into three sections according to voice part.
- Sing the Vocal example focusing on rhythmic syncopations and tuning the three-part chords.

Theory

The Theory section is designed to prepare students to:

- Understand syncopation.
- Perform the syncopated rhythmic patterns found in the music.

Have students:

- March the pulse of the quarter note beat.
- Clap, then chant the rhythm pattern indicated.

Artistic Expression

The Artistic Expression section is designed to prepare students to:

- Understand improvisation.
- Improvise a descant in measures 59–67.

Have students:

- Read the definition of improvisation and discuss common performers that use this technique.
- Sing measures 59–67 as a group, then offer the chance to improvise a descant over these measure to the students.

LESSON PLAN

Suggested Teaching Sequence and Performance Tips

1. Introduce

Direct students to:

- Read and discuss the information found in the Getting Started section on student page 158.
- Practice singing the three-part harmony progressions as shown in the Vocal section on page 159.
- Locate in the score each instance of the harmonic progression. *(measures 11–13, measures 44–46)*
- Practice performing the syncopated rhythm patterns as shown in the Theory section on page 159.
- Locate in the score each instance of the rhythm pattern shown in the Theory section. *(measures 18–21, 22–25, 51–54, 55–58)*

Joshua!
(Fit The Battle Of Jericho)
For TTB and Piano

Adapted and Arranged by
KIRBY SHAW

Traditional Spiritual

160   Intermediate Tenor/Bass

TEACHER *2* TEACHER

Kirby Shaw's arrangement of "Joshua! (Fit the Battle of Jericho)" presents an exciting and fast-paced sequence of rhythms and phrases. Accuracy of rhythms, pitches and diction becomes extremely important when singing at a fast tempo. Students should be encouraged to sing with a full and focused tone that is unforced while at the same time maintaining a high level of energy and vocal agility.

- Chant the rhythms in measures 26–34. March on beats 1 and 3, and maintain a steady tempo. In this section, the arranger employs the technique of call and response.

Progress Checkpoints

Observe students' progress in:

✓ Their ability to sing harmonic progressions in three-part harmony.

✓ Their ability to read syncopated patterns.

✓ Their ability to locate chord progressions and syncopated patterns in the score.

✓ Their ability to identify the compositional technique of call and response in the score.

TEACHING STRATEGY

Performing from Memory

Have students:

1. Memorize this piece by learning shorter phrases at a time.

2. Perform it from memory on a program or in competition.

3. Further develop memorization skills by memorizing other songs and solos to perform for the class informally or at formal concerts.

2. Rehearse

Direct students to:

- Label measures 1–9 as the "Introduction." Chant the rhythms in measures 3–8 with text. Add pitches and rehearse.

- Beginning at rehearsal letter A, carefully clap the rhythms through measure 25. Notice that measures 14–15 are similar to measures 11–12 except that there is a syncopation that occurs on the last beat in measure 13. If necessary, separate Tenor and Bass parts and perform individual parts.

- Sight-sing their parts individually on solfège syllables or on a neutral syllable until parts are secure. Then add the text.

- Sing the three parts together, first on a neutral syllable to check for intonation, then with the text to check for clarity of diction.

- Clap through the B section (measures 26–42). Once the rhythms are secure, add the text. Rehearse Tenor and Bass parts separately to secure pitches, and then add text. Put the parts together at a slow tempo and rehearse until a moderately fast tempo is obtained.

162 Intermediate Tenor/Bass

CURRICULUM CONNECTIONS

Technology in Music

Have students:

1. Identify technology used in music (computer, midi, mp3, CD, audio/video recordings, synthesizer, sound equipment, electronic sounds, and so forth).

2. Discuss what effect technology has on music.

3. Create a musical composition using a form of technology.

4. Perform a solo or small ensemble for the class incorporating technology.

- Beginning at the pickup measure to rehearsal letter D, clap and chant the rhythms found in measures 58–71 (without the descant). Isolate the pickup rhythms to measures 68–69 to make sure that each section knows how to enter the texture.
- Rehearse parts individually until pitches are secure. Then add the text.
- Sing all three parts together in measures 58–71.
- Sight-sing measures 72–76 (pitches, rhythms and text together). Compare this section to the vocal introduction (measures 3–7).
- Learn the descant in measures 59–67 (first Tenors only). Then select a soloist or small group to sing the descant while the rest of the choir sings their parts.

Progress Checkpoints

Observe students' progress in:
- ✓ Their ability to sing with tonal and rhythmic accuracy.
- ✓ Their ability to sing with good diction.
- ✓ Their ability to sing with a solid, focused tone.

Choral Library Joshua! (Fit The Battle Of Jericho) **163**

ENRICHMENT

Narrative Style of Call and Response

The call-and-response style takes on a narrative form if a story from a third person's point-of-view is being told. Often, these stories were scriptural in nature. Locate recordings of other Old Testament-based spirituals and describe if call and response is used to "tell the story." For example, "Go Down, Moses," "Elijah Rock," "Little David, Play on Your Harp," "Daniel, Daniel," "Servant of the Lord," "Witness," "Didn't My Lord Deliver Daniel?"

3. Refine

Direct students to:

- Go back through the piece and circle all the dynamic markings. Chant through the entire piece without pitches, observing all the dynamic markings in the score.

- Reinforce all rhythms.

- Ask any questions about problems with pitches or rhythms.

- Sing the piece from the beginning.

MORE ABOUT...

Spirituals

"Joshua Fit The Battle" is an African American spiritual taken from the Old Testament. References to Old Testament scriptures were common during slavery as one of the purposes of the spiritual was to serve as a form of religious education. Sometimes the biblical references and images were sung as a way of communicating secret messages. For example, in the spiritual "Go Down Moses," the phrase "Tell old Pharaoh 'let my people go'" likened the slave owner to Pharaoh who kept the enslaved Israelites captive in Egypt. The "people" in this instance refers to the African American slaves.

Observe students' progress in:

✓ Singing all rhythms, especially syncopations, with confidence and precision.

✓ Observing and performing all dynamic markings in the score.

TEACHING STRATEGY

Musical Elements of Style

The combination of musical elements determines the style of a piece.

Have students:

1. Compile a list of musical elements that might affect style.

2. Share the lists to compile one master list.

3. Sing known songs, trying out different styles, and then try to describe the musical elements that are characteristic of that style. (For example, try salsa, opera, Broadway, rock, military, lullaby, and so forth.)

4. Select appropriate literature for a particular style.

ASSESSMENT

Informal Assessment

In this lesson, students showed the ability to:

- Sing with diction that is crisp and clear.
- Sing with a choral tone that is supported and focused.
- Sing accurate syncopated rhythms in 4/4 meter.
- Sing accurate pitches in the key of E♭ major.

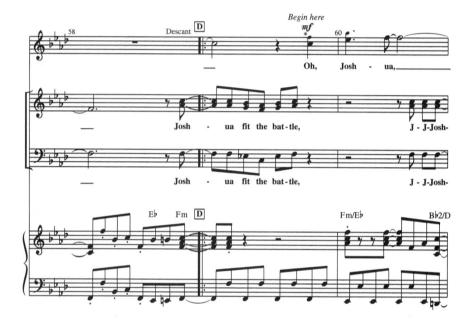

*Cued notes - sing upper or lower notes, not both.

ASSESSMENT
Creating an Assessment Rubric

Have students:

1. Discuss the characteristics of a quality performance of this piece, using all their knowledge of performance techniques.
2. Identify the criteria by which they think an adjudicator might assess the quality of the performance of this piece.
3. For each criterion, decide what characteristics will comprise an adequate, good, very good and excellent quality of the performance.
4. Create a rubric chart.
5. Use the rubric to assess the performance of this song.

Student Self-Assessment

Have students evaluate their individual performances based on the following:

- Posture
- Diction
- Accurate Pitches
- Accurate Rhythms
- Correct Part-Singing

Have each student rate his/her performance of this song in the areas above on a scale of 1–5, 5 being the best.

Individual and Group Performance Evaluation

To further measure growth of musical skills presented in this lesson, direct students to complete the Evaluation section on page 159.

- After each student has located examples of descant, imitation and syncopation in this arrangement, ask for a volunteer to share their findings. Have students describe how these techniques were used in this arrangement. Evaluate their answer.

- Ask for student volunteers to perform an improvised descant in measures 59–67 for the rest of the choir. The choir should evaluate the performances. Was the improvised descant in the style of the piece and did it complement the other parts?

TEACHING STRATEGY

Improvisation

If students are unfamiliar or uncomfortable improvising, have them:

- Echo the teacher in the rhythm or tone set they will be using.
- Echo patterns lead by the teacher, beginning with just quarter notes on the tonal center *do.*
- Continue echoing patterns, as the teacher adds only one rhythmic or melodic element at a time. Rhythmically, use only quarter notes, and eighth notes, and then add one more element at a time. Melodically, move from just the tonic to the tonic triad, *do-mi-do.* Gradually add *la, do',* and *re.* Each new element is a choice, not a requirement.

ENRICHMENT

Concert Etiquette

Have students:

1. Identify appropriate concert etiquette in a variety of settings (formal concerts, informal concerts, large concert halls, small concert halls, and so forth).

2. Attend a variety of live performances.

3. Discuss the appropriate and inappropriate concert behaviors observed.

4. Write a short analysis of appropriate concert etiquette for each setting.

Improvisation

Encourage students to improvise musical melodies while performing. Select an eight-bar phrase from "Joshua." Ask volunteers to improvise a melodic descant above the melody as the choir sings the written notation. Have students take turns improvising.

MUSIC, SOCIETY AND CULTURE

Have students perform additional songs representing diverse cultures, including American and Texas heritage. Go to **music.glencoe.com**, the Web site for Glencoe's choral music programs, for additional music selections students can perform.

168   Intermediate Tenor/Bass

Additional National Standards

The following National Standards are addressed through the Assessment, Extension, Enrichment and bottom-page activities:

4. Improvising melodies, variations and accompaniments. **(c)**

6. Listening to, analyzing, and describing music. **(b, c)**

7. Evaluating music and music performances. **(b)**

SPOTLIGHT

Breath Management

Vocal sound is produced by air flowing between the vocal cords; therefore, correct breathing is important for good singing. Good breath management provides you with the support needed to sing expressively and for longer periods of time.

To experience, explore and establish proper breathing for singing:

- Put your hands on your waist at the bottom of your rib cage.

- Take in an easy breath for four counts, as if through a straw, without lifting your chest or shoulders.

- Feel your waist and rib cage expand all the way around like an inflating inner tube.

- Let your breath out slowly on "sss," feeling your "inner tube" deflating as if it has a slow leak.

- Remember to keep your chest up the entire time.

- Take in another easy breath for four counts before your "inner tube" has completely deflated, then let your air out on "sss" for eight counts.

- Repeat this step several times, taking in an easy breath for four counts and gradually increasing the number of counts to let your air out to sixteen counts.

Sometimes in singing it is necessary to take a quick or "catch" breath.

- Look out the window and imagine seeing something wonderful for the first time, like snow.

- Point your finger at the imaginary something and let in a quick, silent breath that expresses your wonderment and surprise.

- A quick breath is not a gasping breath, but rather a silent breath.

Spotlight *Breath Management* **169**

RESOURCES

Teacher Resource Binder

Vocal Development 13, *Posture & Breathing*

National Standards

1. Singing, alone and with others. **(b)**

BREATH MANAGEMENT

Objectives

- Sing accurately with good breath control.

Suggested Teaching Sequence

Direct students to:

- Read the Spotlight On Breath Management on student page 169 and identify the importance of breath management when singing.
- Perform the exercise described on page 169.
- Practice a "catch" breath as described at the bottom of page 169.
- Compare the concept of proper breath management to effective performance practices.

Progress Checkpoints

Observe students' progress in:

✓ Their ability to perform the breathing exercises described on page 169.

✓ Their ability to discuss the importance of proper breath management when singing.

Leave Her, Johnny

OVERVIEW

Composer: Traditional Sea Chantey, arranged by Emily Crocker

Text: Traditional

Voicing: TB/TTB

Key: F Major

Meter: 4/4

Form: Strophic with Coda

Style: Traditional Sea Chantey

Accompaniment: none

Programming: Contest, Appropriate for large and small ensembles

Vocal Ranges:

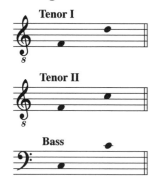

Objectives

After completing this lesson, students will be able to:

- Perform expressively demonstrating fundamental skills, such as staggered breathing.
- Use standard terminology to describe in detail intervals.
- Identify the relationships between the concepts and content of other subjects and those of music.

VOCABULARY

Have students review vocabulary in student lesson. Introduce terms found in the music. A complete glossary of terms is found on page 226 of the student book.

Leave Her, Johnny

Composer: Traditional Sea Chantey, arranged by Emily Crocker

Text: Traditional

Voicing: TB/TTB

VOCABULARY

sea chantey

staggered breathing

dissonance

Focus

- Sing phrases expressively using staggered breathing.
- Identify and describe the music terminology for dissonance.
- Relate music to writing (poetry and short stories).

Getting Started

"Leave Her, Johnny" is another example of a **sea chantey,** or *a song sung by sailors, usually in rhythm with their work.* Although it appears from the title that this is a song about a sailor who must leave his girlfriend, quite the opposite is true. The story is about a sailor leaving his ship ("her") to get married ("tomorrow is your wedding day") to his girlfriend back home.

◆ History and Culture

When researching most sea chanteys, you can find many versions of the same song. This is also true for "Leave Her, Johnny." This song was traditionally sung as the sailors came to port. One can only imagine how anxious the sailors were to leave the ship after many months at sea. The sailors would make up verses to "Leave Her, Johnny" to complain about unpleasant conditions aboard the ship. Perhaps the food had been terrible or the work especially hard. Singing has always been a good way to feel better about your problems.

After you are familiar with this song, try composing a new verse about a good reason to be back in port. As is customary in chanteys, do not change the words in the second or fourth line. "Leave her, Johnny, leave her" and "It's time for us to leave her" should be sung in every verse.

SPOTLIGHT

To learn more about vocal production, see page 215.

RESOURCES

Intermediate Sight-Singing

Sight-Singing in F Major, pages 39–41, 76–77, 112–116

Reading Rhythms in 4/4 Meter, pages 2–6

Reading Quarter Notes and Half Notes, pages 1–9

Reading Eighth Notes, pages 26–27

Teacher Resource Binder

Teaching Master 22, *Letter from the Sea*

Evaluation Master 18, *Sight-Singing Rubric*

Skill Builder 27, *Rhythm Challenge in 4/4 Meter*

Kodály 5, *Music Reading: Pitch*

Interdisciplinary 21–22, *Language Arts*

For additional resources, see TRB Table of Contents.

Links to Learning

◆ **Vocal**

To perform "Leave Her, Johnny" with a continuous, flowing melodic line, it is necessary to use **staggered breathing** (*the practice of planning breaths so that no two singers take a breath at the same time*). This song should be sung in four-bar phrases without a noticeable break in between. With a partner who sings your voice part, plan the breaths so that each four-bar phrase sounds continuous.

◆ **Theory**

Dissonance is *a combination of pitches that clash.* Read and perform the following examples to train your ears to hear and recognize dissonance.

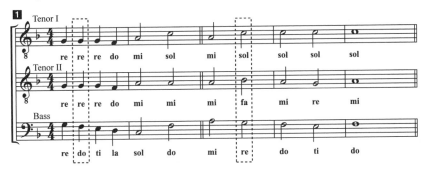

◆ **Artistic Expression**

The storyteller sings, "The trip was hard and the wind was strong." What events made the trip hard? Imagine you are that sailor long ago. Write a story to your family back home about your adventures on the open seas.

Evaluation

Demonstrate how well you have learned the skills and concepts featured in the lesson "Leave Her, Johnny" by completing the following:

- With a partner, perform "Leave Her, Johnny" and plan the staggered breathing. Evaluate how well you were able to create a continuous, flowing line.

- Listen to a recording of "Leave Her, Johnny." Identify the places where dissonance occurs by raising your hand each time you hear it. How well did you do?

Choral Library *Leave Her, Johnny* **171**

RESOURCES

Intermediate Tenor/Bass Rehearsal/Performance CD

CD 2:11 Voices

CD 2:12 Accompaniment Only

CD 3:23 Vocal Practice Track—Tenor I

CD 3:24 Vocal Practice Track—Tenor II

CD 4:17 Vocal Practice Track—Bass

National Standards

1. Singing, alone and with others, a varied repertoire of music **(a, b, c, d)**

6. Listening to, analyzing, and describing music **(a, b, c)**

8. Understanding relationships between music, the other arts, and disciplines outside the arts. **(b)**

LINKS TO LEARNING

Vocal

The Vocal section is designed to prepare students to:

- Understand staggered breathing.
- Plan their breaths for "Leave Her, Johnny."

Have students:

- Read the definition of staggered breathing.
- Read through "Leave Her, Johnny" and plan their breaths with a neighbor that also sings their part, so that no voices breathe at the same time.

Theory

The Theory section is designed to prepare students to understand and perform dissonances.

Have students:

- Read the definition of *dissonance*.
- Divide into three parts according to their voice part and sing the example, emphasizing the dissonance chords.

Artistic Expression

The Artistic Expression section is designed to prepare students to relate to life on the open sea.

Have students:

- Read the text of "Leave Her, Johnny."
- Explain what they think made the trip hard.
- Pretend they are the sailor and write a story to their family back home about their adventures on the open seas.

LESSON PLAN

Suggested Teaching Sequence and Performance Tips

Direct students to:

- Read and discuss the information found in the Getting Started section on student page 170. Then practice the exercises in the Vocal, Theory and Artistic Expression sections on page 171.

- Sight-sing measures 1–8 in each voice part separately. When secure, move to measures 9–20 and learn the remaining pitches.

- Echo the teacher as he/she speaks the text with the desired vowel sound. When speaking the text rhythmically, practice breathing in the marked places.

- Discuss the text and how this song could fit into the life of a sailor. Does the sailor appear to be happy to leave the ship? Do you think the sailor has mixed emotions regarding his situation? Use the ideas to help you sing the text expressively.

Progress Checkpoints

Observe students' progress in:

✓ Their ability to differentiate between a dissonant chord and a chord of resolution.

✓ Reading rhythmic patterns in 4/4 meter with accuracy.

✓ Marking the score with their breath marks and breathing rhythmically.

✓ Singing vowel sounds uniformly as a section and as a choir.

✓ Singing phrases musically with expressive text.

Leave Her, Johnny

For TB or TTB, a cappella

Arranged by
EMILY CROCKER

Traditional Sea Chantey

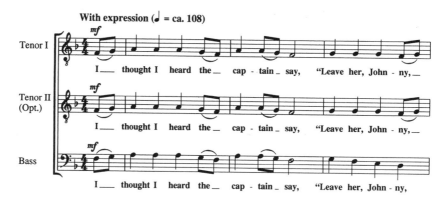

172   Intermediate Tenor/Bass

TEACHER 2 TEACHER

We usually think of sea chanteys as a rollicking work song sung by sailors. This expressive sea chantey, "Leave Her, Johnny," gives us an introspective look at the sailor's love for the sea and how it is often hard to leave the ship even for your own wedding! With easy-to-learn voice parts in two or optional three parts, your students will love putting their own expressive elements into this wonderful setting.

Additional National Standards

The following National Standards are addressed through the Assessment, Extension, Enrichment and bottom-page activities:

6. Listening to, analyzing, and describing music. **(a, c)**

7. Evaluating music and music performances. **(b)**

ASSESSMENT

Informal Assessment

In this lesson, students showed the ability to:

- Sing accurately in three parts with good intonation.
- Recognize chords in the form of dissonance followed by resolution.
- Sing expressively.

Student Self-Assessment

Have students evaluate their individual performances based on the following:

- Breath Management
- Phrasing
- Tall Vowels
- Expressive Singing
- Correct Part-Singing

Have each student rate his/her performance of this song in the areas above on a scale of 1–5, 5 being the best.

Individual and Group Performance Evaluation

To further measure growth of musical skills presented in this lesson, direct students to complete the Evaluation section on page 171.

- After each student has marked their staggered breathing plan, have voice part perform a section for the rest of the class. Did that section create a continuous, flowing line by using staggered breathing?
- While listening to a recording of "Leave Her, Johnny," have students raise their hand each time they hear dissonance. Watch and evaluate. Are the students raising their hands in the correct places?

New River Train

OVERVIEW

Composer: American Spiritual, arranged by Donald Moore

Text: Traditional, with additional words by Donald Moore

Voicing: TB

Key: F major, G♭ major, G major

Meter: 2/2

Form: Verse-Refrain

Style: Spiritual

Accompaniment: Piano

Programming: Concert, Festival

Vocal Ranges:

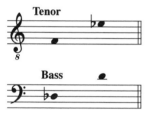

Objectives

After completing this lesson, students will be able to:

• Use standard terminology to describe in detail music notation for rhythm.

• Sight-read music in various keys.

• Relate music to history.

Have students review vocabulary in student lesson. Introduce terms found in the music. A complete glossary of terms is found on page 226 of the student book.

New River Train

Composer: American Spiritual, arranged by Donald Moore
Text: Traditional, with additional words by Donald Moore
Voicing: TB

VOCABULARY
syncopation
scale
major scale

Focus

• Identify standard music symbols for rhythm.

• Sight-sing music.

• Relate music to history.

🎲 SKILL BUILDERS

To learn more about the key of F major, see Intermediate Sight-Singing, *page 39.*

Getting Started

"New River Train" is a fun song to learn and perform because it is very rhythmic. This song repeatedly features syncopated rhythms. **Syncopation** is *the placement of accents on a weak beat or a weak portion of the beat.* The syncopated pattern first appears in measure 5 on the words "ridin' that." Notice that the strong syllable in the word "ridin'" falls off the beat. Again in measure 15, a rest falls on beat 1. This beat of silence brings attention to the syncopated word "brought." When performing "New River Train," accent the syncopated syllables to draw attention to the syncopated rhythm.

◆ History and Culture

The lyrics of many spirituals refer to going home. The mode of transportation in "New River Train" is no longer a horse-drawn chariot, but a steam-engine train! A British inventor named Stephen Trevithick is credited with building the first operational steam locomotive at the beginning of the nineteenth century. The earliest trains were created to haul coal out of mines, but in 1825, the first public passenger railway opened in England. About the same time, trains started to be built in America. By 1835, over a thousand miles of track had been laid, mostly on the East Coast. Trains played a very important role in the westward expansion of the United States throughout the 1880s, capturing the imagination of a nation. So it's natural that trains entered into song lyrics.

RESOURCES

Intermediate Sight-Singing

Sight-Singing in F Major, pages 39–41, 76–77, 112–116

Sight-Singing in G♭ Major, pages 184–185

Sight-Singing in G Major, pages 82–85, 89–90

Reading Rhythms in 2/2 Meter, page 140

Teacher Resource Binder

Evaluation Master 18, *Sight-Singing Rubric*

Skill Builder 1, *Building Harmony*

Skill Builder 12, *Constructing Major Scales*

Skill Builder 24, *Rhythm Challenge Using Syncopation*

Kodály 6, Music Reading: *Rhythm*

For additional resources, see TRB Table of Contents.

Links to Learning

◆ Vocal

This song is in the key of F major and is based on the F major scale. A **scale** is *a group of notes that are sung in succession and are based on a particular keynote, or home tone.* A **major scale** is *a scale that has* do *as its keynote, or home tone.* To locate "F" on a piano, find any set of three black keys. "F" is the white key to the left of the bottom black key. This scale uses the notes F, G, A, B♭, C, D, E, F. Using the keyboard below as a guide, play the F major scale.

Sing the F major scale in the octave that best fits your voice.

◆ Theory

Learning to sight-sing aids in learning new music faster. Follow this procedure to learn to sight-sing. Look at measures 68–95. First use counting syllables to chant the rhythms. When the rhythms are correct, chant these as solfège syllables. Sight-sing the pitches. Even if you make a mistake, keep going! Identify sections that are repeated. Sing your part on solfège syllables or a neutral syllable, and then add the lyrics. Repeat this process as you learn new music.

Evaluation

Demonstrate how well you have learned the skills and concepts featured in the lesson "New River Train" by completing the following:

• Locate in the music examples of syncopation in your part. Remember that notes or rests can be used to place accented syllables on the weak portion of a beat. Share your examples with a classmate and, together, decide how well you were able to identify syncopation in the music.

• Individually sing measures 27–59 to demonstrate your ability to sight-sing music using correct rhythms and pitches. Based on this criteria, rate your performance on a scale of 1 to 5, with 5 being the best.

Choral Library *New River Train* **175**

LINKS TO LEARNING

Vocal

The Vocal section is designed to prepare students to:

• Understand scale and major scale.

• Play and sing the F major scale.

Have students:

• Play the F major scale on the keyboard. If selected students will play the scale on the keyboard, others should follow closely on the keyboard printed on page 175.

• Sing the F major scale on note names.

• Sing the F major scale on solfège syllables.

Theory

The Theory section is designed to prepare students to increase their sight-singing skills.

Have students:

• Look at measures 68–95 and use counting syllables to chant the rhythms.

• Chant the solfège syllables once the rhythms are correct.

• Sight-sing on the solfège syllables until comfortable.

• Sing on the text.

RESOURCES

Intermediate Tenor/Bass Rehearsal/Performance CD

CD 2:13 Voices

CD 2:14 Accompaniment Only

CD 3:25 Vocal Practice Track—Tenor

CD 4:18 Vocal Practice Track—Bass

National Standards

1. Singing, alone and with others, a varied repertoire of music. **(a, b, c, d)**

5. Reading and notating music. **(a, b, c)**

9. Understanding music in relation to history and culture. **(a, b)**

LESSON PLAN

Suggested Teaching Sequence and Performance Tips

1. Introduce

Direct students to:

- Read and discuss the information found in the Getting Started section on student page 174.
- Practice singing the F major scale in the Vocal section on page 175.
- Follow the directions in the Theory section to sight-sing measures 68–95.

Progress Checkpoints

Observe students' progress in:

✓ Their ability to understand the history of this spiritual.

✓ Their ability to play and sing the F major in tune.

✓ Their ability to sight-sing measures 68–95.

New River Train

For TB and Piano

Arranged with Additional Words and Music by
DONALD MOORE

American Spiritual

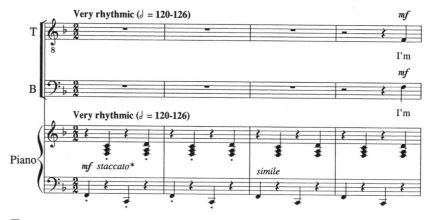

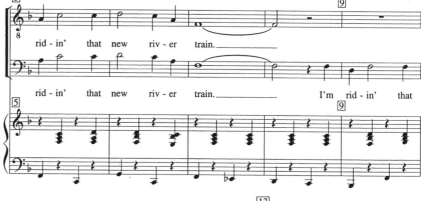

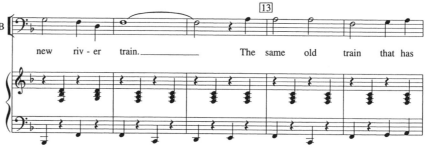

* The accompaniment should simulate the rhythmic sound of a moving train.

176   Intermediate Tenor/Bass

TEACHER 2 TEACHER

"New River Train" is a fast-paced, energetic arrangement that is sure to be a favorite! The repetition of text and musical phrases will allow your group to learn this whole piece rather quickly. Themes in the text—either about trains and travel, or about going home—can be the inspiration for a whole set of songs with lyrics that explore one idea.

2. Rehearse

Direct students to:

- Count the rhythms in measures 5–21, noticing the similarity of this passage to the one that was read in the Theory section.
- When rhythms are correct, sight-sing the pitches on solfège syllables.
- Review the location of do after the key change at measure 32 and continue sight-singing.
- Add the text when rhythms and pitches are accurate, identifying the location of each verse and refrain.

Progress Checkpoints

Observe students' progress in:

✓ Their ability to sight-sing.
✓ Their ability to locate each verse and refrain.

TEACHING STRATEGY

Listening for Form

Discuss verse/refrain form in which each verse is followed by a repeated section (refrain). Have students:

- Listen to "New River Train" and identify the form.
- Discover where each verse begins and when the refrains occur.
- Discuss how each verse or refrain is treated differently with regard to texture, harmony, placement of melody, dynamics, tempo and so forth.

3. Refine

Direct students to:

- Listen for rhythmic energy, especially on syncopated syllables.
- Listen for the Tenor to sustain through the Bass's change in pitch before both parts breathe on the downbeat of measures 50, 54, 84 and 88.
- Apply the dynamic markings provided in the score to give the piece an artistic shaping.
- Maintain tall, round vowels throughout, and in particularly on sustained, longer note values.

Progress Checkpoints

Observe students' progress in:

- ✓ Their ability to sing rhythms energetically.
- ✓ Their ability to sing dynamics as marked.
- ✓ Their ability to sing with proper diction.

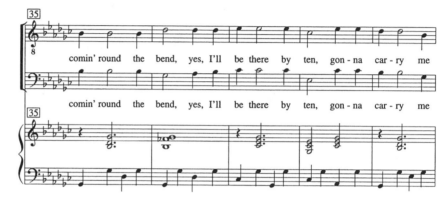

TEACHING STRATEGY

Arranging Musical Melodies

Direct students to:

1. Select one phrase from this song that they know and enjoy singing.
2. Think of creative ways to perform this phrase differently, for example, by using different dynamics, altering the word stress, changing the articulation, and so forth.
3. Create an arrangement of the phrase by adding a descant, adding a simple accompaniment, re-voicing the phrase, adding instruments, writing a new text, changing the meter, and so forth.
4. Have students take turns performing their arrangements for the class.

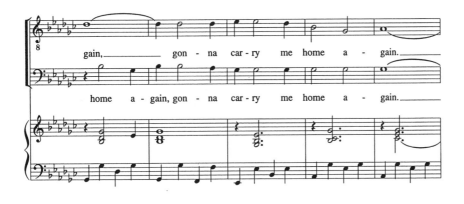

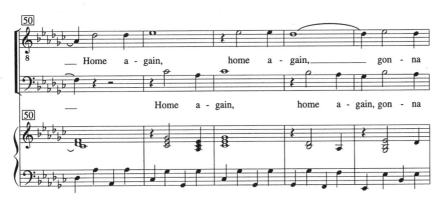

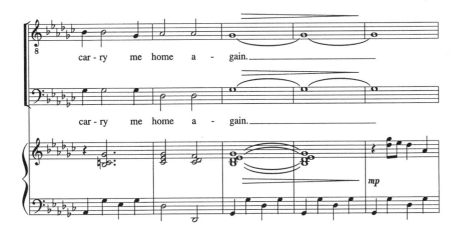

ASSESSMENT

Informal Assessment

In this lesson, students showed the ability to:

- Sing a syncopated rhythm in 2/2 meter.
- Sight-sing rhythms and pitches in the keys of F major, G♭ major and G major.
- Sing an ascending and descending major triad.

Student Self-Assessment

Have students evaluate their individual performances based on the following:

- Posture
- Breath Management
- Tall Vowels
- Accurate Rhythms
- Correct Part-Singing

Have each student rate his/her performance of this song in the areas above on a scale of 1–5, 5 being the best.

TEACHING STRATEGY

Performance Techniques

Have students:

1. Identify appropriate performance techniques to be used in the performance of this song.
2. Either in small ensembles or with the entire choir (large ensemble), perform the song exhibiting these performance techniques.
3. Describe the performance techniques experienced during the performance.
4. Critique the performance based on the observed performance techniques.
5. Repeat this process often in both informal and formal concert settings.

Individual and Group Performance Evaluation

To further measure growth of musical skills presented in this lesson, direct students to complete the Evaluation section on page 175.

- After all students have marked examples of syncopation in their choral score with a checkmark, have them exchange books with a neighbor. Each student should evaluate his neighbor's ability to find the syncopations in this piece.

- Each student should sing measures 27–59 on his own at home or in a practice room. Have them rate their ability to sight-sing these measures on a scale of 1–5, with 5 being the best.

ENRICHMENT

Trains

Research the development of trains in your area. When did trains first arrive? How did the use of trains change the community? Do trains still travel through where you live? Where do they come from and where are they going? What are they carrying? If possible, interview someone who works on a train or who has traveled by train. After gathering some data, ask students to write a paragraph about trains that could be read to the audience before performing "New River Train."

brought me here, gon-na car-ry me home a-gain.

brought me here, gon-na car-ry me home a-gain.

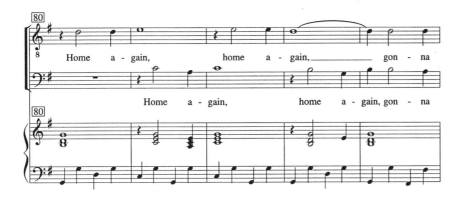

Home a - gain, home a - gain,_____ gon - na

Home a - gain, home a - gain, gon - na

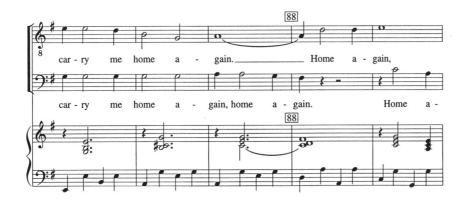

car - ry me home a - gain._____ Home a - gain,

car - ry me home a - gain, home a - gain. Home a -

ENRICHMENT

Concert Etiquette

Have students:

1. Identify appropriate concert etiquette in a variety of settings (formal concerts, informal concerts, large concert halls, small concert halls, and so forth).
2. Attend a variety of live performances.
3. Discuss the appropriate and inappropriate concert behaviors observed.
4. Write a short analysis of appropriate concert etiquette for each setting.

ASSESSMENT

Creating an Assessment Rubric

Have students:

1. Discuss the characteristics of a desirable performance of this piece, using all their knowledge of performance techniques.
2. Identify the criteria by which they think an adjudicator might assess the performance of this piece.
3. For each criterion, decide what characteristics will comprise an adequate, good, very good and excellent performance.
4. Design a rubric chart.
5. Apply the rubric to assess quartets or small ensembles performing all or part of this song.

EXTENSION

Modulation

Modulations are commonly found in arrangements of spirituals and folk songs. "New River Train" passes through three different keys! Develop your students' ability to read in various keys by reading a familiar melody in different keys. Once the melody is memorized, choose a new key and ask students to place the melody on the staff.

MUSIC, SOCIETY AND CULTURE

Have students perform additional songs representing diverse cultures, including American and Texas heritage. Go to **music.glencoe.com**, the Web site for Glencoe's choral music programs, for additional music selections students can perform.

Additional National Standards

The following National Standards are addressed through the Assessment, Extension, Enrichment and bottom-page activities:

6. Listening to, analyzing, and describing music. **(b, c)**

7. Evaluating music and music performances. **(b)**

SPOTLIGHT

Improvisation

Improvisation is *the art of singing or playing music, making it up as you go.* **Scat singing** is *an improvisational style of singing that uses nonsense syllables instead of words.* Sometimes, these nonsense sounds can imitate the sound of an instrument. Scat singing, especially as a solo, can be the scariest part of singing jazz.

Dr. Kirby Shaw, one of the top vocal jazz composers and conductors in the world today, offers some suggestions to help build your confidence in this fun and exciting art form.

Start your scat solo with a short melodic or rhythmic idea from the tune being performed. There is nothing wrong in having a preconceived idea before starting to sing a scat solo! By gradually developing the idea as you sing, you will have an organized solo that sounds completely improvised.

Start with scat syllables like "doo" when singing swing tunes. Try "bee," "dee," and "dn" for occasional accented eighth notes on the *and* of beats (1 *and* 2 *and* 3 *and* 4 *and*). Try "doot" or "dit" for short last notes of a musical phrase.

Be able to imitate any sound you like from the world around you, such as a soft breeze, a car horn or a musical instrument. There might be a place for that sound in one of your solos.

Listen to and imitate, note-for-note, the great jazz singers or instrumentalists. You can be inspired by musicians like Ella Fitzgerald, Jon Hendricks, Louis Armstrong or Charlie Parker.

Learn to sing the blues. You can listen to artists like B. B. King, Stevie Ray Vaughan, Buddy Guy or Luther Allison. There are many types of recordings from which to choose.

In short, learn as many different kinds of songs as you can. The best scat singers quote from such diverse sources as nursery rhymes, African chant and even opera. Above all, have fun as you develop your skills!

RESOURCES

Teacher Resource Binder
Skill Builder 16, *Improvising Melodies*

National Standards
1. Singing, alone and with other, a varied repertoire of music. **(a, b, c)**
3. Improvising melodies, variations and accompaniments. **(a, b, c)**

IMPROVISATION

Objectives
• Create rhythmic and melodic phrases.
• Improvise melodic embellishments and simple rhythmic and melodic variations.

Suggested Teaching Sequence
Direct students to:
• Read the Spotlight On Improvisation on student page 183 and define improvisation and scat singing.
• Identify the steps to follow in learning to scat sing.
• Practice scat singing as described on page 183. Teacher may model, students imitate.
• Apply scat singing techniques to a familiar song.
• Make a list of vocal jazz singers they know and identify characteristics of their singing.
• Apply the techniques presented on this page to the performance of a familiar song that incorporates improvisation.

Progress Checkpoints
Observe students' progress in:
✓ Their ability to define and describe the concept of improvisation.
✓ Their ability to demonstrate scat singing.
✓ Their ability to apply improvisation techniques in the performance of a song.

On The Deep, Blue Sea

OVERVIEW

Composer: Mary Donnelly, arranged by George L. O. Strid

Text: Mary Donnelly

Voicing: TTB

Key: G major

Meter: Cut Time

Form: Verse/Refrain

Style: Contemporary American Chantey

Accompaniment: Piano

Programming: Honor Chorus, Festival

Vocal Ranges:

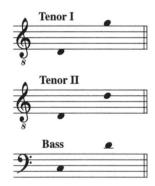

Objectives

After completing this lesson, students will be able to:

- Perform in groups with accurate intonation.
- Describe musical sound.
- Perform expressively a varied repertoire of music representing diverse styles.
- Sight-read music in various meters including cut time.

VOCABULARY

Have students review vocabulary in student lesson. Introduce terms found in the music. A complete glossary of terms is found on page 226 of the student book.

On The Deep, Blue Sea

Composer: Mary Donnelly, arranged by George L. O. Strid
Text: Mary Donnelly
Voicing: TTB

VOCABULARY

sea chantey

chanteyman

chord

cut time

Focus

- Describe and perform chords in tune.
- Sing expressively in a spirited style.
- Read rhythms in cut time.

Getting Started

Have you ever played a game to make the time go by faster? Maybe you've played "I Spy" while traveling by car, or maybe you sang a counting song such as "This Old Man." The song "On The Deep, Blue Sea" is a newly composed piece patterned after **sea chanteys,** *songs sung by sailors, usually in the rhythm of their work.* Singing songs such as this would make the time pass more quickly and raise the sailors' spirits!

◆ History and Culture

Sailors have sung songs of the sea for centuries. The rhythmic flow of the songs helped sailors perform the repetitive jobs while aboard ships. There are two broad categories of sea chanteys based on types of work done.

Hauling chantey – Sung when hauling ropes

Capstan chantey – Sung when raising heavy weights such as the ship's anchor

"On The Deep, Blue Sea" is written in the style of a hauling chantey.

A **chanteyman** was *a soloist who improvised and led the singing of sea chanteys.* He would sing the verses of a chantey and the other sailors would join in on the chorus. A chanteyman was hired with care; his abilities to improvise verses and inspire the men were of prime importance to the captain. The chanteyman was often excused from the heavy work aboard the ship.

SKILL BUILDERS

To learn more about cut time, see Intermediate Sight-Singing, *page 140.*

RESOURCES

Intermediate Sight-Singing

Sight-Singing in G Major, pages 82–85, 89–90

Reading Rhythms in Cut Time, page 140

Teacher Resource Binder

Teaching Master 23, *Text Emphasis in "On the Deep, Blue Sea"*

Evaluation Master 2, *Analyzing Pitch Accuracy*

Evaluation Master 14, *Performance Evaluation: Part Singing*

Skill Builder 1, *Building Harmony*

For additional resources, see TRB Table of Contents.

Links to Learning

◆ **Vocal**

A **chord** *(the combination of three or more notes played together at the same time)* is used to make harmony. Practice the following chords to develop the skill of singing in harmony.

◆ **Theory**

"On The Deep, Blue Sea" is written in **cut time** meter, *a time signature in which there are two beats per measure and the half note receives the beat.* Read and perform the following example to feel the pulse of two beats per measure.

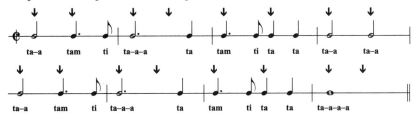

◆ **Artistic Expression**

Contrasts in style give a song interest and variety. In verse 2 (measures 39–55), each section of the choir is featured. Use word stress to add character to the text and strive to make your part the most expressive. Verse 3 (measures 74–90) is more dramatic. The changes in tempo will allow you to be creative in your presentation.

Evaluation

Demonstrate how well you have learned the skills and concepts featured in the lesson "On The Deep, Blue Sea" by completing the following:

- With a small group, perform measures 29–37. Evaluate how well you were able to sing the chords in tune and create harmony.
- Chant the words to verse 2 (measures 74–90) expressively. Exaggerate the changes in tempo, mood and expression. Then sing the verse. In what ways did you perform the verse differently after chanting the words expressively?

Choral Library *On The Deep, Blue Sea* **185**

RESOURCES

Intermediate Tenor/Bass Rehearsal/Performance CD

CD 2:15 Voices

CD 2:16 Accompaniment Only

CD 3:26 Vocal Practice Track—Tenor I

CD 3:27 Vocal Practice Track—Tenor II

CD 4:19 Vocal Practice Track – Bass

National Standards

1. Singing, alone and with others, a varied repertoire of music. **(a, b, c, d)**
5. Reading and notating music. **(a, b, c)**
6. Listening to, analyzing, and describing music. **(a, c)**

LINKS TO LEARNING

Vocal

The Vocal section is designed to prepare students to:

- Understand the meaning of a chord.
- Perform three-part chords in tune creating harmony.

Have students:

- Sing each line independently on solfège syllables either as a full group or as a section divided into voice parts
- Sing the Tenor I line with the Tenor II line.
- Repeat with other combinations of two lines only.
- Sing all three lines together focusing on good intonation.

Theory

The Theory section is designed to prepare students to understand and perform in cut time.

Have students:

- Tap or clap the half note pulse.
- Speak the rhythm pattern while tapping the half note pulse.
- Speak the rhythm pattern as the director conducts in two, while feeling the half note pulse inside.

Artistic Expression

The Artistic Expression section is designed to prepare students to understand the various contrasts in styles between the verses of "On The Deep, Blue Sea."

Have students:

- Examine their music to find the three verses of the song.
- Describe the various features or styles that make the verses different from each other.
- Sing each verse emphasizing the character or the drama of each section.

LESSON PLAN

Suggested Teaching Sequence and Performance Tips

1. Introduce

Direct students to:

- Read and discuss the information found in the Getting Started section on student page 184.
- Practice singing the harmonies in the Vocal section on page 185.
- Practice the rhythm patterns in cut time in the Theory section on page 185.
- Mark their music with breath marks. Direct them to breathe rhythmically. Because of the various entrances, give them the beat number on which to breathe. This will help secure entrances.

On The Deep, Blue Sea

For TTB and Piano

Arranged by
GEORGE L.O. STRID (ASCAP)

Words and Music by
MARY DONNELLY (ASCAP)

186   Intermediate Tenor/Bass

TEACHER 2 TEACHER

It would be fun to program a concert, or a section of a concert with all sea chanteys. This light-hearted original sea chantey by Mary Donnelly would make a clever pairing with "Leave Her, Johnny." "Leave Her, Johnny" (page 170) speaks of leaving the open seas to get married and the other, "On The Deep, Blue Sea," warns sailors to beware of women who want to get married; the sea is the place to be.

- Locate all the cues pitches throughout. Determine if these will be sung and by whom. Have students mark that in their scores.
- Analyze the form of the song. Once they have determined it, tell them to label it in their music.
- Circle the marking at measure 75 that indicates a tempo change. Ask the students to bracket the slower section.
- Circle the *fermata* at measure 86 and star the tempo marking at measure 86–87.

Progress Checkpoints

Observe students' progress in:

✓ Their ability to sing three part chords in tune.

✓ Their ability to read rhythms accurately in cut time.

✓ Their ability to mark their scores with the proper breath marks, pitch changes (cued notes), tempo changes and *fermatas*.

Choral Library *On The Deep, Blue Sea* **187**

2. Rehearse

Direct students to:

- Chant the rhythm of the song. With a metronome to keep from rushing Counting in cut time is ideal, however, if your students experience difficulty, count in 4/4 for the first half of the song while you teach and drill counting in cut time. Count the remainder of the song in cut time.

- Breathe in designated places. Reinforce breathing rhythmically and on the correct beat or part of the beat to secure entrances.

- Sight-sing the first verse on solfège as soon as the rhythms are secure. Ask students to determine which section is unison between the three parts. Have them put parenthesis around those pitches. It would be beneficial to learn this section together and reinforce matching of pitch with good intonation, blending of voices and balancing of sections.

- Continue learning on solfège the harmonic parts of the piece in individual sections until parts are secure and free of mistakes in both pitch and rhythm.
- Check their vocal ranges as to what notes in their part are comfortable for them and what notes are out of their range. Have them mark the notes that are out of their range in their music as a reminder. Taking the time to do so could help with intonation within the section and as a choir.
- Sing the solo section in measures 39–52 checking for consistency in the range of the solos. You may need to add some Tenor II voices to the Tenor I part for tuning of the lower pitches.

Progress Checkpoints

Observe students' progress in:
✓ Breathing with rhythmic accuracy.
✓ Singing with pitch and rhythmic accuracy.
✓ Being familiar with the vocal range to know which notes are out of reach.
✓ Singing three-part chords in tune.

MORE ABOUT...

Expressive Elements of Music

In language, expression is used to communicate mood. The expressive elements of tempo, dynamics, tone color, pitch, articulation and intensity help to convey mood. These same expressive elements are available in performing music and help the performer to establish and communicate the intended mood. It is up to the performer to understand and interpret the intentions of the composer and arranger. In a large group, the conductor frequently helps the group make these decisions, so they are all interpreting the piece in the same way.

3. Refine

Direct students to:

- Begin putting parts together. Isolate chords and sing as a chordal progression on whole notes to tune.

- Speak through the text as you model the desired vowel sounds. Use the metronome to help speak through the text rhythmically without rushing. Emphasize consonants and words that you want stressed at this time and have the students underline them.

- Transfer the solfège syllables to text, phrase by phrase. Try not to move on to the next phrase until the previous phrase is free of mistakes in pitch and rhythm. It could be more beneficial for you to do this transference in sectionals before placing the parts together. You can then solidify each part again before putting them together on the text.

She'll lure you with her lass can throw a net much bet - ter than a fish - er - man.

charms and grant your ev - 'ry wish.

And when you think you've got her

TEACHING STRATEGY

2/2 and 3/2 Meter

These meters may throw students off simply because they might assume that the quarter note should get one beat. Help familiarize everyone with the half note pulse. Place eight "beat bars" (horizontal line each of the same length), on the board, prefaced by a 2/2 meter signature. Have students:

- Pat once for each beat bar as you point.
- Place a half note above each beat bar, and then clap once on each beat as you point.
- Substitute two quarter notes for some of the half notes and clap as you point.
- Substitute other rhythms from the piece into the rhythm, and then clap it.
- Continue to play with the rhythms in 2/2 meter until they become familiar.

- Imitate you as you model the phrases musically how you want them to be sung. Reinforce any rhythmic articulation and word stress taught during the chanting, to add to their expressiveness.
- Add the concept taught in the Artistic Expression section on page 185. Contrasting the verses will add variety and interest both to the students and to the audience.

Progress Checkpoints

Observe students' progress in:

✓ Their accuracy in speaking and singing through text with all parts.

✓ Breathing rhythmically with secure and accurate entrances.

✓ Singing musically and with good intonation in individual parts and as a choir. Listen for students singing the verses in contrast of each other with stressed consonants and words as underlined and practiced during the chanting process.

✓ Their consistency of beginning and ending consonants and rhythmic articulation as directed to clarify the text.

ASSESSMENT

Informal Assessment

In this lesson, students showed the ability to:

- Read and perform music accurately in cut-time meter.
- Sing expressively with good intonation using word stress, uniform vowel sounds and musical phrasing with applied musical contrast.
- Sing three-part chords in tune in the key of G major.

MUSIC, SOCIETY AND CULTURE

Have students perform additional songs representing diverse cultures, including American and Texas heritage. Go to **music.glencoe.com**, the Web site for Glencoe's choral music programs, for additional music selections students can perform.

Have students evaluate their individual performances based on the following:

- Breath Management
- Tall Vowels
- Expressive Singing
- Intonation
- Correct Part-Singing

Have each student rate his/her performance of this song in the areas above on a scale of 1–5, 5 being the best.

Choral Library *On The Deep, Blue Sea* **193**

TEACHING STRATEGY

Extra Help in Tuning Chords

To help students listen to one another, have one student in each group choose a pitch and hold it out until everyone in the group is singing the same pitch, using a neutral syllable such as "oo" or "ah." Point to one student from one of the groups. That student changes the group pitch, and everyone must listen and move to that pitch. Continue to point to individual students in each of the three groups, waiting each time until the group has tuned to the new pitch. The chords will be very interesting, sometimes dissonant, which requires even more careful listening. Encourage soft singing, and very careful listening within and among groups.

Individual and Group Performance Evaluation

To further measure growth of musical skills presented in this lesson, direct students to complete the Evaluation section on page 185.

- After small groups have performed measures 29–37 for the rest of the class, the class should evaluate by asking, "Did these singers sing the chords in tune and create harmony?"

- After chanting the words to verse 2 expressively, have the students sing verse 2, analyzing how the verse was performed differently after adding expression.

CAREERS IN MUSIC

Music as Avocation

Three areas of music that many students may enjoy outside of the classroom are singing in a community or church choir, singing and acting in a musical theater or singing or playing in a band. Ask students if they already participate in an outside musical group. Ask those that are to share their experiences with others. Music can be a lifelong avocation (not related to a job or career) for those who want to continue studying music. Encourage students to explore ways to use their music skills outside of the classroom.

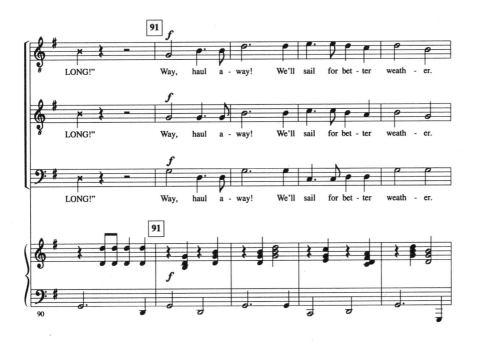

EXTENSION

Vocal Expressiveness

"On the Deep, Blue Sea" is a charming piece because of the text. The text is witty and funny and has a big play on words. How the words are expressed will determine how the audience responds. Ask some of the students to take a phrase and speak it in a manner that would clearly portray to them the thought of the text. Ask them to present it to the class. Have the other students chart the words and mark those that had inflection. Direct the choir to sing the phrases as modeled by the students. Once they have done this with the entire piece, design a pantomime of this song in two or three large groups. Have them come up with a pantomime that will portray the text as the choir is singing. After each group has rehearsed, ask them to present it to the class. The goal of this activity is to act out what is being expressed vocally. Did they feel success in this activity? Ask if it was easier for them to pantomime when a group was expressive.

ENRICHMENT

Concert Performance

After completing the activity in the Extension section, ask the students to determine which group was the best. Stage the best pantomime at your next concert during the performance of this piece. Staging this song with your boys' choir can make this an audience favorite.

Additional National Standards

The following National Standards are addressed through the Assessment, Extension, Enrichment and bottom-page activities:

5. Reading and notating music. **(a)**

6. Listening to, analyzing, and describing music. **(a, c)**

7. Evaluating music and music performances. **(b)**

8. Understanding relationships between music, the other arts, and disciplines outside the arts. **(b)**

 **SPOTLIGHT**

Changing Voice

As we grow in size and maturity, we don't always grow at the same rate. Just look around your school or neighborhood. Some thirteen-year-olds tower over other students, while some are quite small.

As the voice matures, it changes in both pitch and **timbre** *(tone quality)*. The vocal folds or cords are growing longer and thicker. Just like growing in stature, this process is not the same for every person. One person's voice might drop an octave almost overnight, while another person's changes very gradually.

The Male Voice

While every voice change is unique, male singers usually progress through several identifiable stages:

- Before the voice begins to change, the boy's voice has a very light vocal quality, and the tone is pure and clear. Also, the voice is very flexible with the ability to sing in a high range.

- The first sign of voice change is the loss of clarity and richness in the higher pitches. There is a slight decrease in flexibility due to the growth of the vocal folds or cords. As the voice begins to change or mature, the singer will notice that he loses more notes in his top range than he gains in his new, lower voice.

- As the voice lowers, the quality becomes thicker, huskier and sometimes breathy. There may be signs of hoarseness and breaks in the voice when speaking or singing. The voice appears to be weaker and less flexible. Although the vocal range is limited, this is a temporary stage. The more the singer sings during this time, the easier the transition will be. Also, if a singer will continue to sing in his upper range, it will strengthen the vocal cords and help maintain flexibility in the voice.

- As the voice matures, the lower pitches in the speaking voice become evident. The singing voice is lower, firm and clear.

- When the voice has reached full maturity, it has a thicker, heavier voice quality. The tone is consistent. A male singer can move more easily between the lower and upper registers of his voice, including **falsetto** *(the light upper range of the male voice that extends beyond the natural voice)*. The voice will eventually settle into a classification called **tenor** *(the highest-sounding male voice)* or **bass** *(the lowest-sounding male voice)*.

Spotlight *Changing Voice* **197**

RESOURCES

Teacher Resource Binder
Teaching Master 24, *Checking on My Changing Voice*
Reference 7, *Checking on My Voice*

National Standards
1. Singing alone and with others. **(b)**

CHANGING VOICE

Objectives
- Demonstrate characteristic vocal timbre individually and in groups.

Suggested Teaching Sequence
Direct students to:
- Read Spotlight On Changing Voice on student page 197 and identify the five stages of the male changing voice and the characteristics of the voice in each stage.
- Define timbre.
- Test their vocal ranges to determine their highest and lowest comfortable singing note. Check their ranges throughout the year.
- Record themselves singing "America" at the beginning of the year, the middle of the year and at the end of the year. Compare the three recordings and document changes in the voice that have occurred during the course of the year.

Progress Checkpoints
Observe students' progress in:
- ✓ Their ability to identify the five stages of change in the male voice.
- ✓ Their ability to understand timbre.
- ✓ Their ability to discover the progress of change in their individual voice.

Pretty Saro

OVERVIEW

Composer: American Folk Song, arranged by Jennifer B. Scoggin
Text: Traditional
Voicing: TTB
Key: G major (pentatonic melody)
Meter: 3/4
Form: Strophic
Style: American Folk Song
Accompaniment: Piano
Programming: Americana program, Concert, Festival, Large or Small Ensemble

Vocal Ranges:

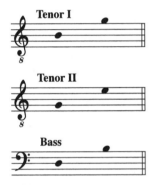

OBJECTIVES

After completing this lesson, students will be able to:

- Read music notation in various meters, including 3/4.
- Notate pitches of the pentatonic scale using standard symbols.
- Perform music representative of diverse cultures, including American heritage.

VOCABULARY

Have students review vocabulary in student lesson. Introduce terms found in the music. A complete glossary of terms is found on page 226 of the student book.

Pretty Saro

Composer: American Folk Song, arranged by Jennifer B. Scoggin
Text: Traditional
Voicing: TTB

VOCABULARY

folk song
pentatonic scale
$\frac{3}{4}$ meter

Focus

- Read music notation in $\frac{3}{4}$ meter.
- Write a pentatonic scale.
- Perform music representing American folk music.

Getting Started

Songs quite often tell a story. What is the story behind this song?

"Down in some lone valley in a lonesome place"

Where is this place? Why is it so lonely? Who else is there?

"Farewell pretty Saro, I bid you adieu."

Why did someone have to say good-bye? Who is pretty Saro?

This American folk song is a story waiting to be told. Finish your story by giving your characters names, ages and circumstances. How will this information change the way you perform this song?

◆ History and Culture

Folk songs are an important part of every culture. They can tell stories of great loves, legends and leaders. **Folk songs** are *songs that are passed down from generation to generation through oral tradition.* They may change with each new generation as each adds its own variation. Make a list of other folk songs you know.

In the early 1900s, many American scholars began to systematically collect and record our folk song literature. Two of our most famous folk song collectors were John and Alan Lomax, a father-and-son team. In 1911 John Lomax published a collection of songs from the Appalachian Mountains. "Pretty Saro" was part of this early collection. Much of the music from Appalachia was handed down from Scottish and Irish ancestors. However, "Pretty Saro" has a third verse that mentions that the girl wants a "freeholder who owns house and land." The term *freeholder* indicates a possible British origin.

SKILL BUILDERS

To learn more about $\frac{3}{4}$ *meter, see* Intermediate Sight-Singing, *page 17.*

198 Intermediate Tenor/Bass

RESOURCES

Intermediate Sight-Singing

Sight-Singing in G Major, page 82–85, 89–90

Reading Rhythms in 3/4 Meter, pages 17–22

Teacher Resource Binder

Teaching Master 25, *Conducting "Pretty Saro"*

Teaching Master 26, *Pentatonic Scales*

Skill Builder 21, *Pitch and Kodály*

Skill Builder 23, *Rhythm and Kodály*

Kodály 6, Music Reading: *Rhythm*

For additional resources, see TRB Table of Contents.

Links to Learning

◆ **Vocal**

A **pentatonic scale** is *a scale based on five pitches (do, re, mi, sol, la).* Notice that in the pentatonic scale the pitches *fa* and *ti* are not used. A pentatonic scale can start on any pitch. For example, the *do* pentatonic scale consists of *do, re, mi, fa, sol.* A *re* pentatonic scale consists of *re, mi, sol, la, do* and so forth. Read and perform the following pentatonic scale to prepare you to sing "Pretty Saro." Sing in the range that best fits your voice.

◆ **Theory**

"Pretty Saro" is written in **¾ meter,** *a time signature in which there are three beats per measure and the quarter note receives the beat.* Read and perform the following rhythmic patterns to establish ¾ meter.

Evaluation

Demonstrate how well you have learned the concepts and skills presented in the lesson "Pretty Saro" by completing the following:

- With a classmate, chant the rhythm and conduct measures 5–20 to show your ability to read music in ¾ meter. Critique each other's performance, and identify areas that need improvement.

- Describe a pentatonic scale. On staff paper or on the computer, write a G pentatonic scale beginning on *do.* Sing the scale that you wrote. How well did you do?

Choral Library *Pretty Saro* **199**

LINKS TO LEARNING

Vocal

The Vocal section is designed to prepare students to:

- Understand a pentatonic scale.
- Sing a pentatonic scale in any key.

Have students:

- Read the definition of a pentatonic scale.
- Sing the pentatonic scale in the key of G as written using solfège syllables.
- Locate these pitches in the melody of "Pretty Saro."

Theory

The Theory section is designed to prepare students to read and perform rhythms in 3/4 meter.

Have students:

- Tap or clap the quarter note pulse in 3/4 meter, emphasizing beat 1.
- Speak the rhythm exercises while continuing to tap the quarter note pulse.
- Speak the rhythm exercises while the director conducts in 3/4 meter still feeling the quarter note pulse inside.

RESOURCES

Intermediate Tenor/Bass Rehearsal/Performance CD

CD 2:17 Voices

CD 2:18 Accompaniment Only

CD 3:28 Vocal Practice Track—Tenor I

CD 3:29 Vocal Practice Track—Tenor II

CD 4:20 Vocal Practice Track—Bass

National Standards

1. Singing, alone and with others, a varied repertoire of music. **(a, b, c, d)**
5. Reading and notating music. **(a, b, c, d)**
9. Understanding music in relation to history and culture. **(b)**

LESSON PLAN

Suggested Teaching Sequence and Performance Tips

1. Introduce

Direct students to:

- Read and discuss the information found in the Getting Started section on student page 198.

- Practice singing the pentatonic scale in the Vocal section on page 199.

- Practice the rhythm patterns in 3/4 time in the Theory section on page 199.

- Locate and identify the melodic line in the score for "Pretty Saro." (Bass/Baritone part)

- Sight-sing a cappella, the bass clef line on solfège syllables in measures 4–12 in their appropriate octave. Determine if this melody uses a major scale or a pentatonic scale. (*pentatonic scale*)

- Identify how many phrases were sung in measures 4–12. (*two phrases*) Sing again on solfège syllables, taking a breath only where there is a comma.

- Sight-sing the bass clef line a cappella, in solfège in measures 13–20 in their appropriate octave. Direct the singers to sing four measure phrases in this section.

- Review measures 4–20, Basses only with text. Emphasize four-measure phrasing. Add accompaniment.

Pretty Saro

For TTB and Piano

Arranged by
JENNIFER B. SCOGGIN

American Folk Song

200   Intermediate Tenor/Bass

This lovely arrangement of "Pretty Saro" will allow your Bass/Baritones to take a lead role, as the melody remains in their part throughout.

- Sight-sing measures 4–12, Tenors only, a cappella, using solfège syllables and hand signs, while the Basses listen and determine why the Tenor parts will lead the ensemble to a more major tonality. *(The arranger's accompaniment and harmonies lend themselves to G major because* fa *(C) is introduced in the tenor line and* ti *(F♯) is used in the accompaniment.)*

- Review the Tenor parts in measures 4–12 by chanting the solfège syllables in 3/4 time. Add accompaniment and continue sight-singing through measure 20.

- Review all parts together through measure 20; first count singing in 3/4, then with lyrics and accompaniment.

Progress Checkpoints

Observe students' progress in:

- ✓ Their ability to locate and identify the G major and pentatonic scales.
- ✓ Their ability to sing accurate intervals, using both solfège syllables and song text.
- ✓ Their ability to sing in three parts.
- ✓ Their ability to create artistic and expressive four-measure phrases.

EXTENSION

Conducting

Have the students practice conducting so they can lead the ensemble. Work on entrance cues and tempo changes until confident. Include dynamic indications in their conducting patterns. Once they are confident, take turns conducting "Pretty Saro" while the ensemble performs.

2. Rehearse

Direct students to:

- Sight-sing measures 23–37. Basses sing the melodic line with text, while Tenors sight-sing using solfège syllables.

- Review parts individually as needed. Sing in four-measure phrases with a *crescendo* to the middle of the phrase and a *decrescendo* to taper the end of the phrase. *(Beautiful phrasing is an important part of artistic singing. Many folk songs lend themselves to a four-measure phrase with the strongest point of the phrase in the middle. The voice then lands gently on the text at the end of the phrase.)*

- Practice drawing the phrase line with your hand in front of your body as you sing. Be expressive!

- Locate and identify the expressive markings of measures 23–37. Discuss why the arranger has marked different dynamic levels for the Bass and Tenor lines. *(mp, mf, tempo change at measures 24, phase markings in Tenor line, ritardando and diminuendo, Bass has the melody and it should be louder than the Tenor harmony.)*

- Sing measures 23–37 using the dynamic and tempo markings as indicated.

- Review measures 1–37 using expressive markings.

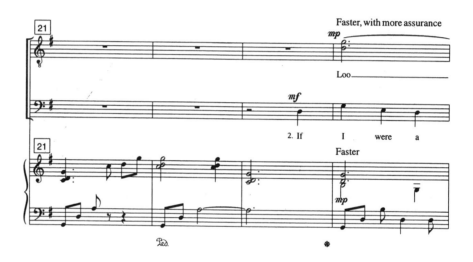

ENRICHMENT

Ballads

The ballad is an important part of the American folk repertoire. These art songs usually have a simple melody that shoulders a story line crossing the ages. Ballads range from simple two- and three-verse songs and poems to those with twenty or more stanzas. Some of our most famous ballads include: "On Top of Old Smokey," "Jeannie with the Light Brown Hair" and "My Darlin' Clementine."

Not all ballads are folk songs. Many modern composers and singers continue the tradition of telling a story through a lyrical song. Investigate and research the popular songs of each decade from the 1950s to the present.

- Locate, identify and define the *a tempo* marking in measures 37 and the *fermata* in measures 39. Practice performing these markings.
- Sight-sing with text the Tenor II part in measures 37 to the end. Evaluate on a scale of one to ten how close the Tenor II voices come to using the appropriate dynamic markings.
- Repeat measures 37–41 with both Tenor parts. Basses listen and score appropriate use of dynamics AND watching the conductor at the *fermata*.
- Sing measures 37–41, Basses only, emphasizing appropriate use of dynamics and *fermata*.

Progress Checkpoints

Observe students' progress in:
- ✓ Their accurate use of dynamic markings.
- ✓ Their ability to follow the conductor's tempo changes at measures 24 and 35.
- ✓ Their ability to sing expressive phrases.
- ✓ Blending their voices and tuning the harmonies accurately.

TEACHING STRATEGY

Singing Dissonant Intervals

To further practice singing this piece in turn, have students:
- Work on voice parts separately until the pitches are solid and secure.
- Sing the piece together, raising a hand when they hear unexpected intervals.
- Return to separate voice parts to reinforce unsure pitches.
- Sing in ensemble several times to become accustomed to the dissonances.

3. Refine

Direct students to:

- Review entire piece, working parts as necessary.
- Secure accurate intonation and vocal blend.
- Sing parts a cappella to check for pitch accuracy vocal independence
- Work toward memorization. Basses sing without music while Tenors use the score and vice versa.
- Use appropriate facial expression to convey the meaning of the text.
- Sing with understandable diction.

Progress Checkpoints

Observe students' progress in:

- ✓ Their ability to balance parts appropriately.
- ✓ Their accuracy and vocal independence.
- ✓ Their ability to sing from memory.
- ✓ Their appropriate facial expression.
- ✓ Singing with understandable diction.

ASSESSMENT

Informal Assessment

In this lesson, students showed the ability to:

- Read music notation in 3/4 meter.
- Identify and sing a pentatonic scale in the key of G.
- Sing expressively with independence of vocal parts.

Intermediate Tenor/Bass

TEACHING STRATEGY

Improvising in the Pentatonic Scale

The Vocal Warm-Up in this lesson requires students to learn tones of the pentatonic scale. To solidify the tones more, have them improvise using these five pitches. At first, it would seem that this would produce a dissonant mess, but the tones of the pentatonic scale, sounding together, avoid the clashes produced by the half steps of *fa* and *ti*, actually sound quite nice together. The more students improvise this way, the more they will realize the safety of exploring in a cacophony of sound. Mistakes are not heard, and good combinations can be remembered for a later time.

Student Self-Assessment

Have students evaluate their individual performances based on the following:

• Posture
• Phrasing
• Diction
• Expressive Singing
• Intonation

Have each student rate his/her performance of this song in the areas above on a scale of 1–5, 5 being the best.

Individual and Group Performance Evaluation

To further measure growth of musical skills presented in this lesson, direct students to complete the Evaluation section on page 199.

• After students have paired up and chanted and conducted measures 5–20 for each other, lead a class discussion on appropriate ways to evaluate and critique classmates.

• After each student has written a G pentatonic scale, have them sing or play it for the class. Evaluate each student by asking, "Did this student exhibit their knowledge of the pentatonic scale by writing and performing it correctly?"

Choral Library *Pretty Saro* **205**

Additional National Standards

The following National Standards are addressed through the Assessment, Extension, Enrichment and bottom-page activities:

2. Performing, alone and with others, a varied repertoire of music. **(a)**

3. Improvising melodies, variations and accompaniments. **(c)**

5. Reading and notating music. **(d)**

7. Evaluating music and music performances. **(a, b)**

Santa Lucia

OVERVIEW

Composer: Teordoro Cottrau (1827–1879), arranged by Henry Leck

Text: Teordoro Cottrau

Voicing: TB

Key: D major

Meter: 3/8

Form: Strophic

Style: Italian Art Song

Accompaniment: Piano

Programming: Multicultural, Men's Showcase

Vocal Ranges:

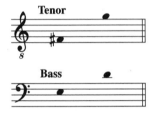

Objectives

After completing this lesson, students will be able to:

- Read and write music notation in 3/8 meter.
- Demonstrate musical artistry by singing expressively using *rubato*.
- Perform music representative of diverse cultures.

Santa Lucia

Composer: Teodoro Cottrau (1827–1879), arranged by Henry Leck

Text: Teodoro Cottrau

Voicing: TB

VOCABULARY

barcarole

⅜ meter

rubato

Focus

- Read and perform rhythmic patterns in ⅜ meter.
- Sing expressively using rubato.
- Perform music that represents the Neopolitan barcarole.

Getting Started

What do these three songs have in common? How are they different?

"You Gentlemen Of England" (see page 216)

"On The Deep, Blue Sea" (see page 182)

"Santa Lucia" (see page 204)

Share your answers with your classmates. It is interesting to see how different cultures express similar ideas through music.

◆ History and Culture

Italian songwriter Teodoro Cottrau (1827–1879) wrote 50 Neapolitan songs, of which "Santa Lucia" is perhaps his most famous. Written in 1850, "Santa Lucia" is an example of a **barcarole,** *a Venetian boating song.* Over the years, it has become the anthem of Naples, Italy, and a favorite among tenors. Cottrau was also a music publisher, lawyer, poet and politician.

"Santa Lucia" is a very popular song with the gondoliers who guide the gondolas (long narrow boats) through the water canals of Venice, Italy. The music expresses the joy of being out in the sea breezes and feeling the flow of the water. It should be sung with a very full and lyric sound, taking liberty with the dynamics and phrasing. While "Santa Lucia" can be sung in English, it is fun and more authentic to sing it in its original language, Italian. Have fun learning this famous Italian boating song.

SKILL BUILDERS

To learn more about ⅜ meter, see Intermediate Sight-Singing, *page 154.*

RESOURCES

Intermediate Sight-Singing

Sight-Singing in D major, pages 99–102.

Sight-Singing in 3/8 meter, pages 154–155.

Teacher Resource Binder

Teaching Master 27, *Pronunciation Guide for "Santa Lucia"*

Skill Builder 31, *Time Signatures in Music*

Reference 16, *My Music Dictionary*

Reference 29, *Zeroing in on IPA*

For additional resources, see the TRB Table of Contents.

Links to Learning

◆ **Theory**

"Santa Lucia" is written in $\frac{3}{8}$ **meter,** *a time signature in which there is one group of three eighth notes per measure and the dotted quarter note receives the beat.* When the tempo is very slow, this meter can be counted as having three beats per measure, with the eighth note receiving the beat.

At the performance tempo, this song should be felt in one. To learn the difference between feeling "Santa Lucia" in one versus three, perform the following examples, first at a slow tempo, feeling the pulse in three. Then repeat the example at the performance tempo, feeling the pulse in one.

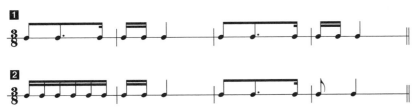

◆ **Artistic Expression**

Rubato, or *the freedom to slow down and/or speed up the tempo without changing the overall pulse of a piece of music,* is an artistic device that is effective in the performance of "Santa Lucia." Look at the music. Where would you use rubato?

Evaluation

Demonstrate how well you have learned the skills and concepts featured in the lesson "Santa Lucia" by completing the following:

- Alone or in a small group, clap the rhythms in measures 25–32. Check your performance for showing a clear distinction between the eighth note and sixteenth note patterns.

- Select one person to come forward and serve as a "rubato leader." As a class, perform "Santa Lucia," following the leader. How well was the class able to follow the leader?

Choral Library *Santa Lucia* **207**

RESOURCES

Intermediate Tenor/Bass Rehearsal/Performance CD

CD 2:19 Voices

CD 2:20 Accompaniment Only

CD 3:30 Vocal Practice Track—Tenor

CD 4:21 Vocal Practice Track—Bass

National Standards

1. Singing, alone and with others, a varied repertoire of music. **(b, c, e)**

5. Reading and notating music **(b)**

LINKS TO LEARNING

Theory

The Theory section is designed to prepare students to:

- Read and perform rhythmic patterns in 3/8 meter.

Have students:

- Chant each example at a slow tempo using rhythm syllables. Repeat several times until they are secure in the reading the rhythms.

- Change the tempo to a faster tempo and chant the rhythms again. Feel the pulse in one.

- Discuss the difference between feeling the pulse with three beats per measures versus feeling the pulse with one beat per measure.

Artistic Expression

The Artistic Expression section is designed to prepare students to make decisions about how to use rubato appropriately in the performance of "Santa Lucia."

Have students:

- Define *rubato*.

- Sing a familiar song ("America," for example) and experiment with rubato.

- Look at the music of "Santa Lucia" and decide where it would be appropriate to add *rubato*.

LESSON PLAN

Suggested Teaching Sequence and Performance Tips

1. Introduce

Direct students to:

- Read and discuss the information in the Getting Started section on page 206. Compare the three songs. *(They are all songs of the sea. They are from three different cultures: English, American, and Italian.)*

- Share what they know about Italy, Venice, gondoliers, and barcaroles. Locate Venice, Italy, on the map.

- Practice reading the rhythmic patterns in the Theory section on page 207. Read them at a slower tempo in three, and then again at a faster tempo in one.

- Read the rhythm of the song one phrase at a time.

- Sing the melody on a neutral syllable or on solfège syllables.

Progress Checkpoints

Observe students' progress in:

✓ The ability to read rhythms in 3/8 meter.

✓ The ability to read notation in D major.

Santa Lucia

For TB and Piano*

Arranged by
HENRY LECK

Words and Music by
TEODORO COTTRAU (1827–1879)

*Accompaniment CD has a four-measure introduction.

208   Intermediate Tenor/Bass

"Santa Lucia" is a fun, showcase piece for male singers that may also be used to develop tone and vocal technique. It is an excellent tool for teaching open Italian vowels and for developing a full, lyric, vocal style.

2. Rehearse

Direct students to:

- Chant the Italian text in rhythm in an exaggerated manner. Use tall Italian vowels.
- Discover the flow of the melody line by having the Tenors sing measures 9–12 in unison followed by the Basses singing measures 13–16. Discuss which parts have the melody and which parts sing the harmony. Emphasize that the melody line should be heard over the harmony line at all times.
- Sing the melody with the Italian text.
- Learn measures 9–16.
- Learn their respective parts on measures 17–24 (melody too high for most basses).
- Discover that once they have learned measures 1–24, they will have learned the entire song.
- Sing measures 1–24 in Italian in two parts.
- Figure out the "road map" of the piece including the D. C. marking.

Progress Checkpoints

Observe students' progress in:

- ✓ The ability to distinguish between who sings melody and who sings harmony.
- ✓ The ability to sing in two parts and balance the parts between melody and harmony.
- ✓ The ability to sing with correct Italian diction.

EXTENSION

Italian Tenors

Singing is an important element in the Italian culture. Famous tenors such as Luciano Pavarotti are known worldwide. Collect recordings of famous Tenors singing "Santa Lucia." Compare and contrast the various recordings.

3. Refine

Direct students to:

- Read the Artistic Expression section on page 207 to learn about *rubato.* Have students look in music and find places where they could add *rubato. (Answers may vary)*
- Sing each phrase experimenting with changes in tempo.
- Add the dynamics indicated in the score. Show contrast.
- Add the articulation markings indicated. Sing with strong accents in measures 17–20. Note: These accents are connected, not separated, in a more Romantic style.
- Sing measures 21–24 in a contrasting smooth and *legato* style.

Progress Checkpoints

Observe students' progress in:

- ✓ The ability to add expressive nuances to their performance—*rubato,* dynamic contrast, articulation.
- ✓ The ability to show contrast between accented and *legato* passages.
- ✓ Sing with correct Italian diction.

210   Intermediate Tenor/Bass

ENRICHMENT

Listening for Form

Form relates to the structure or musical design of a composition. If students can identify and analyze the form of a composition, they are able to perform with greater comprehension and understanding. Listen to a recording of this song. Direct students to:

- Identify the form of "Santa Lucia" as strophic—a form in which the melody repeats while the words change from verse to verse.
- Discuss how each verse is sung differently to match the words.
- Listen to and identify other songs in strophic form in this book, such as "Dauntem Tale" (page 94) and "Red River Valley" (page 22).

San - ta Lu - ci - a!
San - ta Lu - ci - a!
San - ta Lu - ci - a!
San - ta Lu - ci - a!

San - ta Lu - ci - a!
San - ta Lu - ci - a!
San - ta Lu - ci - a!
San - ta Lu - ci - a!

Additional National Standards

The following National Standards are addressed through the Assessment, Extension, Enrichment and bottom-page activities:

6. Analyzing and describing music. **(b)**

7. Evaluating music and music performances. **(a)**

ASSESSMENT

Informal Assessment

In this lesson, students showed the ability to:

- Sing expressively using *rubato*.
- Read and perform rhythmic patterns in 3/8 meter.
- Perform a Neapolitan barcarole.

Student Self-Assessment

Have students evaluate their individual performances based on the following:

- Intonation
- Rhythm
- Expressive Singing
- Articulation
- Italian diction

Have each student rate his/her performance of this song in the areas above on a scale of 1–5, with 5 being the best.

Individual Performance and Group Evaluation

To further measure growth of musical skills presented in this lesson, direct students to complete the Evaluation section on page 207.

- Individually clap the rhythms in measures 25–32. Teacher will listen for accurate performance of the eighth- and sixteenth-note patterns.
- Encourage students to serve as the conductor. Evaluate how well the leader understands *rubato* and uses it appropriately while conducting.

Sing To The Lord

OVERVIEW

Composer: Emily Crocker
Text: Based on the Psalms
Voicing: TTB
Key: G major
Meter: 4/4
Form: ABA
Style: Contemporary American Anthem
Accompaniment: None
Programming: Contest, Appropriate for large and small ensembles

Vocal Ranges:

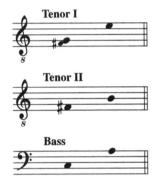

Objectives

After completing this lesson, students will be able to:

- Describe and analyze musical sound.
- Read and perform independently with accurate rhythms.
- Identify relationship between the content and concepts of other subjects and those of music.

VOCABULARY

Have students review vocabulary in student lesson. Introduce terms found in the music. A complete glossary of terms is found on page 226 of the student book.

Sing To The Lord

Composer: Emily Crocker
Text: Based on the Psalms
Voicing: TTB

VOCABULARY

ABA form

unison

part-singing

▲ SPOTLIGHT

To learn more about the dotted quarter notes, see Intermediate Sight-Singing, page 45.

Focus

- Distinguish between unison singing and part-singing.
- Read and perform rhythmic patterns that contain dotted quarter notes.
- Relate music to other subjects.

Getting Started

A Japanese haiku is a form of poetry that uses seventeen syllables of text divided into three lines. Commonly, the first line consists of five syllables, the second seven, and the last five. In describing the subject matter, the poem should also reflect the Japanese philosophy of lightness, simplicity, openness and depth.

Have you ever written a poem? Complete this haiku.

Voices resounding

All joined together as one

Singing, _____ _____ _____.

◆ History and Culture

Although not written in the style of a haiku, the text to "Sing to the Lord" is poetry. It is loosely based on Psalm 150 and describes singing as jubilant and joyful. Just as there are many different ways to write poetry, there are many different ways to write music. The music to "Sing To The Lord" is written in ABA form. **ABA form** is *the design in which the opening phrase (section A) is followed by a contrasting phrase (section B), which leads to a repetition of the opening phrase (section A).* The opening eight measures beginning with "Sing to the Lord" is section A. Find where section A appears again. The contrasting middle section B ("Praise Him with sounding brass") is different in texture, style and phrasing. By discovering the form or organization of the music, you will find that learning a song may become easier. For example, once you have learned the opening eight measures of "Sing To The Lord," you will already know two-thirds of the song!

RESOURCES

Intermediate Sight-Singing

Sight-Singing in G Major, page 82–85, 89–90

Reading Rhythms in 4/4 Meter, pages 2–6

Reading Quarter Notes and Half Note, pages 1–9

Reading Dotted Notes, pages 45, 48, 49

Teacher Resource Binder

Evaluation Master 2, *Analyzing Pitch Accuracy*

Evaluation Master 11, *Group Performance Evaluation*

Skill Builder 27, *Rhythm Challenge in 4/4 Meter*

Skill Builder 30, *Solfège Hand Signs*

Interdisciplinary 21–22, *Language Arts*

For additional resources, see TRB Table of Contents.

Links to Learning

◆ **Vocal**

In "Sing To The Lord," the choir often sings in **unison** (*all parts singing the same notes*), then moves into **part-singing** (*two or more parts singing an independent line at the same time*), and finally returns to unison singing. Perform the following example to practice moving between unison singing and part-singing. Listen carefully to match the unison pitches.

◆ **Theory**

A **dot** is *a symbol that increases the length of a given note by half its value.* It is placed to the right of the note. A dotted quarter note receives one and a half beats. Read and perform the following rhythmic patterns that contain dotted quarter notes.

Evaluation

Demonstrate how well you have learned the skills and concepts featured in the lesson "Sing To The Lord" by completing the following:

- Locate in the music (measures 1–8) the places where the voice parts are singing in unison. In a trio with one singer on a part, sing measures 1–8 and hold the unison notes. Evaluate how well your group was able to match pitch on the unison notes.

- Sing measures 1–7 to show your ability to read music that contains dotted quarter notes. Rate your performance on a scale of 1 to 5, with 5 being the best.

RESOURCES

Intermediate Tenor/Bass Rehearsal/Performance CD

CD 2:21 Voices

CD 2:22 Accompaniment Only

CD 3:31 Vocal Practice Track—Tenor I

CD 3:32 Vocal Practice Track—Tenor II

CD 4:22 Vocal Practice Track—Bass

National Standards

1. Singing, alone and with others, a varied repertoire of music. **(a, b, c, d)**

5. Reading and notating music. **(a)**

6. Listening to, analyzing, and describing music. **(a, b)**

8. Understanding relationships between music, the other arts, and disciplines outside the arts. **(b)**

LINKS TO LEARNING

Vocal

The Vocal section is designed to prepare student to:

- Understand the difference between unison and part-singing.

- Sing with vocal independence when moving from a unison pitch to harmony.

Have students:

- Read and discuss the definitions of unison and part-singing.

- Examine the example and circle all unison pitches between parts.

- Sing each line independently on solfège syllables either as a full group or as a section divided into voice parts.

- Sing the Tenor I line with the Tenor II line.

- Repeat with other combinations of two lines only.

- Sing all three lines together focusing on good intonation on the unison pitches and three-part chords.

Theory

The Theory section is designed to prepare students to:

- Understand the purpose of a dot in music.

- Read rhythmic patterns containing dotted quarter notes.

Have students:

- Read the definition and function of a dot in music notation.

- Tap or clap the quarter note pulse.

- Speak the rhythm pattern while tapping the quarter note pulse.

LESSON PLAN

Suggested Teaching Sequence and Performance Tips

1. Introduce

Direct students to:

- Read and discuss the information found in Getting Started on page 210.
- Mark the form of the composition. Mark the A section (measures 1–8), B section (measures 9–16) and the return to the A section (measures 17–end).
- Mark places the choir will breathe together in the music. Practice breathing rhythmically to secure the entrances.
- Place brackets around notes and measures that contain unison pitches between two or three parts.
- Practice the chords in the Vocal section on page 213, carefully tuning the unison pitches.
- Practice the rhythm pattern in the Theory section on page 213 to reinforce dotted rhythms.

Progress Checkpoints

Observe students' progress in:

- ✓ Marking the music to indicate form and unison passages.
- ✓ Reading rhythmic patterns with dotted quarter notes.
- ✓ Singing common intervals in G major in tune individually, as a section, and as a choir.

Sing To The Lord

For TTB, a cappella

Based on the Psalms

Words and Music by
EMILY CROCKER

214   Intermediate Tenor/Bass

TEACHER 2 TEACHER

"Sing To The Lord" presents an opportunity for your young men's ensemble to experience the straightforward homophonic choral style, listening for moving parts and the relationship of their vocal line to the harmony.

EXTENSION

Syllabic Word Stress

To demonstrate syllabic word stress, use this physical movement while singing: Pat your foot to indicate a stressed syllable of a word and lift the front part of your foot for the unstressed syllable. Discuss how this is much like tapping your foot while listening to the radio or your favorite CD. How does this activity affect the singing of the text? Does the physical activity make you more aware of the word stress in the composition? When singing with word stress be sure to remember to sing the accented part of the word with a fuller, richer tone.

2. Rehearse

Direct students to:

- Chant the rhythm in measures 1–8. Practice the measures that move together rhythmically before adding the part that is different. Repeat the same process while learning the B section and the final A' section.
- Sight-sing the A section using solfège syllables.
- Secure the rhythm of the entrances and breaths in the B section (measures 9–16).
- Sight-sing the final section.

Progress Checkpoints

Observe students' progress in:

- ✓ Singing the rhythms with precision.
- ✓ Singing the correct pitches independently in their own part.

3. Refine

Direct students to:

- Speak the text using tall vowel sounds and crisp beginning and ending consonants.
- Discuss the various ways to contrast the B section. Sing it first in a straightforward, *marcato* manner and then with a more lyrical, connected phrasing. Decide the interpretation that best fits your group.

Progress Checkpoints

Observe students' progress in:

- ✓ Performing with uniform vowel sounds while using percussive consonants.
- ✓ Singing with expressive musical phrasing while contrasting the A and B sections.

215

ASSESSMENT

Informal Assessment

In this lesson, students showed the ability to:

- Analyze the form of the text and the music.
- Read dotted quarter note rhythms correctly in 4/4 meter.
- Establish a key and demonstrate vocal independence when singing harmony.
- Sing with tall vowel sounds and crisp consonants.

Student Self-Assessment

Have students evaluate their individual performances based on the following:

- Breath Management
- Diction
- Tall Vowels
- Intonation
- Correct Part-Singing

Have each student rate his/her performance of this song in the areas above on a scale of 1–5, 5 being the best.

Individual and Group Performance Evaluation

To further measure growth of musical skills presented in this lesson, direct students to complete the Evaluation section on page 213.

- After the choir has divided into small groups, have each small group perform measures 1–8 for the rest of the class. The class should evaluate. How well did these singers match pitch on the unison notes?
- Have each student sing measures 1–7. They should each evaluate their own ability to read music that contains dotted quarter notes.

216   Intermediate Tenor/Bass

Additional National Standard

The following National Standards is addressed through the Assessment activities:

7. Evaluating music and music performances. **(a, b)**

SPOTLIGHT

Vocal Production

There are many ways we can use our voices to communicate. We can speak, shout, laugh, whisper, sigh and sing. This lesson will focus on your singing voice. It is best to think of singing as extended speech so you do not put too much physical effort into it.

Perform the following exercises to experience, explore and establish singing as extended speech.

- Say the phrase "Hello, my name is _____" as if you were greeting someone enthusiastically.

- Say the phrase again, but speak all of it on the same pitch as the first syllable.

- Repeat the phrase, making sure you take a singer's breath before you start.

- Feel the flow of the breath as it smoothly connects each word to the next.

- Try the phrase several times, starting on different pitches, seeing how long you can hold out your name.

- Remember to keep your chest high and your "inner tube" inflated for as long as you can. (It will feel like a belt is tightening around your waist the longer you hold it.)

Explore your **head voice** (*the singer's higher singing voice*) and your **chest voice** (*the singer's lower singing voice*) by performing the following exercises.

- Place your upper teeth on your lower lip as if you were going to say the letter "v."

- Make a singing tone on a lower pitch for a few seconds, keeping your teeth on your lower lip.

- Now, take a singer's breath and start the "v" sound on a lower pitch, but immediately move the pitch upward as high as you can go.

- Repeat the last step, this time bringing the voice back down low again.

- Notice the stretching feeling you have in your throat as you go higher and lower.

Objectives

- Demonstrate proper fundamental skills.

Suggested Teaching Sequence

Direct students to:

- Read the Spotlight On Vocal Production on student page 217.

- Perform the exercises in the order listed to establish singing as extended speech. Check for proper posture.

- Discuss the difference between head voice and chest voice. Demonstrate the difference with their voices.

- Perform the exercises in the order listed to explore their head voices and chest voices.

Progress Checkpoints

Observe students' progress in:

- ✓ Their ability to establish singing as extended speech.
- ✓ Their ability to sing with proper posture.
- ✓ Their ability to know and demonstrate the difference between head voice and chest voice.

RESOURCES

Teacher Resource Binder

Vocal Development 1-6, *Developing the Voice*

National Standards

1. Singing, alone and with others, a varied repertoire of music. **(b)**

You Gentlemen of England

OVERVIEW

Composer: Time of Elizabeth, arranged by Barry Talley
Text: Martin Packer
Voicing: TB
Key: E major
Meter: 4/4
Form: Verse/Refrain
Style: British Renaissance Song
Accompaniment: Piano
Programming: Concert, Renaissance Festival

Vocal Ranges:

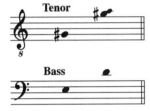

Objectives

After completing this lesson, students will be able to:
- Perform expressively from memory.
- Interpret music terms and symbols referring to dynamics when performing.
- Use standard terminology to describe in detail music notation.

VOCABULARY

Have students review vocabulary in student lesson. Introduce terms found in the music. A complete glossary of terms is found on page 226 of the student book.

You Gentlemen Of England

Composer: Time of Elizabeth, arranged by Barry Talley
Text: Martin Packer
Voicing: TB

VOCABULARY

dynamics

sequence

contrary motion

SPOTLIGHT

To learn more about concert etiquette, see page 137.

Focus

- Perform expressively from memory.
- Interpret music symbols referring to dynamics when performing.
- Define musical symbols and writing techniques found in music.

Getting Started

The dates April 14, 1912, and September 1, 1985, are linked in history. The first is the day that the ocean liner Titanic sank, and the second is the day that explorers found the wrecked ship located about 2.5 miles beneath the surface of the waters far off the coast of Newfoundland. Rumored to be an unsinkable ship, the Titanic serves as a reminder that life at sea can be both adventurous and dangerous. The lyrics in "You Gentlemen Of England" ask those "who live at home at ease" to remember those who experience "the danger of the seas."

◆ History and Culture

The tune of "You Gentlemen Of England" dates from the time of England's Queen Elizabeth I, who ruled from 1558 to 1603. Like her father, the popular King Henry VIII, she was musically gifted and had a passion for the arts. Moreover, she was a wise ruler. During her reign, England prospered politically and economically, which created favorable conditions for the arts to flourish. Music was a popular entertainment. A good education included learning to play musical instruments and to compose simple tunes. This era, referred to as the Elizabethan Age, also produced great literature. The most famous author from this time is William Shakespeare.

218   Intermediate Tenor/Bass

RESOURCES

Intermediate Sight-Singing

Sight-Singing in A Major, pages 152–163

Reading Rhythms in 4/4 Meter, pages 2–6

Reading Quarter Notes and Half Notes, pages 1–9

Teacher Resource Binder

Evaluation Master 7, *Evaluating Musical Expression*

Reference 1, At-a-Glance: *Music Terms and Symbols*

Reference 16, *My Music Dictionary*

Links to Learning

◆ Vocal

Sing the following example to practice performing a variety of dynamic levels. **Dynamics** are *symbols used in music that indicate how loud or soft to sing.* The first time, sing *f* (loud or full). Repeat the example several times, singing it *p* (soft), *mp* (medium soft), or *mf* (medium loud). Try it different ways.

◆ Theory

Perform the following example to practice singing a sequence. A **sequence** is *a pattern that, when repeated, starts on a different pitch.* Here, the music for the words "and the fears" is a sequence of "all the cares." Also, notice that on the words "All the" and "and the," the Tenor and Bass parts move in **contrary motion,** *a technique in which one part moves up while the other moves down.*

◆ Artistic Expression

The text in measures 16–19 repeats in measures 20–23. Although the melody remains the same, the dynamics change and the Tenors sing a different harmony part. Locate all the dynamic markings. In rehearsal and in performance, sing the contrasting dynamic markings.

Evaluation

Demonstrate how well you have learned the skills and concepts featured in the lesson "You Gentlemen Of England" by completing the following:

- Sing from memory measures 27–46 to reveal your ability to sing expressively by performing all the dynamics as marked. Evaluate how well you were able to sing expressively.

- Record yourself singing measures 12–23. Listen to the recording and evaluate how well you were able to sing with varied dynamics.

Choral Library You Gentlemen Of England **219**

RESOURCES

Intermediate Tenor/Bass Rehearsal/Performance CD

CD 2:23 Voices
CD 2:24 Accompaniment Only
CD 3:33 Vocal Practice Track—Tenor
CD 4:33 Vocal Practice Track—Bass

National Standards

1. Singing, alone and with others, a varied repertoire of music. **(a, b, d)**
5. Reading and notating music. **(c)**
6. Listening to, analyzing, and describing music. **(a)**

LINKS TO LEARNING

Vocal

The Vocal section is designed to prepare students to:

- Understand dynamics.
- Sing various dynamic levels.

Have students:

- Read the definition of dynamics.
- Sing the two-part example *forte*.
- Sing the example *piano*, then *mezzo piano*.
- Try it a various dynamic levels.

Theory

The Theory section is designed to prepare students to:

- Understand a sequence and contrary motion.
- Sing sequences and contrary motion in the music they are singing.

Have students:

- Read the definitions of a sequence and contrary motion.
- Sing the example in two parts, noting the contrary motion and sequences as marked.

Artistic Expression

The Artistic Expression section is designed to prepare students to locate and sing all the various dynamic levels in "You Gentlemen Of England."

Have students locate all the dynamic markings in this piece and perform the piece singing all the contrasting dynamic levels.

LESSON PLAN

Suggested Teaching Sequence and Performance Tips

1. Introduce

Direct students to:

- Read and discuss the information found in the Getting Started section on page 218.
- Practice the exercise in the Vocal section on page 217 to reinforce singing on various dynamic levels.
- Sing and study the excerpt in the Theory section on page 217 to learn about sequences and contrary motion.

Progress Checkpoints

Observe students' progress in:

- ✓ Singing with audible differences in dynamic levels.
- ✓ Singing a sequence pattern with another part making contrary motion.

You Gentlemen Of England

For TB and Piano

Arranged by
BARRY TALLEY

Music by MARTIN PACKER
Music, time of Elizabeth

TEACHER 2 TEACHER

"You Gentlemen Of England" is a hearty song for young men to sing and one full of teaching opportunities. The unison beginning to each verse is an ideal means of learning to sing in parts.

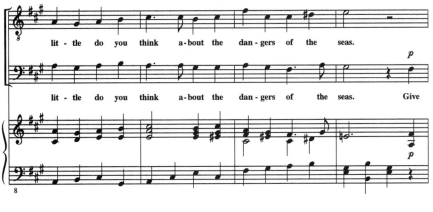

little do you think a-bout the dan-gers of the seas.

little do you think a-bout the dan-gers of the seas. Give

Ear to mar-i-ners, they will show,— All— the—

ear un-to the mar-i-ners, and they will plain-ly show,— All— the

cares and— the fears when the— storm-y winds do blow.

cares and— the fears when— the storm-y winds do blow. All— the

Choral Library *You Gentlemen Of England* **221**

Direct students to:

- Count the rhythms. Notice where the two parts share the same rhythm and where they do not.
- Read the pitches each part individually and phrase-by-phrase. Combine the parts, noting where unisons occur.
- Identify the passage beginning midway through measures 15 and 38 as that in the Theory section on page 219.
- Learn measures 48 to the end, noticing that while it begins like the first phrase, the melody shifts from the bass to the tenor and the final two measures are newly composed. This part is a coda (special ending) section.
- Add the text, taking care to sing with tall vowel sounds and crisp consonants and accurate releases.

Progress Checkpoints

Observe students' progress in:

- ✓ Counting and performing rhythms accurately.
- ✓ Singing pitches accurately, particularly through the chromatic passages and unisons.
- ✓ Singing with tall, rounded vowels and clean releases.
- ✓ Locating and performing the coda.

EXTENSION

Thirds

Often, the easiest way to create harmony is with the third above or below the melody. Arranger Barry Talley uses thirds, particularly when coming out of a unison, as in measures 6–7, 8–9, and 18. Identify these intervals as thirds. Locate other places where the parts sing in thirds. (such as the downbeats of measures 15–17, and 19–22) Direct the choristers to listen for correct intonation with all of these thirds.

3. Refine

Direct students to:

- Create four-measure phrases, sustaining energy from the beginning through the final consonant. Where a half note occurs mid-point in a phrase, keep the airflow moving forward.
- Rehearse the phrase break between beats 2 and 3 in measures 15 and 38. Allow time to end one phrase gracefully before starting the next, without sounding rushed.
- Apply the dynamic markings provided in the score to give an artistic shape to the whole piece.

Progress Checkpoints

Observe students' progress in:

- ✓ Their ability to sing four-measure phrases artistically.
- ✓ Their ability to make an audible difference between dynamic levels.

222   Intermediate Tenor/Bass

ENRICHMENT

Military Might

In modern warfare, control of air space is often the determining factor in who wins a battle. During the Elizabethan Age, however, military might was measured by marine maneuverability. Whoever controlled the seas held power, because naval strength meant that commercial ships were safe to travel in the waters. In the late 1500s, rival powers Spain and England both wanted naval superiority. Spain gathered its fleet, named the Spanish Armada, to attack Britain. In the late summer of 1588, the British navy established its superiority over the Spanish Armada, ending Spain's bid as a world ruler.

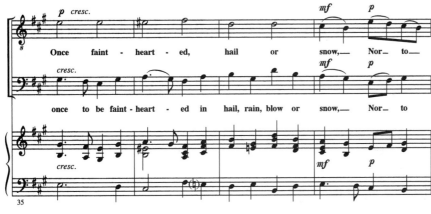

ASSESSMENT

Informal Assessment

In this lesson, students showed the ability to:

- Locate and perform a sequence in the key of A major.
- Locate and sing in contrary motion in two parts.
- Sing contrasting dynamic levels.
- Sing with vocal independence.
- Phrase artistically.

Student Self-Assessment

Have students evaluate their individual performances based on the following:

- Breath Management
- Phrasing
- Tall Vowels
- Intonation
- Correct Part-Singing

Have each student rate his/her performance of this song in the areas above on a scale of 1–5, 5 being the best.

TEACHING STRATEGY

Dynamics

Have students identify the term *dynamics* as relating to the loudness or softness of a sound.

pp—*pianissimo*—very soft
p—*piano*—soft
mp—*mezzo piano*—medium soft
mf—*mezzo forte*—medium loud
f—*forte*—loud
ff—*fortissimo*—very loud
crescendo—gradually going from soft to loud
decrescendo—gradually going from loud to soft.

Individual and Group Performance Evaluation

To further measure growth of musical skills presented in this lesson, direct students to complete the Evaluation section on page 219.

- Have each student sing measures 27–46 from memory at home or in a practice room. They should evaluate their ability to perform expressively.
- Have students record themselves singing measures 12–23. Have students listen to their recordings and evaluate how well they were able to sing with varied dynamics.

ENRICHMENT

Listening for Form

Discuss verse/refrain form in which each verse is followed by a repeated section (refrain). Have students:

- Listen to "You Gentlemen of England" and identify the form.
- Discover where each verse begins and when the refrains occur.
- Discuss how each verse or refrain is treated differently with regard to texture, harmony, placement of melody, dynamics, tempo and so forth.

224 Intermediate Tenor/Bass

Additional National Standards

The following National Standards are addressed through the Assessment, Extension, Enrichment and bottom-page activities:

6. Listening to, analyzing, and describing music. **(a)**

7. Evaluating music and music performances. **(a, b)**

Glossary

CHORAL MUSIC TERMS

2/2 meter   A time signature in which there are two beats per measure and the half note receives the beat.

2/4 meter   A time signature in which there are two beats per measure and the quarter note receives the beat.

3/2 meter   A time signature in which there are three beats per measure and the half note receives the beat.

3/4 meter   A time signature in which there are three beats per measure and the quarter note receives the beat.

3/8 meter   A time signature in which there is one group of three eighth notes per measure and the dotted quarter note receives the beat. When the tempo is very slow, this meter can be counted as having three beats per measure, with the eighth note receiving the beat.

4/4 meter   A time signature in which there are four beats per measure and the quarter note receives the beat.

5/8 meter   A time signature in which there are five beats per measure and the eighth note receives the beat.

6/4 meter   A time signature in which there are two groups of three quarter notes per measure and the dotted half note receives the beat. When the tempo is very slow, this meter can be counted as having six beats per measure, with the quarter note receiving the beat.

6/8 meter   A time signature in which there are two groups of three eighth notes per measure and the dotted quarter note receives the beat. When the tempo is very slow, this meter can be counted as having six beats per measure, with the eighth note receiving the beat.

9/8 meter   A time signature in which there are three groups of three eighth notes per measure and the dotted quarter note receives the beat. When the tempo is very slow, this meter can be counted as having nine beats per measure, with the eighth note receiving the beat.

12/8 meter   A time signature in which there are four groups of three eighth notes per measure and the dotted quarter note receives the beat.

A

a cappella *(ah-kah-PEH-lah)*   [It.] A style of singing without instrumental accompaniment.

a tempo *(ah TEM-poh)*   [It.] A tempo marking which indicates to return to the original tempo of a piece or section of music.

ABA form   A form in which an opening section (A) is followed by a contrasting section (B), which leads to the repetition of the opening section (A).

accelerando *(accel.) (ah-chel-leh-RAHN-doh)* [It.] A tempo marking that indicates to gradually get faster.

accent   A symbol placed above or below a given note to indicate that the note should receive extra emphasis or stress. ($\overset{>}{\bullet}$)

accidental   Any sharp, flat or natural that is not included in the key signature of a piece of music.

adagio *(ah-DAH-jee-oh)*   [It.] Slow tempo, but not as slow as *largo*.

ad libitum *(ad. lib.)*   [Lt.] An indication that the performer may vary the tempo or add or delete a vocal or instrumental part.

Aeolian scale *(ay-OH-lee-an)*   [Gk.] A modal scale that starts and ends on *la*. It is made up of the same arrangement of whole and half steps as a natural minor scale.

al fine *(ahl FEE-neh)*   [It.] To the end.

aleatory music *(AY-lee-uh-toh-ree)*   A type of music in which certain aspects are performed randomly. Also known as chance music.

alla breve   Indicates cut time; a duple meter in which there are two beats per measure, and half note receives the beat. *See* cut time.

allargando (*allarg.*) *(ahl-ahr-GAHN-doh)* [It.] To broaden, become slower.

allegro *(ah-LEH-groh)* [It.] Brisk tempo; faster than *moderato*, slower than *vivace*.

allegro non troppo *(ah-LEH-groh nohn TROH-poh)* [It.] A tempo marking that indicates not too fast. Not as fast as *allegro*.

altered pitch Another name for an accidental.

alto *(AL-toh)* The lowest-sounding female voice.

andante *(ahn-DAHN- teh)* [It.] Moderately slow; a walking tempo.

andante con moto *(ahn-DAHN- teh kohn MOH-toh)* [It.] A slightly faster tempo, "with motion."

animato Quickly, lively; "animated."

anthem A choral composition in English using a sacred text.

arpeggio *(ahr-PEH-jee-oh)* [It.] A chord in which the pitches are sounded successively, usually from lowest to highest; in broken style.

arrangement A piece of music in which a composer takes an existing melody and adds extra features or changes the melody in some way.

arranger A composer who takes an original or existing melody and adds extra features or changes the melody in some way.

art song A musical setting of a poem.

articulation The amount of separation or connection between notes.

articulators The lips, teeth, tongue and other parts of the mouth and throat that are used to produce vocal sound.

avocational Not related to a job or career.

B

barbershop A style of *a cappella* singing in which three parts harmonize with the melody. The lead sings the melody while the tenor harmonizes above and the baritone and bass harmonize below.

barcarole A Venetian boat song.

baritone The male voice between tenor and bass.

barline A vertical line placed on the musical staff that groups notes and rests together.

Baroque period *(bah-ROHK)* [Fr.] The historical period in Western civilization from 1600 to 1750.

bass The lowest-sounding male voice.

bass clef A clef that generally indicates notes that sound lower than middle C.

basso continuo *(BAH-soh cun-TIN-you-oh)* [It.] A continually moving bass line, common in music from the Baroque period.

beat The steady pulse of music.

bebop style Popular in jazz, music that features notes that are light, lively and played quickly. Often the melodic lines are complex and follow unpredictable patterns.

blues scale An altered major scale that uses flatted or lowered third, fifth and seventh notes: *ma* (lowered from *mi*), *se* (lowered from *sol*) and *te* (lowered from *ti*).

blues style An original African American art form that developed in the early twentieth century in the Mississippi Delta region of the South. The lyrics often express feelings of frustration, hardship or longing. It often contains elements such as call and response, the blues scale and swing.

body percussion The use of one's body to make a percussive sound, such as clapping, snapping or stepping.

breath mark A symbol in vocal music used to indicate where a singer should take a breath. (**,**)

breath support A constant airflow necessary to produce sound for singing.

C

cadence A melodic or harmonic structure that marks the end of a phrase or the completion of a song.

call and response A derivative of the field hollers used by slaves as they worked. A leader or group sings a phrase (call) followed by a response of the same phrase by another group.

calypso A style of music that originated in the West Indies and which features syncopated rhythms and comical lyrics.

canon A musical form in which one part sings a melody, and the other parts sing the same melody, but enter at different times. Canons are sometimes called rounds.

cantabile *(con-TAH-bee-leh)* [It.] In a lyrical, singing style.

cantata *(con-TAH-tah)* [It.] A large-scale musical piece made up of several movements for singers and instrumentalists. Johann Sebastian Bach was a prominent composer of cantatas.

cantor *(CAN-tor)* A person who sings and/or teaches music in a temple or synagogue.

canzona [It.] A rhythmic instrumental composition that is light and fast-moving.

chamber music Music performed by a small instrumental ensemble, generally with one instrument per part. The string quartet is a popular form of chamber music, consisting of two violins, a viola and a cello. Chamber music was popular during the Classical period.

chantey *See* sea chantey.

chanteyman A soloist who improvised and led the singing of sea chanteys.

chest voice The lower part of the singer's vocal range.

chorale *(kuh-RAL)* [Gr.] Congregational song or hymn of the German Protestant Church.

chord The combination of three or more notes played or sung together at the same time.

chromatic scale *(kroh-MAT-tick)* [Gk.] A scale that consists of all half steps and uses all twelve pitches in an octave.

Classical period The historical period in Western civilization from 1750 to 1820.

clef The symbol at the beginning of a staff that indicates which lines and spaces represent which notes.

coda A special ending to a song. A concluding section of a composition. (⊕)

common time Another name for 4/4 meter. Also known as common meter. (**C**)

composer A person who takes a musical thought and writes it out in musical notation to share it with others.

compound meter Any meter in which the dotted quarter note receives the beat, and the division of the beat is based on three eighth notes. 6/8, 9/8 and 12/8 are examples of compound meter.

con moto *(kohn MOH-toh)* [It.] With motion.

concert etiquette A term used to describe what is appropriate behavior in formal or informal musical performances.

concerto *(cun-CHAIR-toh)* [Fr., It.] A composition for a solo instrument and orchestra.

concerto grosso *(cun-CHAIR-toh GROH-soh)* [Fr., It.] A multimovement Baroque piece for a group of soloists and an orchestra.

conductor A person who uses hand and arm gestures to interpret the expressive elements of music for singers and instrumentalists.

conductus A thirteenth-century song for two, three or four voices.

consonance Harmonies in chords or music that are pleasing to the ear.

Contemporary period The historical period from 1900 to the present.

countermelody A separate melodic line that supports and/or contrasts the melody of a piece of music.

counterpoint The combination of two or more melodic lines. The parts move independently while harmony is created. Johann Sebastian Bach is considered by many to be one of the greatest composers of contrapuntal music.

contrary motion A technique in which two melodic lines move in opposite directions.

crescendo *(creh-SHEN-doh)* [It.] A dynamic marking that indicates to gradually sing or play louder. ◁—

cut time Another name for 2/2 meter. (¢)

D

da capo *(D.C.)* *(dah KAH-poh)* [It.] Go back to the beginning and repeat; *see also* dal segno *and* al fine.

dal segno *(D.S.)* *(dahl SAYN-yah)* [It.] Go back to the sign and repeat.

D. C. al Fine *(FEE-nay)* [It.] A term that indicates to go back to the beginning and repeat. The term *al fine* indicates to sing to the end, or *fine*.

decrescendo *(DAY-creh-shen-doh)* [It.] A dynamic marking that indicates to gradually sing or play softer. —▷

descant A special part in a piece of music that is usually sung higher than the melody or other parts of the song.

diatonic scale *(die-uh-TAH-nick)* A scale that uses no altered pitches or accidentals. Both the major scale and the natural minor scale are examples of a diatonic scale.

diction The pronunciation of words while singing.

diminished chord A minor chord in which the top note is lowered one half step from *mi* to *me*.

diminuendo *(dim.)* *(duh-min-yoo-WEN-doh)* [It.] Gradually getting softer; *see also* decrescendo.

diphthong A combination of two vowel sounds.

dissonance A combination of pitches or tones that clash.

dolce *(DOHL-chay)* [It.] Sweetly.

dominant chord A chord built on the fifth note of a scale. In a major scale, this chord uses the notes *sol, ti* and *re*, and it may be called the **V** ("five") chord, since it is based on the fifth note of the major scale, or *sol*. In a minor scale, this chord uses the notes *mi, sol* and *ti* (or *mi, si* and *ti*), and it may be called the **v** or **V** ("five") chord, since it is based on the fifth note of the minor scale, or *mi*.

Dorian scale *(DOOR-ee-an)* [Gk.] A modal scale that starts and ends on *re*.

dot A symbol that increases the length of a given note by half its value. It is placed to the right of the note.

dotted half note A note that represents three beats of sound when the quarter note receives the beat. ♩.

double barline A set of two barlines that indicate the end of a piece or section of music.

D. S. al coda *(dahl SAYN-yoh ahl KOH-dah)* [It.] Repeat from the symbol (𝄋) and skip to the coda when you see the sign. (𝄌)

duet A group of two singers or instrumentalists.

dynamics Symbols in music that indicate how loud or soft to sing or play.

E

eighth note A note that represents one half beat of sound when the quarter note receives the beat. Two eighth notes equal one beat of sound when the quarter note receives the beat. ♪ ♫

eighth rest A rest that represents one half beat of silence when the quarter note receives the beat. Two eighth rests equal one beat of silence when the quarter note receives the beat. 𝄾

expressive singing To sing with feeling.

F

falsetto [It.] The register in the male voice that extends far above the natural voice. The light upper range.

fermata *(fur-MAH-tah)* [It.] A symbol that indicates to hold a note or rest for longer than its given value. (⌒)

fine *(fee-NAY)* [It.] A term used to indicate the end of a piece of music.

flat A symbol that lowers the pitch of a given note by one half step.(♭)

folk music Music that passed down from generation to generation through oral tradition. Traditional music that reflects a place, event or a national feeling.

folk song A song passed down from generation to generation through oral tradition. A song that reflects a place, event or a national feeling.

form The structure or design of a musical composition.

forte *(FOR-tay)* [It.] A dynamic that indicates to sing or play loud. (*f*)

fortissimo *(for-TEE-see-moh)* [It.] A dynamic that indicates to sing or play very loud. (*ff*)

fugue *(FYOOG)* A musical form in which the same melody is performed by different instruments or voices entering at different times, thus adding layers of sound.

fusion Music that is developed by the act of combining various types and cultural influences of music into a new style.

G

gospel music Religious music that originated in the African American churches of the South. This music can be characterized by improvisation, syncopation and repetition.

grand staff A staff that is created when two staves are joined together.

grandioso [It.] Stately, majestic.

grave *(GRAH-veh)* [It.] Slow, solemn.

grazioso *(grah-tsee-OH-soh)* [It.] Graceful.

Gregorian chant A single, unaccompanied melodic line sung by male voices. Featuring a sacred text and used in the church, this style of music was developed in the medieval period.

H

half note A note that represents two beats of sound when the quarter note receives the beat. ♩

half rest A rest that represents two beats of silence when the quarter note receives the beat. ▬

half step The smallest distance (interval) between two notes on a keyboard; the chromatic scale is composed entirely of half steps.

harmonic minor scale A minor scale that uses a raised seventh note, *si* (raised from *sol*).

harmonics Small whistle-like tones, or overtones, that are sometimes produced over a sustained pitch.

harmony A musical sound that is formed when two or more different pitches are played or sung at the same time.

head voice The higher part of the singer's vocal range.

homophonic *(hah-muh-FAH-nik)* [Gk.] A texture where all parts sing similar rhythm in unison or harmony.

homophony *(haw-MAW-faw-nee)* [Gk.] A type of music in which there are two or more parts with similar or identical rhythms being sung or played at the same time. Also, music in which melodic interest is concentrated in one voice part and may have subordinate accompaniment.

hushed A style marking indicating a soft, whispered tone.

I

imitation The act of one part copying what another part has already played or sung.

improvisation The art of singing or playing music, making it up as you go, or composing and performing a melody at the same time.

International Phonetic Alphabet (IPA) A phonetic alphabet that provides a notational standard for all languages. Developed in Paris, France, in 1886.

interval The distance between two notes.

intonation The accuracy of pitch, in-tune singing.

Ionian scale *(eye-OWN-ee-an)* [Gk.] A modal scale that starts and ends on *do*. It is made up of the same arrangement of whole and half steps as a major scale.

J

jazz An original American style of music that features swing rhythms, syncopation and improvisation.

jongleur [Fr.] An entertainer who traveled from town to town during medieval times, often telling stories and singing songs.

K

key Determined by a song's or scale's home tone, or keynote.

key signature A symbol or set of symbols that determines the key of a piece of music.

L

ledger lines Short lines that appear above, between treble and bass clefs, or below the bass clef, used to expand the notation.

legato *(leh-GAH-toh)* [It.] A connected and sustained style of singing and playing.

lento *(LEN-toh)* [It.] Slow; a little faster than *largo*, a little slower than *adagio*.

lied *(leet)* [Ger.] A song in the German language, generally with a secular text.

liturgical text A text that has been written for the purpose of worship in a church setting.

lute An early form of the guitar.

Lydian scale *(LIH-dee-an)* [Gk.] A modal scale that starts and ends on *fa*.

lyrics The words of a song.

M

madrigal A poem that has been set to music in the language of the composer. Featuring several imitative parts, it usually has a secular text and is generally sung *a cappella*.

maestoso *(mah-eh-STOH-soh)* [It.] Perform majestically.

major chord A chord that can be based on the *do, mi,* and *sol* of a major scale.

major scale A scale that has *do* as its home tone, or keynote. It is made up of a specific arrangement of whole steps and half steps in the following order: W + W + H + W + W + W + H.

major tonality A song that is based on a major scale with *do* as its keynote, or home tone.

mangulina A traditional dance from the Dominican Republic.

marcato *(mar-CAH-toh)* [It.] A stressed and accented style of singing and playing.

Mass A religious service of prayers and ceremonies originating in the Roman Catholic Church consisting of spoken and sung sections. It consists of several sections divided into two groups: proper (text changes for every day) and ordinary (text stays the same in every mass). Between the years 1400 and 1600, the Mass assumed its present form consisting of the Kyrie, Gloria, Credo, Sanctus and Agnus Dei. It may include chants, hymns and psalms as well. The Mass also developed into large musical works for chorus, soloists and even orchestra.

measure The space between two barlines.

medieval period The historical period in Western civilization also known as the Middle Ages (400–1430).

medley A collection of songs musically linked together.

melisma (*muh-LIZ-mah*) [Gk.] A group of notes sung to a single syllable or word.

melismatic singing (*muh-liz-MAT-ik*) [Gk.] A style of text setting in which one syllable is sung over many notes.

melodic contour The overall shape of the melody.

melodic minor scale A minor scale that uses raised sixth and seventh notes: *fi* (raised from *fa*) and *si* (raised from *sol*). Often, these notes are raised in ascending patterns, but not in descending patterns.

melody A logical succession of musical tones.

meter A way of organizing rhythm.

meter signature *See* time signature.

metronome marking A sign that appears over the top line of the staff at the beginning of a piece or section of music that indicates the tempo. It shows the kind of note that will receive the beat and the number of beats per minute as measured by a metronome.

mezzo forte (*MEH-tsoh FOR tay*) [It.] A dynamic that indicates to sing or play medium loud. (*mf*)

mezzo piano (*MEH-tsoh pee-AH-noh*) [It.] A dynamic that indicates to sing or play medium soft. (*mp*)

mezzo voce (*MEH-tsoh VOH-cheh*) [It.] With half voice; reduced volume and tone.

minor chord A chord that can be based on the *la, do,* and *mi* of a minor scale.

minor scale A scale that has *la* as its home tone, or keynote. It is made up of a specific arrangement of whole steps and half steps in the following order: W + H +W + W + H + W + W.

minor tonality A song that is based on a minor scale with *la* as its keynote, or home tone.

mixed meter A technique in which the time signature or meter changes frequently within a piece of music.

Mixolydian scale (*mix-oh-LIH-dee-an*) [Gr.] A modal scale that starts and ends on *sol*.

modal scale A scale based on a mode. Like major and minor scales, each modal scale is made up of a specific arrangement of whole steps and half steps, with the half steps occurring between *mi* and *fa*, and *ti* and *do*.

mode An early system of pitch organization that was used before major and minor scales and keys were developed.

modulation A change in the key or tonal center of a piece of music within the same song.

molto [It.] Very or much; for example, *molto rit.* means "much slower."

motet (*moh-teht*) Originating as a medieval and Renaissance polyphonic song, this choral form of composition became an unaccompanied work, often in contrapuntal style. Also, a short, sacred choral piece with a Latin text that is used in religious services but is not a part of the regular Mass.

motive A shortened expression, sometimes contained within a phrase.

music critic A writer who gives an evaluation of a musical performance.

music notation Any means of writing down music, including the use of notes, rests and symbols.

musical A play or film whose action and dialogue are combined with singing and dancing.

musical theater An art form that combines acting, singing, and dancing to tell a story. It often includes staging, costumes, lighting and scenery.

mysterioso [It.] Perform in a mysterious or haunting way; to create a haunting mood.

N

narrative song A song that tells a story.

national anthem A patriotic song adopted by nations through tradition or decree.

nationalism Patriotism; pride of country. This feeling influenced many Romantic composers such as Wagner, Tchaikovsky, Dvořák, Chopin and Brahms.

natural A symbol that cancels a previous sharp or flat, or a sharp or flat in a key signature. (♮)

natural minor scale A minor scale that uses no altered pitches or accidentals.

no breath mark A direction not to take a breath at a specific place in the composition. (N.B.)

non troppo (*nahn TROH-poh*) [It.] Not too much; for example, *allegro non troppo*, "not too fast."

notation Written notes, symbols and directions used to represent music within a composition.

O

octave An interval of two pitches that are eight notes apart on a staff.

ode A poem written in honor of a special person or occasion. These poems were generally dedicated to a member of a royal family. In music, an ode usually includes several sections for choir, soloists and orchestra.

opera A combination of singing, instrumental music, dancing and drama that tells a story.

optional divisi (*opt.div.*) Indicating a split in the music into optional harmony, shown by a smaller cued note.

oral tradition Music that is learned through rote or by ear and is interpreted by its performer(s).

oratorio (*or-uh-TOR-ee-oh*) [It.] A dramatic work for solo voices, chorus and orchestra presented without theatrical action. Usually, oratorios are based on a literary or religious theme.

ostinato (*ahs-tuh-NAH-toh*) [It.] A rhythmic or melodic passage that is repeated continuosly.

overture A piece for orchestra that serves as an introduction to an opera or other dramatic work.

P

palate The roof of the mouth; the hard palate is at the front, the soft palate is at the back.

parallel motion A technique in which two or more melodic lines move in the same direction.

parallel sixths A group of intervals that are a sixth apart and which move at the same time and in the same direction.

parallel thirds A group of intervals that are a third apart and which move at the same time and in the same direction.

part-singing Two or more parts singing an independent melodic line at the same time.

patsch The act of slapping one's hands on one's thighs.

pentatonic scale A five-tone scale using the pitches *do, re, mi, sol* and *la*.

perfect fifth An interval of two pitches that are five notes apart on a staff.

perfect fourth An interval of two pitches that are four notes apart on a staff.

phrase A musical idea with a beginning and an end.

Phrygian scale *(FRIH-gee-an)* [Gk.] A modal scale that starts and ends on *mi*.

pianissimo *(pee-ah-NEE-see-moh)* [It.] A dynamic that indicates to sing or play very soft. (*pp*)

piano *(pee-AH-noh)* [It.] A dynamic that indicates to sing or play soft. (*p*)

pitch Sound, the result of vibration; the highness or lowness of a tone, determined by the number of vibrations per second.

pitch matching In a choral ensemble, the ability to sing the same notes as those around you.

piu *(pew)* [It.] More; for example, *piu forte* means "more loudly."

poco *(POH-koh)* [It.] Little; for example *poco dim.* means "a little softer."

poco a poco *(POH-koh ah POH-koh)* [It.] Little by little; for example, *poco a poco cresc.* means "little by little increase in volume."

polyphony *(pah-LIH-fun-nee)* [Gk.] Literally, "many sounding." A type of music in which there are two or more different melodic lines being sung or played at the same time. Polyphony was refined during the Renaissance, and this period is sometimes called "golden age of polyphony."

polyrhythms A technique in which several different rhythms are performed at the same time.

presto *(PREH-stoh)* [It.] Very fast.

program music A descriptive style of music composed to relate or illustrate a specific incident, situation or drama; the form of the piece is often dictated or influenced by the nonmusical program. This style commonly occurs in music composed during the Romantic period.

Q

quarter note A note that represents one beat of sound when the quarter note receives the beat.

quarter rest A rest that represents one beat of silence when the quarter note receives the beat.

quartet A group of four singers or instrumentalists.

R

rallentando *(rall.)* *(rahl-en-TAHN-doh)* [It.] Meaning to "perform more and more slowly." *See also* ritard.

refrain A repeated section at the end of each phrase or verse in a song. Also known as a chorus.

register, vocal A term used for different parts of the singer's range, such as head register, or head voice (high notes); and chest register, or chest voice (low notes).

relative minor scale A minor scale that shares the same key signature as its corresponding major scale. Both scales share the same half steps, between *mi* and *fa*, and *ti* and *do*.

Renaissance period The historical period in Western civilization from 1430 to 1600.

repeat sign A symbol that indicates that a section of music should be repeated. (:‖)

repetition The restatement of a musical idea; repeated pitches; repeated "A" section in ABA form.

requiem *(REK-wee-ehm)* [Lt.] Literally, "rest." A mass written and performed to honor the dead and comfort the living.

resonance Reinforcement and intensification of sound by vibration.

rest A symbol used in music notation to indicate silence.

rhythm The combination of long and short notes and rests in music. These may move with the beat, faster than the beat or slower than the beat.

ritard *(rit.)* *(ree-TAHRD)* [It.] A tempo marking that indicates to gradually get slower.

Romantic period The historical period in Western civilization from 1820 to 1900.

rondo form A form in which a repeated section is separated by several contrasting sections.

rote The act of learning a song by hearing it over and over again.

round *See* canon.

rubato *(roo-BAH-toh)* [It.] The freedom to slow down and/or speed up the tempo without changing the overall pulse of a piece of music.

S

sacred music Music associated with religious services or themes.

scale A group of pitches that are sung or played in succession and are based on a particular home tone, or keynote.

scat singing An improvisational style of singing that uses nonsense syllables instead of words. It was made popular by jazz trumpeter Louis Armstrong.

sea chantey A song sung by sailors, usually in rhythm with their work.

secular music Music not associated with religious services or themes.

sempre *(SEHM-preh)* [It.] Always, continually.

sempre accelerando *(sempre accel.)* *(SEHM-preh ahk-chel)* [It.] A term that indicates to gradually increase the tempo of a piece or section of music.

sequence A successive musical pattern that begins on a higher or lower pitch each time it is repeated.

serenata [It.] A large-scale musical work written in honor of a special occasion. Generally performed in the evening or outside, it is often based on a mythological theme.

sforzando *(sfohr-TSAHN-doh)* [It.] A sudden strong accent on a note or chord. (*sfz*)

sharp A symbol that raises the pitch of a given note one half step.

shekere An African shaker consisting of a hollow gourd surrounded by beads.

sight-sing Reading and singing music at first sight.

simile *(sim.)* *(SIM-ee-leh)* [It.] To continue the same way.

simple meter Any meter in which the quarter note receives the beat, and the division of the beat is based on two eighth notes. 2/4, 3/4 and 4/4 are examples of simple meter.

singing posture The way one sits or stands while singing.

sixteenth note A note that represents one quarter beat of sound when the quarter note receives the beat. Four sixteenth notes equal one beat of sound when the quarter note receives the beat.

sixteenth rest A rest that represents one quarter beat of silence when the quarter note receives the beat. Four sixteenth rests equal one beat of silence when the quarter note receives the beat.

skip-wise motion The movement from a given note to another note that is two or more notes above or below it on the staff.

slur A curved line placed over or under a group of notes to indicate that they are to be performed without a break.

solfège syllables Pitch names using *do, re, mi, fa, sol, la, ti, do*, etc.

solo One person singing or playing an instrument alone.

sonata-allegro form A large ABA form consisting of three sections: exposition, development and recapitulation. This form was made popular during the Classical period.

soprano The highest-sounding female voice.

sostenuto *(SAHS-tuh-noot-oh)* [It.] The sustaining of a tone or the slackening of tempo.

sotto voce In a quiet, subdued manner; "under" the voice.

spirito *(SPEE-ree-toh)* [It.] Spirited; for example, *con spirito* ("with spirit").

spiritual Songs that were first sung by African American slaves, usually based on biblical themes or stories.

staccato *(stah-KAH-toh)* [It.] A short and detached style of singing or playing.

staff A series of five horizontal lines and four spaces on which notes are written. A staff is like a ladder. Notes placed higher on the staff sound higher than notes placed lower on the staff.

stage presence A performer's overall appearance on stage, including enthusiasm, facial expression and posture.

staggered breathing In ensemble singing, the practice of planning breaths so that no two singers take a breath at the same time, thus creating the overall effect of continuous singing.

staggered entrances A technique in which different parts and voices enter at different times.

stanza A section in a song in which the words change on each repeat. Also known as a verse.

step-wise motion The movement from a given note to another note that is directly above or below it on the staff.

strophe A verse or stanza in a song.

strophic A form in which the melody repeats while the words change from verse to verse.

style The particular character of a musical work; often indicated by words at the beginning of a composition, telling the performer the general manner in which the piece is to be performed.

subdominant chord A chord built on the fourth note of a scale. In a major scale, this chord uses the notes *fa, la* and *do,* and it may be called the **IV** ("four") chord, since it is based on the fourth note of the major scale, or *fa.* In a minor scale, this chord uses the notes *re, fa* and *la,* and it may be called the **iv** ("four") chord, since it is based on the fourth note of the minor scale, or *re.*

subito (sub.) *(SOO-bee-toh)* [It.] Suddenly.

suspension The holding over of one or more musical tones in a chord into the following chord, producing a momentary discord.

swing rhythms Rhythms in which the second eighth note of each beat is played or sung like the last third of triplet, creating an uneven, "swing" feel. A style often found in jazz and blues. Swing rhythms are usually indicated at the beginning of a song or section.

syllabic *See* syllabic singing.

syllabic singing A style of text setting in which one syllable is sung on each note.

syllabic stress The stressing of one syllable over another.

symphonic poem A single-movement work for orchestra, inspired by a painting, play or other literary or visual work. Franz Liszt was a prominent composer of symphonic poems. Also known as a tone poem.

symphony A large-scale work for orchestra.

syncopation The placement of accents on a weak beat or a weak portion of the beat, or on a note or notes that normally do not receive extra emphasis.

synthesizer A musical instrument that produces sounds electronically, rather than by the physical vibrations of an acoustic instrument.

tempo Terms in music that indicate how fast or slow to sing or play.

tempo I or tempo primo *See a tempo.*

tenor The highest-sounding male voice.

tenuto *(teh-NOO-toh)* [It.] A symbol placed above or below a given note indicating that the note should receive stress and/or that its value should be slightly extended. (♩)

text Words, usually set in a poetic style, that express a central thought, idea or narrative.

texture The thickness of the different layers of horizontal and vertical sounds.

theme A musical idea, usually a melody.

theme and variation form A musical form in which variations of the basic theme make up the composition.

third An interval of two pitches that are three notes apart on a staff.

tie A curved line used to connect two or more notes of the same pitch together in order to make one (♩♩♩) longer note.

tied notes Two or more notes of the same pitch connected together with a tie in order to make one longer note.

timbre The tone quality of a person's voice or musical instrument.

time signature The set of numbers at the beginning of a piece of music. The top number indicates the number of beats per measure. The bottom number indicates the kind of note that receives the beat. Time signature is sometimes called meter signature.

to coda Skip to (✛) or CODA.

tone color That which distinguishes the voice or tone of one singer or instrument from another; for example, a soprano from an alto, or a flute from a clarinet. *See also* timbre.

tonic chord A chord built on the home tone, or keynote of a scale. In a major scale, this chord uses the notes *do, mi* and *sol*, and it may be called the **I** ("one") chord, since it is based on the first note of the major scale, or *do*. In a minor scale, this chord uses the notes *la, do* and *mi*, and it may be called the **i** ("one") chord, since it is based on the first note of the minor scale, or *la*.

treble clef A clef that generally indicates notes that sound higher than middle C.

trio A group of three singers or instrumentalists with usually one on a part.

triplet A group of notes in which three notes of equal duration are sung in the time normally given to two notes of equal duration.

troppo *(TROHP-oh)* [It.] Too much; for example, *allegro non troppo* ("not too fast").

tutti *(TOO-tee)* [It.] Meaning "all" or "together."

twelve-tone music A type of music that uses all twelve tones of the scale equally. Developed in the early twentieth century, Arnold Schoenberg is considered to be the pioneer of this style of music.

two-part music A type of music in which two different parts are sung or played.

unison All parts singing or playing the same notes at the same time.

variation A modification of a musical idea, usually after its initial appearance in a piece.

vivace *(vee-VAH-chay)* [It.] Very fast; lively.

vocal jazz A popular style of music characterized by strong prominent meter, improvisation and dotted or syncopated patterns. Sometimes sung *a cappella*.

W

whole note   A note that represents four beats of sound when the quarter note receives the beat.   o

whole rest   A rest that represents four beats of silence when the quarter note receives the beat.   ▬

whole step   The combination of two successive half steps.

word painting   A technique in which the music reflects the meaning of the words.

word stress   The act of singing important parts of the text in a more accented style than the other parts.

Y

yoik   A vocal tradition of the Sámi people of the Arctic region of Sampi that features short melodic phrases that are repeated with slight variations.

Classified Index

A Cappella

The Battle Cry Of Freedom 122

Festival Procession 34

Leave Her, Johnny 170

Now Is The Month Of Maying 66

Red River Valley 22

Sing To The Lord 212

Soldier's Hallelujah 42

Composers

Thomas Morley (1557–1602)
Now Is The Month Of Maying 66

Johann Sebastian Bach (1685–1750)
Der Herr segne euch 74

Wolfgang Amadeus Mozart (1756–1791)
Ave Verum Corpus 86

George Frederick Root (1825–1895)
The Battle Cry Of Freedom 122

Teodoro Cottrau (1827–1879)
Santa Lucia 206

Johannes Brahms (1833–1897)
Da unten im Tale 94

Bob Chilcott (b. 1955)
Be Cool 14

Folk

African American Spiritual
Joshua! (Fit The Battle Of Jericho) . . 158

New River Train 174

The Shepherd's Spiritual 56

American
Frog Went A-Courtin' 140

Pretty Saro 198

Red River Valley 22

Cuban
Guantanamera 152

German
Da unten im Tale 94

Foreign Language

German
Da unten im Tale 94

Der Herr segne euch 74

Italian
Santa Lucia 206

Latin
Ave Verum Corpus 86

Festival Procession 34

Spanish
Guantanamera 152

Instruments

Percussion
Festival Procession 34

Frog Went A-Courtin' 140

Soldier's Hallelujah 42

Music & History

Medieval
Festival Procession 34

Renaissance
Now Is The Month Of Maying 66

You Gentlemen Of England 218

Baroque
Der Herr segne euch 74

Classical
Ave Verum Corpus 86

Romantic
The Battle Cry Of Freedom 122

Da unten im Tale 94

Santa Lucia 206

Contemporary
Be Cool 14

Poetry

Come Travel With Me 128

Guantanamera 152

Sea Chantey

Codfish Shanty 26

Leave Her, Johnny 170

On The Deep, Blue Sea 184

Seasonal, Patriotic

The Battle Cry Of Freedom 122

Festival Procession 34

Light The Candles Of Hanukkah . . . 48

Now Is The Month Of Maying 66

This Land Is Your Land 2

The Shepherd's Spiritual 56

Soldier's Hallelujah 42

Vocal Jazz

Be Cool 14

Joshua! (Fit The Battle Of Jericho) . . 158

Listening Selections

As Vesta Was Descending
    Thomas Weelkes 103

"Three Voltas" from *Terpsichore*
    Michael Praetorius 103

"Gloria in excelsis Deo"
    from *Gloria in D Major*
    Antonio Vivaldi 107

"The Arrival of the Queen of Sheba"
    from *Solomon*
    George Frideric Handel 107

"The Heavens Are Telling"
    from *Creation*
    Franz Joseph Haydn 111

Eine Kleine Nachtmusik, First Movement
    Wolfgang Amadeus Mozart 111

"Toreador Chorus" from *Carmen*
    Georges Bizet 115

The Moldau (excerpt)
    Bedrich Smetana 115

Joshua Fit the Battle
    arr. Moses Hogan 119

"Infernal Dance of King Kaschei"
    from *The Firebird*
    Igor Stravinsky 119

Index of Songs and Spotlights

Ave Verum Corpus 86
The Battle Cry Of Freedom 122
Be Cool 14
Codfish Shanty 26
Come Travel With Me 128
Da unten im Tale 94
Der Herr segne euch 74
Festival Procession 34
Frog Went A-Courtin' 140
Guantanamera 152
Joshua! (Fit The Battle Of Jericho) 158
Leave Her, Johnny 170
Light The Candles Of Hanukkah 48
New River Train 174
Now Is The Month Of Maying 66
On The Deep, Blue Sea 184
Pretty Saro 198
Red River Valley 22
Santa Lucia 206
Sing To The Lord 212
Soldier's Hallelujah 42
The Shepherd's Spiritual 56
This Land Is Your Land 2
You Gentlemen Of England 218

Spotlights

Arranging 21
Breath Management 169
Careers In Music 127
Changing Voice 197
Concert Etiquette 139
Diction 120
Improvisation 183
Posture 13
Vocal Production 217
Vowels 65

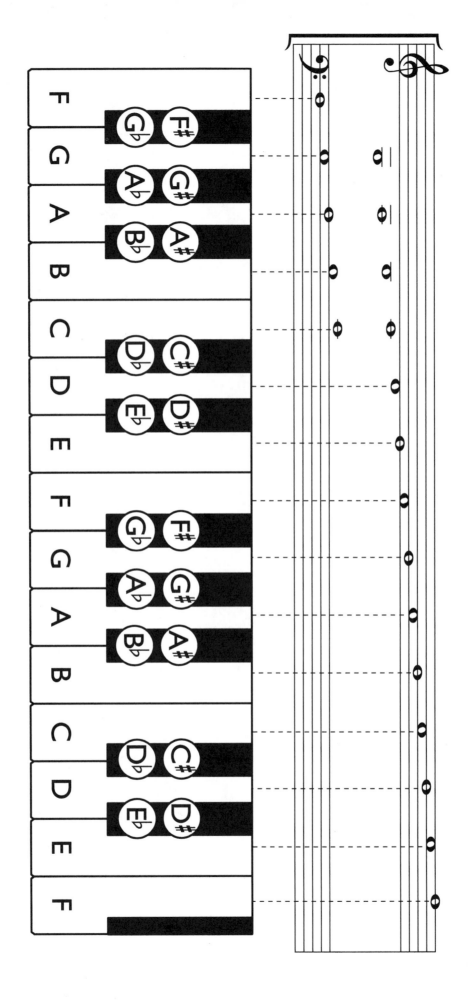